BEOWULF

BEOWULF

a new verse translation by R. M. Liuzza

broadview literary texts

Canadian Cataloguing in Publication Data

Beowulf. English
  Beowulf

(Broadview literary texts)
Includes bibliographical references.

ISBN 155111-189-6

I. Liuzza, R. M.   II. Title.   III. Series.
PR1583.L58 1999   829'.3   C99-932632-5

Broadview Press Ltd., is an independent, international publishing house,
incorporated in 1985.

North America:
P.O. Box 1243, Peterborough, Ontario, Canada K9J 7H5
3576 California Road, Orchard Park, NY 14127
TEL: (705) 743-8990; FAX: (705) 743-8353;
E-MAIL:customerservice@broadviewpress.com

United Kingdom: Turpin Distribution Services Ltd.,
Blackhorse Rd., Letchworth, Hertfordshire SG6 1HN
TEL: (1462) 672555; FAX (1462) 480947; E-MAIL: turpin@rsc.org

Australia: St. Clair Press, P.O. Box 287, Rozelle, NSW 2039
TEL: (02) 818-1942; FAX: (02) 418-1923

www.broadviewpress.com
Broadview Press is grateful to Professor Eugene Benson for advice on
editorial matters for the Broadview Literary Texts series.

Broadview Press gratefully acknowledges the financial support of the
Ministry of Canadian Heritage through the Book Publishing Industry
Development Program.

Text design and composition by George Kirkpatrick

PRINTED IN CANADA

Contents

Acknowledgements

My thanks are due to David Johnson, J.R. Hall, Molly Rothenberg, and Myra Seaman for their comments on an early draft of the introduction. I am grateful to my students at Tulane University for their reading of the text during several semesters.

Selections from Saxo Grammaticus, *The History of the Danes*, tr. Peter Fisher and ed. H. Ellis Davidson, ©1979 D.S. Brewer, are reprinted with the permission of Boydell and Brewer Ltd. Selections from *Bede's Ecclesiastical History of the People*, edited and translated by Bertram Colgrave and R. A. B. Mynors, ©1969 Oxford University Press, are reprinted with the permission of Oxford University Press. Selections from *Beowulf: A Dual-Language Edition*, edited and translated by Howell D. Chickering, ©1977 Anchor Books, are reprinted by permission of Doubleday. Selections from *Beowulf*, tr. Kevin Crossley-Holland, are from *The Anglo-Saxon World: An Anthology*, ©1982 Boydell Press, and are reprinted with the permission of Boydell and Brewer Ltd. Selections from *Beowulf: A New Prose Translation*, translated by E. Talbot Donaldson, translation copyright ©1966 by W.W. Norton and Company, are reprinted by permission of W.W. Norton and Company Inc. Selections from *A Readable Beowulf: The Old English Epic Newly Translated* by Stanley B. Greenfield, ©1982 by the Board of Trustees, Southern Illinois Press, are reprinted by permission of Southern Illinois University Press. Selections from *Beowulf* by Marc Hudson, ©1990 Bucknell University Press are reprinted by permission of Bucknell University Press. Selections from *Beowulf: The Oldest English Epic*, translated by Charles W. Kennedy, translation copyright 1940 by Oxford University Press Inc., renewed 1968 by Charles W. Kennedy, are used by permission of Oxford University Press Inc. Selections from *Beowulf: An Imitative Translation*, translated by Ruth P. M. Lehmann, copyright ©1988, appear courtesy of the author and the University of Texas Press. Selections from *Beowulf*, translated by Edwin Morgan (Berkeley: University of California Press, 1962), have been reprinted by permission of

Edwin Morgan. Selections from *Beowulf: A New Verse Translation*, translated by Frederick Rebsamen (San Francisco: Harper-Collins, 1991), are ©1991 Frederick Rebsamen and reproduced by permission of Frederick Rebsamen. Selections from *Beowulf*, translated by S.A.J. Bradley, are from *Anglo-Saxon Poetry*, ©1982 Everyman, and are reprinted with the permission of Everyman Publishers PLC. Selections from *Beowulf* by Burton Raffel, ©1963 by Burton Raffel, Afterword ©1963 by New American Library, are reprinted with the permission of Dutton Signet, a division of Penguin Putnam Inc.

The illustration of folio 129r of Cotton Vitellius A. xv is from a digital image prepared by the Electronic *Beowulf* project, editor Kevin S. Kiernan; it is reproduced by permission of the British Library Board.

The epigraphs in the introduction are excerpts from "Burnt Norton" in *Four Quartets*, ©1943 by T. S. Eliot and renewed 1971 by Esme Valerie Eliot, reprinted by permission of Harcourt Brace and Company and Faber and Faber Limited.

Preface

Adeo sanctum est vetus omne poema. — Horace.

Beowulf is one of the earliest full-scale works of English literature and is still sometimes regarded as a straightforward heroic poem, an uncomplicated point of origin (for good or ill) of the "English Literary Tradition." But most serious readers of the poem have come to recognize that *Beowulf* is a complex product of Anglo-Saxon cultural tensions, itself a work of long gestation and mixed heritage born of melancholy and nostalgia. Fueled by these relatively new readings of a classic text, interest in *Beowulf* continues unabated: new student editions by Jack, Alexander, and Mitchell and Robinson; publications such as Bjork and Niles' *Beowulf Handbook*, an updated reprint of Colin Chase's collection *The Dating of Beowulf*, and a reissue of Kevin Kiernan's groundbreaking *Beowulf and the Beowulf Manuscript*; new book-length studies by Davis, Deskis, Earl, and Hill, and new anthologies of *Beowulf* criticism by Baker and Fulk all indicate that scholars and students are still intrigued by the poem, still active in its interpretation, and still struggling towards some understanding of its complexity. These new works offer a depth of study and breadth of context not formerly available to the non-specialist reader, and I hope that a new translation that has benefited from their influence may not be an unworthy companion to them.

The present work is intended to bring together a readable and reliable translation with adequate notes, a collection of supporting texts and commentary, and an introduction that situates the poem in a literary history. For those who do not wish to learn Old English, I believe I have provided a fluent and accurate text; for those who already know *Beowulf* in its original language, I hope I can offer a kind of reading of the poem at close range in the form of a translation, a record of the poem's effect on me, and an account of my sense of its context and meaning. Like most readers of *Beowulf*, I have often been struck by the many ways translations of the poem fail to capture its peculiar beauty. My own work, I know well, does little better, but I hope my love for the poem has not been entirely unrequited, and that some sense of the *Beowulf* I have read and continue to read with such pleasure is conveyed in my work.

The supporting texts were chosen to illustrate the poem's background and context, but since the date and place of composition of *Beowulf* are unknown and the subject of much debate, and the critical history of the poem has linked it to both pagan Germanic and Latin Christian sources, I have felt free to include works of various kinds and dates: analogues from Old Norse and Latin, poems in Old English, references in Latin chronicles to characters appearing in the poem, letters from an eighth-century English missionary saint, and sermons from the turn of the millennium. All are meant to suggest, sometimes obliquely, the richness of the cultural milieu in which *Beowulf*, the story and the text, circulated.

A study guide for *Beowulf* can be found online at www.tulane.edu/~beowulf.

New Orleans

Introduction

Only one copy of the Old English poem which modern editors call *Beowulf* has survived, and it is likely that it has survived only by accident. A manuscript containing *Beowulf* and a small collection of other texts – a poetic treatment of the deuterocanonical Old Testament story of Judith, a prose life of St. Christopher, and two treatises of fantastical geography now known as *The Wonders of the East* and *Alexander's Letter to Aristotle* – was copied by two scribes, probably in the decade after 1000, in a monastic center somewhere in the south of England. It is an eclectic anthology containing prose and verse, hagiography and secular heroism, oriental and biblical and Germanic lore; its contents baffle our modern expectations of genre. The texts are from different sources, and the prose pieces are all translations of Latin works. What unites them, apparently, is an interest in monsters and marvels, faraway places and long-distant ages, and fantastic beings of extraordinary size; Andrew Orchard has described its contents as "Pride and Prodigies." Whatever its original purpose or audience, the book was abandoned to obscurity in the centuries after the Norman Conquest and its later history is unknown until 1563, when the English antiquary Laurence Nowell signed his name on the first page of *St. Christopher*. The Nowell Codex, as it is sometimes called, later came into the library of the collector Sir Robert Cotton (1571-1631); the present-day shelfmark of the manuscript (British Library MS Cotton Vitellius A. xv) recalls the arrangement of Cotton's library, in which books were stored in shelves surmounted by busts of Roman emperors. Cotton bound the manuscript with an unrelated 12th-century copy of Augustine's *Soliloquies* and other works. In 1731, while Cotton's collection was stored at Ashburnam House in Westminster awaiting donation to the future British Museum, a disastrous fire damaged or destroyed hundreds of volumes and nearly consumed the *Beowulf* manuscript as well (the damage to the library is surveyed by Prescott 1997 and 1998).

Apart from an entry in an early manuscript catalogue by Humphrey Wanley in 1705, it was not until the end of the 18th century that scholars began to appreciate the contents of this scorched and charred manuscript. The romantic nationalism of the time expected – indeed, more or less required – a national epic analogous to the Greek *Iliad* at the beginning of every nation's literature. The French had the *Chanson de Roland*, the Germans the *Nibelungenlied*; *Beowulf*, the earliest full-length heroic poem in any Germanic language, was claimed by the English (because of its language), Danes (because of its subject), and Germans (because of its setting in the pre-Christian north). The first printed notice of the poem, along with some badly-translated passages, was in Sharon Turner's second edition of his *History of the Anglo-Saxons* (1805), where it is called "a composition most curious and important.... [I]t may be called an Anglo-Saxon epic poem." In 1787 a copyist who was probably commissioned by the scholar Grímur Thorkelin, an Icelander in the service of Denmark, made a transcription of the poem; later Thorkelin himself went to the British Library to make another (see Kiernan, *Thorkelin Transcripts*). Like Turner, Thorkelin's inability to read Old English did not prevent him from admiring *Beowulf*. He was convinced that the poem was originally composed in Danish, though surviving in an English translation, and that its author had been an eyewitness to the funeral of the hero Beowulf, which he placed in the year 340 (Bjork, "Thorkelin's Preface"). Thorkelin's transcripts are still invaluable evidence for many readings now lost from the crumbling edges of the manuscript's pages. His first edition of the poem (with a Latin translation) in 1815, however, was a task somewhat beyond his powers, and was quickly superseded by other and better editions, including that of J. M. Kemble in 1833, Benjamin Thorpe in 1855, and C. W. M. Grein in 1857. The poem was translated into Danish verse by N. F. S. Gruntvig in 1820, and long passages appeared in English in J. J. Conybeare's *Illustrations of Anglo-Saxon Poetry* in 1826; a full English prose translation was produced by J. M. Kemble in 1837. In this way the poem gradually reached a wider audience; eventually more reliable scholarly editions and more accurate translations became available. The standard modern edition of the poem is that of Friedrich Klaeber, which appeared in several revisions between 1922 and 1950.

Beowulf Between Myth and History

> *If all time is eternally present*
> *All time is unredeemable.*

Although like other Old English poems *Beowulf* is copied in its manuscript as prose, from margin to margin, the poem consists of 3,182 extant lines of alliterative verse, divided into 43 numbered sections of varying length with an unnumbered prologue. Its language is allusive and embellished and its plot digressive and complex, but its story is relatively straightforward. The Danish king Hrothgar, descendant of the legendary Scyld, has built a magnificent hall Heorot, but the hall is invaded night after night by a marauding beast or demon named Grendel (sec. I-II). A young warrior of the tribe of the Geats named Beowulf hears of Hrothgar's troubles and comes to his rescue; after a series of challenges and boasts he faces the monster unarmed, and tears off his arm in a wild wrestling match (III-XII). Celebration is lively but short-lived; the next night the monster's mother attacks the hall in revenge for the death of her son, killing one of Hrothgar's most trusted retainers (XIII-XIX). Undaunted, Beowulf follows her tracks to an underwater lair and after a difficult fight kills her with an extraordinary sword which he finds in her cave (XX-XXIII). He returns to the Danish hall to much praise, celebration, and giftgiving; soon he returns to his native land and recounts his adventures to his own king and uncle Hygelac (XXIV-XXXI).

Fifty years are passed over in a few verses, and Beowulf is now himself an aged king. His kingdom is attacked by a dragon who has been roused from his underground barrow when his horde of ancient treasure is plundered (XXXII-XXXIII). Beowulf, although old, ventures forth to fight the dragon, armed with a fireproof shield and accompanied by a troop of men. His companions flee in terror, but a young warrior named Wiglaf comes to the king's aid; together they kill the dragon, but in the fight Beowulf is mortally wounded (XXXIV-XXXVIII). He dies beside the heap of treasure he has won for his nation; amid gloomy predictions of the impending downfall of the Geats, he is buried with mourning and sad ceremony (XXXIX-XLIII).

In such bare outline, the story has an almost archetypal symmetry and simplicity, and scholars have not failed to notice parallels between the hero's combats and various elements of northern folklore and world mythology.[1] The story of Beowulf in Denmark – a young man of great strength who kills a monster in single combat without the aid of weapons – conforms to the pattern of a traditional folktale identified by Friedrich Panzer in 1910 as the "Bear's Son Tale" or "The Three Stolen Princesses" (see also Stitt). Although Grendel is described by the narrator as a demonic descendant of Cain, his closest narrative relatives are the trolls which inhabit Scandinavian folktales (see Appendix B.1) such as the *draugr*, a kind of restless and violent zombie. The dragon, on the other hand, may be an emblem of Satan in the Biblical Book of Revelation, but in this poem he acts more like a creature of the natural world, malevolent but not necessarily demonic; he is not called the "foe of mankind" (164) or the "ancient adversary" (1776), as Grendel is. The *Cotton Maxims*, a collection of Old English proverbs about the nature of the world, state that "A dragon will be in his barrow, ancient and proud in his treasures" (Dobbie 55-7, line 26). A similar sort of dragon appears in the narrative of Danish historian Saxo Grammaticus (Appendix B.2), and the slaying of a dragon is an ancient motif (though adapted in *Beowulf* to a particular and tragic purpose) of which the poem's own account of Sigemund (875-98) is both analogue and foreshadowing. The story of Beowulf follows the narrative patterns of a folktale: a hero who quests and fights in isolation from friends and family, fabulous battles against monstrous foes, the theme of a

---

1   Good examples of this approach can be found in Page and Cassidy, Nagler, Damico, Barnes (with a response by Rosenberg); general reflections may be found in Niles, "Myth and History."

young man who was thought to be lazy (lines 2183-89) but later becomes a mighty hero, even the concatenation of three challenges in ascending order of difficulty. The fabulous outlines of the story equally recall the broad brushstrokes of myth: the mighty Beowulf may be a distant echo of Thor (Lerer); his descent into the mere may dimly depict a shamanistic initiation (Gloseki 152-210); his death may contain a hint of Ragnarok, the northern apocalypse (Dronke). *Beowulf*, then, appears to be a reflex of an ancient and universal plot.

Certainly the ultimate roots of the story, unknown and probably unknowable, are deep in the common soil of all story-telling, in the archetypal story Joseph Campbell (using a term borrowed from James Joyce) has called the 'monomyth.'[1] Joseph Fontenrose has pointed out that the hero's struggles have something in common even with the battles of Hercules or Theseus or Apollo. Such mythic and folkloric analogues are generally strongest, however, in inverse proportion to the clarity with which the details of the story are remembered; in the mythopoeic night, all cats are gray. Whatever its underlying structural patterns, *Beowulf* is neither myth nor folktale; its stories of dragon-slaying and nocturnal struggles are set against a complex background of legendary history. The action of the poem unfolds on a roughly-recognizable map of Scandinavia: Hrothgar's hall Heorot has been plausibly placed in the village of Lejre on the Danish island of Zealand, and we may tentatively identify Beowulf's tribe of Geats with the historical Gautar of Southern Sweden.[2] The mythical figure of Scyld soon yields to the historical figure of Hrothgar, and a number of the poem's characters – among them Heremod, Hrothgar, Ingeld and Hygelac – are mentioned in other sources and were

1 Campbell's description of "the nuclear unit of the monomyth" might well be applied to much of story line of *Beowulf*: "A hero ventures forth from the world of common day into a region of supernatural wonder: fabulous forces are there encountered and a decisive victory is won: the hero comes back from this mysterious adventure with the power to bestow boons on his fellow man (30)."

2 Historical background may be found in Chambers; the identity of the Geats is discussed in Malone and Farrell, but Leake argues that they are instead to be identified with the legendary Getae, a tribe of no fixed geographical abode.

certainly regarded as figures of history rather than fable. The Frankish historian Gregory of Tours (d. 594) mentions the disastrous raid of Hygelac (whom he calls Chlochilaicus and describes as a Danish king) and dates it around the year 520 (see Appendix A.1). And like its characters and setting, the concerns of the poem are historical. Behind the drama of autonomous and isolated hand-to-hand encounters against monstrous adversaries, *Beowulf* is an intensely political poem; the poet is as intrigued by Danish diplomacy and the bitter feud between the Geats and Swedes as he is by the hero's battles. Kingdoms and successions, alliances and truces, loyalties and the tragically transient stability of heroic society are the poem's somber subtext, a theme traced less in the clashes of the battlefield than in the patterns of marriage and kin, in stories remembered and retold, in allusion and digression and pointed foreshadowing.

Whatever historical interests may be found in *Beowulf*, however, it is difficult to read the poem with anything like a modern expectation of historical accuracy. Like many medieval works, *Beowulf* is frustratingly ambivalent — it is not quite mythical enough to be read apart from the history it purports to contain, nor historical enough to furnish clear evidence for the past it poetically recreates. The action of the poem is set in a somewhat vague heroic *geardagum* ("bygone days," line 1), an age not meant to be counted on a calendar, nor its kingdoms and tribes marked on a map; nor, undoubtedly, were the monstrous races of Grendels and dragons so clearly distinct in the poet's mind from the real dangers of the real world just beyond the margins of the known. While medieval authors certainly made distinctions between *historia* and *fabula*, the boundaries between these terms are not nearly as impermeable as those of our modern categories "history" and "fable"; this unruly poem, like the manuscript in which it survives, does not stay within the framework of our generic expectations. Moreover, the poem itself is a monumental exercise of the historical imagination, poetically re-creating a past which is itself multilayered and temporally complex. Inside the story a sense of time past and time passing is evoked by reference to earlier events such as the reign of Heremod and the death of Herebeald, and by forecast of future ones such as the burning of Heorot or the conquest of the Geats (the scene in which Wealhtheow gives Beowulf a necklace, lines 1192-1214, is a striking instance of the poem's historical depth of field) and by the carefully allusive interweaving of historical and political concerns into the main plot, suggesting the context in which the hero's exploits occur and the consequences they entail.[1] In many respects the poem already contains its own background and foreground, a fictionalized matrix of past and present within the text; our modern efforts to explain *Beowulf*'s origins or context or even to place the hero's actions into some perspective can only mimic or mirror the poem's own contextualizing impulses. Fred C. Robinson has noted,

> the average reader of English literature often comes to *Beowulf* with the naive expectation that reading this early poem will bring him face to face with the collective unconscious of English culture, will allow him to experience at first hand what is primordial, elemental and primitively powerful in it. But the experience is more complex than that, for the Anglo-Saxons who wrote and read *Beowulf* were themselves exploring the unconscious of their culture by returning to dark beginnings in an age long antecedent to theirs. If reading *Beowulf* is an exploration of our primal selves, we are led on that exploration by a refined, reflective, Christian Anglo-Saxon poet whose curiosity about the remote origins of his people is perhaps not unlike our own (*"Beowulf"* 142-3).

The poet looks back on a world long vanished, imaginatively bringing its textures and values to life; his own complex sense of the past prevents us from reading his work as either a transhistorical and transcultural fragment of primordial myth or a transparent window onto the cultural or material conditions of a lost heroic age.

---

1   The poem's historical interests are examined by Hanning, Frank "Sense of History," Dean, and Helterman.

This interweaving of legendary history and fabulous tales in *Beowulf*, the political intrigues of battles, feuds, marriages, and successions and the archetypal combat of a solitary hero against a supernatural foe, has caused much critical anxiety throughout the history of *Beowulf* studies. Klaeber, the editor of the standard edition, echoed the sentiments of most of his contemporaries when he lamented that the poet's poor taste had caused him to spend so much time on childish matters like monsters and dragons and less on the more interesting and dignified subjects of wars and alliances: "we may well regret that those subjects of intensely absorbing interest play only a minor part in our epic, having to serve as a foil to a story which in itself is of decidedly inferior weight" (lv). J. R. R. Tolkien's 1936 essay, "*Beowulf*: the Monsters and the Critics," is usually credited with re-establishing the fabulous elements and heroic combats at the center of the modern reader's appreciation of the poem. In many respects, however, the separation of the poem into "mythical" and "historical" elements is a false dichotomy. If, as many modern scholars maintain, it is the business of myth to condense and contain the most fundamental sources of cultural tension, those areas in which the self and the world are in greatest friction, and to validate current ideologies by dramatizing them and retrojecting their contours into the past, then the hero's "mythic" combats equally reflect an interest in the social order, an authorization of certain cultural conditions and practices; the placing of these combats in a context of legendary history indicates the poem's desire to examine these cultural tensions in relation to the passage of time. Beowulf's fabulous adversaries perform strenuous cultural work: Grendel can be regarded as a monstrous embodiment of the principle of fratricide, his mother a manifestation of the harsh economy of revenge and the even darker powers of the primal claims of tribal kinship against the masculine world of the warrior band or comitatus, and the dragon a kind of perverse king hoarding his wealth in a dark anti-hall. Without detracting from the poet's delight in the physical reality of Beowulf's battles – his depictions are richly textured, from the terror of Grendel's fiery eyes to the coiling and belching of the dragon – each combat can be read as a dramatized locus of cultural anxiety, pitting the hero against some aspect of his own society drawn in grotesque caricature. The monsters outside the hall are projections of the evils within the hall – the implied treachery of Hrothulf (hinted in lines 1013-19 and 1163-65, though not all scholars have read them so), the remembered treachery of Unferth, the predicted treachery of Ingeld, the fatal treachery of Beowulf's cowardly retainers. These battles against the inhuman forces of destruction outside the hall, no matter how praiseworthy and heroic, however, do nothing to prevent the blossoming and flourishing of all-too-human evil within the hall. The order that is restored by the slaying of Grendel and his mother is not permanent, and the destruction of the dragon requires the death of Beowulf himself, a loss which appears to inaugurate the destruction of his whole nation. As Joyce Lionarons has noted, the "mythic" elements of *Beowulf* portray the labor required to create and sustain a civilized social order, threatened within and without by a culture of violence; its monsters are narrative manifestations of the forces of disorder and chaos which an orderly society must hold at bay but which will, in the dark world of the poem, inevitably triumph. This sad triumph is made possible by the debilitating effects of the passage of time and the failure of the social order successfully to channel the human passions. In this sense the poem springs, quite precisely, from the intersection of myth and history, the individual psyche and its cultural milieu, the desire to authorize the present by means of the past – in effect denying the passage of time – and the necessity of accepting the inevitable contingency and loss such passing brings.

Beowulf Between Song and Text

> *Words, after speech, reach*
> *Into the silence. Only by the form, the pattern,*
> *Can words or music reach*
> *The stillness, as a Chinese jar still*
> *Moves perpetually in its stillness.*

Both the ultimate and the proximate origins of *Beowulf* are unknown. Most scholars assume that the surviving manuscript is a copy of an earlier written text, and is probably the last in a long chain of copies.[1] Moreover, the poem begins with the assumption that we are hearing a familiar story, or a least a story from a familiar milieu: "We have heard of the glory ... of the folk-kings of the spear-Danes," the poet asserts, and his cryptic allusions throughout the poem suggest that his audience was already familiar with a larger repertoire of songs and stories of kings and heroes. A poem such as *Widsith* (Appendix A.6) assumes that heroic history was considered a fit subject for secular entertainment, and a surviving fragment of a poem about the fight at Finnesburh (Appendix A.5) proves that at least some Anglo-Saxons had heard stories like the ones in *Beowulf;* the complaint of Alcuin (Appendix A.3) indicates that even churchmen enjoyed stories about the adventures of ancient heroes like Ingeld. In the poem itself we are given several scenes of poetic entertainment – a poet sings of the wonders of creation (90-8), Beowulf is praised by songs about Sigemund (867-915), the Danes are entertained by a story of Finn and Hengest (1065-1160) – and it is often assumed that such scenes reflect the real circumstances of the composition and reception of *Beowulf:* the poem originated as an oral performance rather than a text. The poem begins *Hwæt, we ... gefrunon* (in the present translation, "Listen! We have heard" – the opening word is a call for attention), and always remains firmly in the realm of listening and hearing rather than reading and writing. When

---

1   A notable dissenter from this scholarly consensus is Kevin Kiernan, *'Beowulf' and the 'Beowulf' Manuscript.*

the narrator affirms the truth of his story he uses expressions such as "I have never heard" (38, 1011, etc.) or "as I have heard" (74, 838, etc.), rather than, as later medieval narrators might say, "as books tell us" or "as my *auctor* alleges"; this is a poem of fame and familiar story, with no indication that the narrator relies on written documents or regards them as the bearers of truth about the past.

The practice of oral poetry in early medieval cultures is naturally invisible; all surviving evidence is in writing. Scholars have analyzed the repetitions in Homeric and other bodies of early verse, however, and made field studies of oral-traditional poetry performed by singers of traditional poetry in the early twentieth century, and these have offered models and analogies for imagining the practice of the Anglo-Saxon scop or singer-poet. They suggest that he would have worked from a collection of traditional stories improvised in performance from a repertoire of formulaic elements, groups of words which met the demands of meter and sense and could be used and reused according to the needs of the poem.[1] Traditional phrases and descriptive tags would contribute to the singing of a tale, and recurring scenes and motifs (approaching the hall, donning armor, the threat of battle, etc.) could be added in variable combinations at each performance; the core of the story and elements of poetic style remained the same but the surface changed with each new telling. Such a traditional method of oral composition, employing a collection of metrical formulae, stock scenes and narrative patterns, probably existed as part of the common heritage of the Germanic peoples, and the Angles and Saxons may have brought songs of kings and heroes to Britain from their continental homeland. Such traditional stories, told and retold over centuries, may have contributed to both the narrative form and the diction of *Beowulf* as it survives today.

---

1   The literature on the "oral-formulaic" theory is vast: among the most useful introductions to methods and problems are Lord, Magoun "Oral-Formulaic Character," Creed, Calder, and the many works of John Miles Foley, including "Tradition and the Collective Talent," *Theory of Oral Composition*, *Oral-Formulaic Theory and Research*, and *"Texts That Speak."*

The expectation of striking originality from a work of art is a modern phenomenon; metrical formulae and narrative set-pieces were the building-blocks of traditional poetry, a highly-patterned language for a highly formal narrative style. A delight in recurrence-with-variation in language and story is one of the deepest aesthetic principles of Old English poetry, and many of the individual lines of *Beowulf* can be found repeated in the poem itself and in other Old English poems. The expression *weox under wolcnum* "grew under heaven" (literally, "under the clouds") in line 8 appears, with variations, in other poems and elsewhere in *Beowulf* (Grendel comes *wan under wolcnum* "pale under the clouds" in line 651; later we are told he *wod under wolcnum* "went under the clouds" 714; Hrothgar says that he *weold under wolcnum* "ruled under the clouds" in 1770). We can assume, then, that the formula "X *under wolcnum*" was one of the poet's ready-made metrical packages. Likewise the expression *ofer hronrade* "over the whale's-riding" (10) formed a metrically-correct periphrasis for "the sea," and it is found elsewhere in expressions such as "over the swan's-riding" and "over the sail-road" (*Beowulf* 1429) – the formula might be expressed as "*ofer* X-*rad*," with "X" variable according to mood, tone, and the needs of alliteration. The line introducing the hero's speech, *Beowulf maþelode, bearn Ecgþeowes* ("Beowulf spoke, son of Ecgtheow") is repeated in lines 529, 631, 957, 1383, 1473, 1651, 1817, 1999, and 2425, and a similar formula is used to introduce speeches of other characters (e.g., *Wiglaf maðelode, Weohstanes sunu* "Wiglaf spoke, son of Weohstan," lines 2862 and 3076). A modern reader must learn to hear such outright repetitions not as stylistic defects but rather as aspects of the traditional craft of the singer; in the hands of a good poet like the author of *Beowulf* such repeated formulae are not deployed unfeelingly or automatically according to some principle of compositional thrift, but are used to enhance and elaborate the poem's stately and formal art.

Recurring narrative moments such as sea-voyages, arrival at a hall, arming, or funeral obsequies could be crafted out of a stock of appropriate formulae and built according to a pattern of expected elements; these "themes" – the equivalent on the level of narrative of the formula on the level of diction – are used to produce an artful interaction between a particular moment in the poem and an audience's expectations.[1] Speech situations which are parallel in organization and narrative function, such as Beowulf's three introductory boasts in Denmark, are characterized by elaborate variation and differences in detail and effect; their recurrence establishes a kind of motif, elaborated in a slightly different register at each retelling. Francelia Clark has drawn attention to the fact that each recurrence of a repeated element in *Beowulf*, such as the mention of Hygelac's ill-fated raid on Frisia (reference to it appears in lines 1202-14, 2200-02, 2354-60, 2910-21, and possibly 2499-2507), generally offers new information and new emphasis in each re-telling; the amount of direct verbal repetition is dramatically small. Even Beowulf's re-telling of his own adventures (1999-2151) offers a number of striking new perspectives on the events we have already witnessed: we learn of Grendel's strange glove and Ingeld's predicted attack, and interestingly enough we do not hear anything about Unferth's verbal challenge to Beowulf. The whole structure of the poem offers a large-scale example of such a repeated motif, an old king supported by a young champion; here too it is recurrence-with-variation, the tension between structural similarity and narrative difference, that drives the poem's art and meaning.

The formulaic diction and narrative style of traditional poetry was "an instrument of enormous, and absolutely singular, sensitivity" (Foley, *Immanent Art* 193) which was employed even by thoroughly literate poets such as the author of the OE *Phoenix* (a verse translation of a Latin original) and the translators of the OE *Metrical Psalms*. The fact that such traditional diction is masterfully used in *Beowulf* is no certain indication of its origins as an oral performance – though the highly-polished craft of the poem is no argument against it either.[2] A theory of

---

1 Two classic studies of the theme in OE poetry are Greenfield, "Formulaic Expression" and Magoun, "Theme of the Beasts of Battle"; and see, more recently, Amodio's "Affective Criticism."

2 For discussion of this topic see Benson, "Literary Character," and Russom.

oral formulaic composition, however, though it helps us appreciate the artistry of a work like *Beowulf*, has interesting consequences for the scholar who seeks the origins, context, and meaning of the poem. The concept of "traditional poetry" tends to encourage a sense of a body of poetry without individual authorship or historical roots; it minimizes the role of individual intention and artistry in the creation of a given work. By blurring the boundary between tradition and the individual talent, the idea of oral composition complicates, if it does not altogether preclude, the discovery of a particular place and specific time for the production of a given work. Carol Braun Pasternak argues that readers of Old English poetry ought to consider the "implied tradition" rather than the "implied author" of a work. If *Beowulf* is simply condensed from the always-already-present tradition of oral Old English poetry, composed in formulae and inherited narrative building-blocks, then the specific circumstances of its creation are all but irrecoverable; a literary work in oral circulation is always new, recreated at each performance; in effect it has no history, no matter how ancient its traditional narrative or style may be.

Even if the ultimate roots of *Beowulf* are in performance, however, we can still seek its origins as a text. Writing fixes a literary work in a particular form – relatively speaking, for manuscript copies are subject to scribal alteration in the course of their transmission[1] – and this form should bear the marks of its context, whether linguistic or historical. Earlier critical opinion on the date of *Beowulf* placed the genesis of the poem in the late seventh or early eighth century, relatively early in Anglo-Saxon literary history. In 1982 a volume of essays on *The Dating of Beowulf* (edited by Colin Chase) offered a series of vigorous challenges to this received opinion, and since then scholars have drifted away from their earlier consensus. Though a growing number of critics have favored a later date (ninth or tenth century) for the poem's composition, the range of modern opinion is wide, and seems to be limited only by the

---

1 This fundamental fact of manuscript textuality is discussed by Sisam, "Authority of Old English Poetical Manuscripts," and O'Keeffe, *Visible Song*.

absolute limits of the poem's possible date, 520 (when Gregory of Tours says the raid of Hygelac took place) and c. 1000 (when the surviving manuscript was written). The dialect of the poem offers no indication of its origins: like most surviving works of Old English poetry, the language of *Beowulf* is largely late West-Saxon, with some element of Anglian (northern) vocabulary, a kind of poetic mixture not easily traced to one time or place. Moreover, Old English orthographic habits were somewhat fluid, and scribes might well have modernized and altered the dialect of an older poem in the course of their copying. The poem's meter, even if it derived from an inherited traditional practice, would have been relatively fixed when the poem was committed to writing, and various metrical-linguistic features (the use or avoidance of definite articles with certain forms of adjectives, the use of contracted or uncontracted forms of some words, and the distribution of certain metrical patterns) have been analyzed, most thoroughly in R. D. Fulk's *History of Old English Meter*, in the hopes of correlating their appearance in *Beowulf* to some chronology outside the poem. Such efforts have been strenuous but have remained inconclusive. As Ashley Crandell Amos argued in 1981, the reliance of formal poetic language on traditional diction and phrase, the uncertain nature of linguistic and metrical tests, and the limits of our knowledge of Old English dialect chronology all preclude certainty.[1]

Details of story and scene which might have been relatively fluid in performance would have been relatively fixed when the poem was written down, and these too might offer clues to the poem's context. Archaeological and sociological approaches to the dating of the poem, however, have been scarcely more fruitful than metrical and linguistic ones. The poem's material culture, its cups and swords and ships and halls, appears to reflect sixth- or seventh-century reality, but this may be deliberate archaism or poetic license on the part of the poet; in *Beowulf*,

---

1   Janet Bately also offers an important discussion of this topic. A general overview of the issues at stake in the controversy over the dating of *Beowulf* can be found in Liuzza, "On the Dating of *Beowulf*."

the antiquity of heirloom weapons is a large part of their value. Moreover, the poet's sense of material reality, unlike his sense of the social and moral order, is not particularly historical. He makes no distinction between the antique artifacts unearthed from the dragon's hoard – the poem's most ancient event – and the trappings of warriors like Beowulf himself. When it comes to material objects, everything for the poet is old: either old and bright, or old and rusty. From this we may infer that his descriptions of material objects are not to be trusted as a criterion for dating the poem. Similarly, the forms of social organization found in the poem are those, more or less, of all heroic poetry – a generous warrior-chief surrounded by a band of both loyal and treacherous retainers who fight for gold and glory; the poem's "lived reality" offers only vague indications of its origins. Most other aspects of the social world – economic dependency, labor and service, and perhaps most strikingly to the modern reader, romantic love – are outside the poet's interest. The historical allusions in *Beowulf* have also been mined for possible clues to the poem's context. An apparently gratuitous passage of praise for the continental king Offa (1931-62) was regarded by Dorothy Whitelock as possible evidence that the poem was composed in the late eighth-century court of the Mercian king of the same name (58-64); Sam Newton revives the theory that the poem's Wylfings (461) are a reference to the East Anglian royal line of Wuffings. The spectacular seventh-century ship burial found at Sutton Hoo in East Anglia in 1939 has often been linked to *Beowulf*, not just for the richness of its artifacts and its apparent blending of Christian and pagan symbols and customs, but for the connections it suggests between eastern England and southern Sweden.[1]

It may be argued that the casual nature of the poem's historical allusions implies a poet who expects his audience to recognize a whole array of characters, large and small, from northern legend, and may thus argue for a relatively earlier date, but the

---

[1] A general review of archaeological approaches to the poem is found in Hills. On Sutton Hoo in particular see Evans, Bruce-Mitford, Carver, and the essays in Farrell and Neuman de Vegvar; an elegant caution is sounded by Frank, "*Beowulf* and Sutton Hoo."

extent of Anglo-Saxon knowledge of such matters is not really known. Indeed the general setting and interest of the poem needs some explanation: any opinion on the date of *Beowulf* must account for the oddity of an English poem so peculiarly sympathetic to the Danes and their history, and so intimately interested in the details of the feuds of Scandinavian tribes, a pack of dark-age Hatfields and McCoys. Why did an English poet feel drawn to work this old material into such a powerful story?

Relations between the Anglo-Saxons and the northern continent were complex at all periods in early English history. On the one hand the English endured a devastating century of Viking raids, beginning spectacularly with the sacking of the monastery of Lindisfarne in 793 and becoming earnest and incessant after 830. These raids destroyed churches, farms, and villages, disrupted ecclesiastical and intellectual life, and brought down nearly all the kings of England until peace was reached in the reign of Alfred the Great in the 890s; a later reminiscence of the terror of this period can be found in Ælfric's account of the martyrdom of King Edmund of East Anglia (Appendix D.2). A century later the utter demoralization of the nation in the face of another wave of northern invasion is movingly recorded in the *Anglo-Saxon Chronicle*; Wulfstan's *Sermo Lupi* considers the "Danes" (a generic name for all the northern tribes) a manifestation of the wrath of God (Appendix D.1). Dorothy Whitelock's 1951 *The Audience of Beowulf* argued that the poem's praise of the Danes could not have been written after the beginning of these Viking raids; no English audience, she believed, would have willingly listened to a poem celebrating the success of its enemies. R. I. Page, however, notes that it would be wrong to assume "an unsophisticated audience for a sophisticated poem" (113) – and in any case it must be said that the poem's praise of the Danes is, at best, qualified. More recently, scholars such as Nicholas Howe have argued that the Anglo-Saxons throughout their history maintained a lively interest in their pre-migration past, and kept a clear sense of the difference between the "Danes" of legend and the Danes who were their foes, neighbors, and compatriots.

The West-Saxon royal house traced its ancestry back through Woden to Scyld and Heremod, legendary Danish kings mentioned in *Beowulf* (Appendix A.4); apparently the Christian West-Saxon kings thought it worthwhile to note their descent from the same legendary heroes as the pagan Danes. When the English were converted to Christianity they sent missionaries to save the souls of their continental cousins (Appendix C.3), and virtuous pagans were held up as a rebuke to evil English kings (Appendix C.4). From Alfred's time onward the English lived and worked alongside Danish settlers in the eastern and northern regions of the country, known as the Danelaw, and such mixed Anglo-Danish milieus, where integration and assimilation coexisted with distinction, division, and hostility, may have fostered an interest in the legendary history of the northern tribes. On strictly historical grounds, then, there is no period in Anglo-Saxon history in which a poem like *Beowulf* might not have been written or appreciated.

There is a great deal at stake in these argument over the poem's origins. *Beowulf* will be read differently if it is imagined to have been produced in the time of Bede (c. 725) or Alfred (c. 880) or Ælfric (c. 1000). The earlier we think the poem to be, the more potentially authentic its historical material; a later *Beowulf*, more openly fictional, is a more complex work. Moreover, the more closely we try to assign a date and place of origin to the poem, the more closely we read it as a text, the intention of a single author or a reflection of a particular ideology, rather than a product of an oral poetic art whose composition may have been collective and whose traditional roots are beyond discovery. Unfortunately there is no consensus, and little hope for one, on the question of the poem's origins. In the final analysis it may be useful, as John Niles has suggested, to divide the question into two parts: "first, what is the probable origin of the discourse, the collective heroic verse-making tradition, that finds textual expression in *Beowulf*? And second, what is the probable origin of this individual poem, in the shape that we now have it?" ("Locating *Beowulf*" 91-2). In its most elementary structures the story of Beowulf may be as old as the migration to Britain itself. Recent works by James Earl and Craig Davis have noted how the poem asserts the dominance of the warrior band or comitatus, organized around the men's hall, over the tribe, organized around agriculture and family groups; it celebrates the warrior in heroic isolation – fighting for honor and fame rather than hearth and home, rewarded with riches by his kings and patrons but rootless, unmarried, without progeny. The shift in cultural balance from tribe to hall probably began before the migration period, but the migration to Britain reinforced a social order founded on military kingship and must have contributed to the force and popularity of stories like *Beowulf* which endorsed and celebrated this new social order. In the course of its telling and retelling the poem may have taken on something like its present shape, but constant refinement and adjustment must have been made throughout its growth: its story reimagined in light of later spiritual and historical concerns, allusive tributes to English kings like Offa woven into its narrative fabric, its adventures placed in the framework of Christian history and set against the background of the Scylding dynasty from which the West-Saxons claimed their descent. Finally, as the tradition of aristocratic oral storytelling was declining, replaced even in the vernacular by books of history and chronicle, the poem was committed to writing (Niles, "Oral Poetry Acts"). *Beowulf* may thus reflect the interests of several different eras, its traditional materials coalescing into a rough form before being shaped by the hand of its final author; it may respond to diverse moments of cultural crisis and triumph in early and later Anglo-Saxon society, whether the secularized aristocratic monasteries of Bede's day (as Patrick Wormald suggests) or the nation-building of Athelstan or the reign of Æthelred "the Unready" where stories of generous and noble heroes like Beowulf may have served as a kind of "invention of tradition" (in Eric Hobsbawm's phrase) for the demoralized English nation in the face of Danish attack. In each case the poem's force derives from its projecting into the past of values and attitudes sought in the present, but the values sought in the poem may have been different from one age to the next, from one reader to another.

Obscure in its origins, inarticulate in its purposes, enigmatic in its history: given these ambiguities, and the poem's allusive complexity, is it possible to read *Beowulf* with modern expectations of unity and coherence? Can the various threads of the poem be gathered into a single pattern? When the poem was first read some scholars contended that it was a collection of 'lays' or *Lieder*; scholars such as Ludwig Ettmüller and Karl Müllenhoff were eager to separate *Beowulf* into different layers from different sources. Woven into the main narrative are numerous "digressions" which most early scholars regarded as structural flaws.[1] The stories of Finn and Sigemund, the long "sermon" of Hrothgar to the triumphant Beowulf (1700-84), the hero's verbal sparring with Unferth, the somewhat murky story of Thryth, even the prologue concerning Scyld Scefing, have all been regarded at one time or another as detachable parts of a composite structure, in need of explanation and apology. Others, such as Tolkien and Adrien Bonjour, resisted this diachronic view of the poem's structure and argued for the unity of the poem as it now stands; most modern critics assume that the poem should be read as a unified work, however elusive its principles of unity may sometimes be.[2] The poem's shaping aesthetic principles, as Jonathan Evans argues, do not derive from an Aristotelian emphasis on structure and closure; rather they give rise to a work which is episodic, digressive, and recursive. Edward B. Irving has described this as an "emotional" rather than a structural unity, "a unity based on the very fact of diversity" (193). Even the term "digression" may be misleading if it implies that the reader ought to expect a single narrative strand, with some dangling irrelevancies which are merely decorative or detachable from the main plot. It may be better to follow the lead of John Leyerle, who examined the complex "interlace" structure of the poem's interlocking motifs and stories and concluded that "there are no digressions in *Beowulf*"

---

1 See the survey of earlier scholarship by Shippey, and Bjork, "Digressions and Episodes."

2 But the desire to dissect the poem into its component parts did not vanish; F. P. Magoun wrote two articles ("*Beowulf* A" and "*Beowulf* B") arguing for the disunity of the poem, and Kenneth Sisam's *Structure of Beowulf* dismisses the idea that the poem is unified in any modern sense.

(13). Every piece of the poem can be read alongside every other piece as an adumbration or refraction of some larger theme: the story of Sigemund reflects on the relation of the heroic individual to his society; the story of Finn foregrounds the tragic insufficiency of marriages and truces to effect lasting peace; the prologue concerning Scyld Scefing sounds the first note of a repeated motif, the mystery of divine providence, and provides a long foreshadowing of the poem's melancholy conclusion. To say that the various parts of *Beowulf* work together towards an overarching effect, however, is not to say that it is entirely the product of one poet's mind or pen. Like an Anglo-Saxon church made from the salvaged stones of a Roman temple, the structure of *Beowulf* may reveal complex layers of source and context; built perhaps by many hands over many years but according to an ancient plan and with a single purpose, it is unified by use and time rather than pre-formed design.

Beowulf Between Court and Cloister

> ...both a new world
> and the old made explicit, understood
> in the completion of its partial ecstasy,
> the resolution of its partial horror.

Critics of Beowulf are divided on many issues, but none is more important than the significance of the poem's religious elements. Though it is still sometimes argued that the poem's origin and ethos are essentially pagan, with only a veneer of Christianity or an imperfect grasp of the principal tenets of the Christian faith,[1] Christine Fell pointedly observes that "Rome had been officially Christian only a couple of centuries before Pope Gregory sent his missionaries to the Anglo-Saxons yet we accept that these missionaries came with a full understanding of Christian teaching. We are curiously reluctant however to accept that within another couple of hundred years the Anglo-

---

1   See, for example, Moorman, Cherniss.

Saxon educated mind was equal in understanding and commitment" (14). Most critics agree that the heroic action of the
poem is thoroughly accommodated to a Christian paradigm;
they disagree, however, on the meaning and purpose of that
accommodation. Scholars such as Alan Cabaniss and M. B.
McNamee have argued that Beowulf, who gives his life for his
people, should be seen as a type of Christ, while others, most
notably Margaret Goldsmith, have read *Beowulf* as a condemnation of pagan pride, greed and violence. These two extreme
positions capture quite dramatically the dilemma caused by
what can be regarded as the poem's deliberate ambivalence:
Beowulf is a secular Christian poem about pagans which avoids
the easy alternatives of automatic condemnation or enthusiastic
anachronism. While early scholars tried to find a single source
for the poem's complex and peculiar texture – whether in pure
Germanic paganism or orthodox Augustinian Christianity –
more recent work recognizes that *Beowulf*, like the culture of
the Anglo-Saxons themselves, reflects a variety of interdepen-
dent and competing influences and attitudes, even a certain
tension inherent in the combination of biblical, patristic, secular
Latin, and popular Germanic material. The search for a single
"audience" of *Beowulf*, and with it a sense of a single meaning,
has given way to a recognition of a plurality of readers and
interests in Anglo-Saxon England.

The author of the poem (for the sake of argument, let us say
the person who was responsible for its commitment to parch-
ment) was certainly a Christian: the technology of writing in
the Anglo-Saxon period was almost entirely confined to
monastic scriptoria. The manuscript in which *Beowulf* is preserved contains a saint's legend and a versified Bible story.
Moreover the poet indicates a clear familiarity with the Bible
and expects the same from his audience – Grendel and his
mother are said to be descended from Cain (104-8; 1258-65; cf.
Genesis 4:8-16), and apocryphal Old Testament legend is alluded to in the story of the giants who perished in the flood
(1688-91).[1] Some of the details of Grendel's lair seem to derive

---

1 These legends, and the possibility of their being known among the Anglo-Saxons,
   are discussed by Mellinkoff.

from descriptions of Hell in the Old English homiletic tradition (see Appendix B.5). Words borrowed from Latin such as *candel* (1572), *gigant* "giant" (113, 1562), and *non* "the ninth hour" (1600) suggest an easy cohabitation between the heroic story and the vocabulary of the Church. The poem depicts a God who watches over history and secures even the safety of the Danes who do not know Him (14-18; 700-02; 1553), and the narrator laments the religious ignorance of his characters (183-88). Equally clearly, however, these characters are pagan — they practice cremation and burial with lavish treasure, foretell the future with auguries (204), make occasional and desperate sacrifice to their deities (recognized by the narrator as devils, 175-88), repeatedly stress their belief in fate, and cling to fame as the only afterlife. The narrator acknowledges that "they did not know the Lord God" (181).

This explicit admission appears only once, however; the paganism of the characters is otherwise presented in a curiously muted way. None of the more offensive pagan practices is mentioned explicitly. Characters speak of "the Lord" or "the Almighty," using terms which overlap with Christian epithets for God, and they never name any particular pagan deity; their natural piety is evident in the way they thank God for their victories and worry about having offended the Creator. The poet's Christianity neither sets itself against the paganism of his characters in a posture of condemnation (except in the one passage noted above) nor obscures his sense of their difference from his audience. There is no intrusive or anachronistic reference to Christian doctrine, nothing about Christ's mercy, the veneration of Mary, the loving self-sacrifice of the martyrs, the ascetic devotion of the desert fathers, or the miracles of the saints. There is, one might say, an Old Testament feeling about the poem's religiosity, appropriate for the kind of story it tells and the kind of world it represents, in which a somber and hidden King of Heaven battles his demonic foes through the power of such men as Beowulf. Thomas Hill argues that "the religious language of the poem reflects the religious knowledge of those patriarchs who lived before the covenants and the creation of Israel" (67-8); following Robert Kaske, he describes the poem's spiritual atmosphere as "Noachite." Even the "judgment of the righteous" to which Beowulf's soul goes (line 2820) can be found in the Old Testament book of Ecclesiastes 3:17: "I said in my heart, God will judge the righteous and the wicked, for he has appointed a time for every matter and for every work" (NRSV translation). The poem's religion is tailored to its heroic action and scene.

Though the paganism of Beowulf's world is downplayed, however, it is not denied; his age is connected to that of the audience but separated by the gulf of conversion as much as by the seas of migration. The religious atmosphere in *Beowulf* is an aspect of the author's sense of history, his appreciation that the past is different from yet prologue to the present, his exploration of the meaning of individual action in the framework of possibilities and limitations imposed by time and place. For some Anglo-Saxons no connection could be tolerated between the Christian present and the pagan past; the heroes of legend and history were unbaptized, unsaved, and unworthy of remembrance. Alcuin's caustic rebuke (Appendix A.3) indicates that, for at least one prominent churchman, tales of the pagan past were of no value whatsoever: we may lament the ignorance and sinfulness of our pagan forebears, but hardly celebrate or emulate their heroic deeds. Other Anglo-Saxons, such as the archbishop Wulfstan at the turn of the millennium, railed against paganism as a religious system (Appendix C.5) and sought to suppress its traces in folk customs or "superstitions" (Appendix C.6). As Larry Benson argues, however, there is evidence that not all Anglo-Saxons felt such automatic condemnation for the people who were, after all, their ancestors ("Pagan Coloring"). Theological speculation on the salvation of the "naturally good" pagans may have reached England from Ireland, as Charles Donahue has argued; this opens the possibility of imagining a kind of spiritual solidarity between the pagan past and the Christian present. Pope Gregory advised the missionaries to the English to make churches out of the shrines and temples of the heathens, and preserve their celebrations while changing their meaning (Appendix C.1); it is easy to imagine a poem like *Beowulf* arising from the same impulse to preserve the past while re-interpreting it in the light of a fuller revelation. The Anglo-Saxons managed to use their inherited traditional poetic modes to write verse saints' lives and biblical history; there must have been some impulse among them to salvage their old stories of kings and heroes as well. *Beowulf* seeks to explore both the bridges and the chasms between the pagan past and the Christian present; it teaches secular readers how to be pious, moral, and thoughtful about their own history, mindful of fame and courage while aware of its limitations and dangers. The poem is a Christian author's imaginative recreation of a pagan mentality, similar in some respects to Bede's eloquent simile of the sparrow, which he places in the mouth of one of King Edwin's retainers in the *Ecclesiastical History* I.30 (Appendix C.2) – the warm but fleeting pleasures of life are placed against the somber background of its ultimate meaninglessness, and without the hope of conversion or salvation all that is available to make sense of the world is courage, honor, and a stoical acceptance of one's fate, whether good or bad.

The question of the spiritual status of pagans is not avoided in *Beowulf*, but the possibility of any easy answer to the question is foreclosed in the poem's prologue. The fate of Scyld after his death, the narrator states, is unknown; the shift into the present tense insists on our own suspension of judgment:

Men do not know
how to say truly – not trusted counselors,
nor heroes under the heavens – who received that cargo
(50-52).

It could be said that the poem teaches us how to answer this question; the answer comes, mournfully triumphant and shadowed with a certain ambiguity, in lines 2817-20, at the death of Beowulf himself:

That was the last word of the old warrior,
his final thought before he chose the fire,
the hot surging flames – from his breast flew
his soul to seek the judgment of the righteous.

Later (line 3155) we are told of his funeral pyre, "Heaven swallowed the smoke." Is this a sign of divine favor? If so, it is a strikingly pagan one (see Appendix B.3).

Framed by these moments of metaphysical speculation, the action of *Beowulf* unfolds, and for most of the poem pains are taken to assert the distant yet connected relationship between the world of the pagan past and the Christian present, a connection heard most clearly in the repeated phrase "in those days of this life" (197, 790, 806). Clearly we are meant to admire the hero's actions and accept that his world and ours share certain norms for judging these actions. Susan Deskis has recently discussed the poem's numerous generalizing gnomic passages – the first begins at line 20 – which link the world of the characters to that of the audience; we are explicitly told to admire and imitate their heroic courage and restraint, and at the end of the poem we are told again that "it is proper" to praise the dead and celebrate their memory (3174). Hospitality, readiness for defense, generosity, vengeance, courage, loyalty, are all presented in the mirror of the poem as virtues which we, too, ought to practice, the common ground of pagan and Christian secular life. The rewards of heroic success – rings, cups, swords, horses, feasts, and above all fame – are held up, lovingly, for our admiration; they are the good things of this world, the just and desirable accoutrements of a warrior's achievements. Moreover, Beowulf fights with God's help against God's enemies; he does God's work and enjoys God's favor. Grendel is a "fiend from hell" (101) descended from the archcriminal Cain; he is "God's adversary" (786), he bears "God's anger" (711), and lives among "a host of devils" (756). It could hardly be more plain: Beowulf, whether he knows it or not, is on God's side.

For all that, however, Beowulf dies, and his death has none of the triumphant sanctification of the death of a martyr like King Edmund, or a Christian hero like Charlemagne's champion in the French *Chanson de Roland*. In the last third of the poem the dazzling picture of the hero's exploits grows darker and sadder; the glittering of treasure and the sweet songs of fame, all the values celebrated in the earlier episodes, are questioned and finally abandoned. The good things of the world and the virtues of heroic nobility they represent are, finally, not enough to save Beowulf's people from destruction. Linda Georgianna has eloquently described how in the poem's long conclusion the possibility of action gives way to the limitations of action; we may feel that even the possibility of telling a true tale is called into question as the narrative weaves in and out of the complex history of Swedish/Geatish relations, the story coils around on itself like a serpent, and the reader is lost in the narrative maze of a history that finally seems to consume even the Geats themselves. It might be that killing monstrous opponents is easier than building a stable society on the volatile values of gold, pride, and violent self-assertion; the world of Beowulf, however noble and attractive, is consumed by its own force, reduced to ashes by the long-smoldering history of raids, feuds, failed truces, and unpaid debts of honor. The so-called "Lay of the Last Survivor" marks the tone of the poem's long twilight as surely as Beowulf's stirring call to action "Sorrow not, wise one!" (1384-96) marks the tone of its earlier clear day:

> "Hold now, o thou earth, for heroes cannot,
> the wealth of men – Lo, from you long ago
> those good ones first obtained it! Death in war,
> and awful deadly harm have swept away
> all of my people who have passed from life,
> and left the joyful hall. Now have I none
> to bear the sword or burnish the bright cup,
> the precious vessel – all that host has fled.
> Now must the hardened helm of hammered gold
> be stripped of all its trim; the stewards sleep
> who should have tended to this battle-mask;
> so too this warrior's coat, which waited once
> the bite of iron over the crack of boards,
> molders like its owner. The coat of mail
> cannot travel widely with the war-chief,
> beside the heroes. Harp-joy have I none,
> no happy song; nor does the well-schooled hawk
> soar high throughout the hall, nor the swift horse
> stamp in the courtyards. Savage butchery
> has sent forth many of the race of men!" (2247-66)

The speech, pronounced over a hoard of treasure which has outlasted its owners and is being consigned to a burial mound, is an elegy for all the bright world of the poem's early sections, all the feasts, all the rewards, all the honor and fame, all now lost to the inevitability of decline and death. The lines recall the biblical injunction against "storing up treasures on earth" (Matthew 6:19) as well as the classical and Germanic tradition of lament for lost times; it is perhaps the poem's most characteristic moment, and would surely have been accepted even by a monastic audience as an expression of worldly wisdom. But the wisdom of *Beowulf* is only that – worldly – and that is its tragedy. At the end of the poem, after the hero has bravely met his fate, we are left with only the possibility of mourning and the commemoration of values we have been forced to recognize as inadequate. Beowulf, however brave, is unable to secure lasting peace and safety for his people even at the cost of his own life; his fame may endure but things look grim indeed for the rest of the Geats. *Beowulf* is a Christian poet's bittersweet elegy for the doomed heroic life, the futility of forging peace by the works of war, the instability of the bonds formed by gifts and exchange and inter-tribal marriage, and the impossibility of permanence in a world whose knowledge is tragically limited.

It would be wrong to imply, however, that the elegiac turn at the end of *Beowulf* is unexpected; even the brightest moments in the poem are set against a darkening awareness of the inevitable end of things. The poem's characteristic word is "until"; the poem continually looks forward from present happiness to future catastrophe. As soon as the great hall Heorot is raised the narrator says "it awaited hostile fires, / the surges of war" (82-3); when Hrothgar and his nephew Hrothulf are seated together we are told that "Heorot within was / filled with friends – no *false* treacheries / did the people of the Scyldings plot *at that time*" (1017-19, emphasis added). No happiness is permanent; uncertain and dangerous sleep must follow every feast. This theme of mutability is sounded throughout the poem, and so the ending of *Beowulf* seems inevitable rather than surprising. The career of the hero is depicted against a recognition that his triumph is limited and his defeat unavoidable; all the great works of the poem – the hall, the peace of Hrothgar's kingdom, the gifts of Wealhtheow, perhaps the fame of Beowulf himself – are doomed to fall. Because this realization never quite reaches the hero himself, the poem is suffused with intense and poignant dramatic irony. Characters in *Beowulf* clearly believe in the values of feuding, boasting, gift-giving, thaneship and peace-weaving, but they do so because their world, at least as the poem constructs it, offers no other choice.[1] As Eric Stanley has observed, the pagan heroic ideal is noble, but in comparison to the higher ideal of the Christian world, it is insufficient. At the moment of his death a martyr like Edmund of East Anglia renounces the heroic ideal in favor of a higher ideal whose exemplar is Christ; his reward is not only long-lasting fame, but eternal life.

And yet the poem's encroaching sense of the tragic limitations of the heroic life does not negate its recognition and celebration of its beauty and value. Whatever attitude the reader may take towards the poem must somehow respect both the overwhelming honor paid to Beowulf and his deeds and the overwhelming sadness with which the poem ends – the hero and his world are precious but precarious, noble but impossible. Our sympathetic suspension of judgment on the doomed world of Beowulf is never quite allowed to resolve itself; the poem's last word praises the hero for being *lofgeornost*, "most eager for fame," and even after nearly 3200 lines we cannot tell whether this is admiration or condemnation. Perhaps it is both. What else do the pagans have but fame? Richard Schrader (492) has pointed out the relevance to *Beowulf* of a haunting passage from Augustine's *City of God*: "since the Romans were in an earthly city...and a kingdom, not in heaven but in earth – not in the sphere of eternal life, but in the sphere of demise and succession, where the dead are succeeded by the dying – what else but glory should they love, by which they wished even after death to live in the mouths of their admirers? (*City of God* V:xiv)" But it is the poem *Beowulf* itself which creates and sustains the fame of the hero Beowulf. The Christian poet peers

---

1   A well-argued dissent from this critical consensus may be found in Hill, *Cultural World*.

into the pagan past, remembers, seeks connection, celebrates, questions, forswears, recollects, mourns, and finally, by his very participation in the continuum of poetic fame and praise, endorses the values of a lost heroic world.

Nor, in some ways, are the values of a work like Ælfric's Life of St Edmund – a text nearly contemporary with the manuscript of *Beowulf* – entirely antithetical to those of the poem. The Christian idea of heroic martyrdom is obviously quite different from the heroism of Beowulf's death – his last thoughts are of treasure and his people, not Christ and His angels – and the demonizing of the Danes in Ælfric's work stands in sharp contrast to the historical sympathy of the Beowulf-poet. Yet despite these obvious differences many similarities of form and content between the two works can be noted: the rhetoric of challenging speeches and formal promises, a concern with the afterlife (whether of reputation or of Christian salvation), a belief that fidelity to one's ideals is more important than victory or long life, a memorializing of the body, a pattern of reference to other stories of similar people who form a kind of constellation of figures of exemplary value. One work encourages praise of God and His saints, the other praise of secular deeds, heroic integrity, and a hero's sad but noble courage in the face of inevitable defeat, but both present noble figures from the past; both celebrate ideals which are worthy of emulation. Both draw on a similar stock of narrative themes and patterns to present a hero who is at the same time exemplary – available for emulation and contemporary appropriation – and historically rooted. In the end it is not impossible to imagine an Anglo-Saxon reader of a historical turn of mind, interested in stories worthy of remembrance and tales of kings and heroes of whatever nation and lineage, enjoying both works with attention and profit.

Beowulf Between Old and Modern English

> *Words strain,*
> *Crack and sometimes break, under the burden,*
> *Under the tension, slip, slide, perish,*
> *Decay with imprecision, will not stay in place,*
> *Will not stay still.*

Early in the poem the technique of a court poet is described:

> At times the king's thane,
> full of grand stories, mindful of songs,
> who remembered much, a great many
> of the old tales, found other words
> truly bound together; he began again
> to recite with skill the adventure of Beowulf
> adeptly tell an apt tale,
> and weave his words. (867–74)

To many readers the expressions "weaving" and "binding" suggest the structural principles of Old English verse. Each line of *Beowulf* consists of two half-lines containing (usually) two stressed syllables each and a varying number of unstressed syllables. The half-lines are linked by alliteration between one or both stressed syllables in the first half-line and the first stressed syllable of the second half-line; the most common pattern is aa:ax. Alliteration and stress held the lines of an Old English poem together, as meter and rhyme hold together the lines of a Shakespearean sonnet; they were not decorative, as they are in modern poetry, but necessary structural elements.

The opening lines of the poem in Old English illustrate this alliterative structure (the letters þ and ð represent the *th* sound in *thin* and *then*; sc in Old English is pronounced like *sh* in *ship* or *shield*; most words are accented on the first syllable):

> Hwæt! We Gardena   in geardagum,
> þeodcyninga   þrym gefrunon,
> hu ða æþelingas ellen fremedon.

Oft Scyld Scefing sceaþena þreatum,
monegum mægþum, meodosetla ofteah,
egsode eorlas. Syððan ærest wearð
feasceaft funden, he þæs frofre gebad,
weox under wolcnum, weorðmyndum þah,
oðþæt him æghwylc þara ymbsittendra
ofer hronrade hyran scolde,
gomban gyldan. Þæt wæs god cyning.

Though the passage of time has placed a thorough disguise upon it, Old English can still be recognized as the ancestor of Modern English. The most stable words through the intervening millennium have been the grammatical function-words: pronouns such as "we," "he," "him" and (despite orthographical differences) "that," prepositions such as "in" and "under" and "ofer" (Modern English "over" has changed its spelling, but is still pronounced the same), adverbs such as "hu" (how) and "oft." Other words are related to modern English words: *geardagum* is almost recognizable as "yore-days," i.e. "days of yore" and *wolcnum* survives as the archaic "welkin," i.e., "the heavens"; *funden* is not too far from the participial adjective "found," *hyran* is related to modern "hear" (though it means "obey" as well as "hear" in Old English), and *god* is only an older spelling of "good." Still other words, especially those in an aristocratic or poetic register, vanished from the language soon after the arrival of the Normans – *æþelingas* "noblemen," *ellen* "(deeds of) valor," *þrym* "glory," *frofre* "consolation."

Other important differences between Old and Modern English are found in word-order and inflection. A literal translation into Modern English (words in italics are grammatical particles required in Modern English but expressed by inflectional endings in Old English) clearly reveals this:

What! We *of the* Spear-Danes   in days-of-yore
of the people-kings   glory heard,
how the noblemen   valor did.
Often Scyld, son-of-Sceaf   from enemies' troops
from many tribes mead-benches took away

terrified nobles.   After first he was
destitute found,   he for-that comfort awaited,
grew under *the* skies,   *in* honors prospered
until *to* him each   *of the* surrounding ones
over *the* whale-riding   obey had to,
tribute yield.   That was *a* good king.

Old English tended to place verbs after direct objects (as in
lines 2, 3, 5, 7, 8, 11), while Modern English requires a fairly
strict Subject-Verb-Object order. Old English could express
grammatical relationships by inflection, but Modern English
require grammatical particles like prepositions and definite articles.

Other differences, however, reflect features peculiar to the
Old English poetic style.[1] One feature which is difficult to
reproduce in translation is the profusion of synonyms. Alliterative poetry required a number of different ways of saying the
same thing in different lines: depending on the meter, context,
and the necessity of making an alliterative link, a king might be
called a *cyning, dryhten, hyrde, ræswa, sigedryhten, þeodcyning, weard,*
or *wine.* Of course these words are not quite synonyms, any
more than their nearest equivalents in Modern English ("king,"
"lord," "shepherd," "prince," "victorious lord," "king of the people," "guardian," "friend"), but it is hard to avoid the suspicion
that their use in Old English is only partly determined by the
nuances of their connotations. At times metrical necessity must
have played a decisive role. The aged and ineffectual king
Hrothgar, for example, is called *helm Scyldinga* "protector of the
Scyldings" in lines 371, 456, and 1321, presumably not because
he is such a great protector of his people – under the circumstances, the title could at best be regarded as a courtesy – but
because *helm* alliterates with *Hrothgar.* But the elaboration of
synonyms is part of what gives the poem its notable formality,
another instance of the recurrence-with-variation that is the
essence of its art.

One of the most striking features of Old English poetry is

---

1   Good introductions to Old English poetic style are found in O'Keeffe, "Diction,"
    and Schaefer.

the restatement and repetition of subjects, predicates, and objects, the use of several different words, grammatically parallel, for the same referent. This "appositive style" (as Fred C. Robinson calls it), also known as "variation" (Brodeur), involves a kind of multiplication of reference: a simple example is the line "Beowulf spoke, son of Ecgtheow" (631 and elsewhere). Elsewhere its use is more complex; a grammatical analysis of the sentence beginning in line 4, for example, reveals a series of restatements with carefully-nuanced connotations:

> Often Scyld Scefing (1) took away meadbenches from troops of enemies, (2) terrified nobles from many tribes.

> After he first was found destitute, he (1) awaited comfort for that, (2) grew under the skies, (3) prospered in honors,

> until each of the surrounding tribes over the whale's-riding had to (1) obey him, (2) pay him tribute.

Variants can move from greater to lesser specificity (Scyld "took away meadbenches," that is, deprived his enemies of their halls, and by so doing he "terrified nobles from many tribes") or from lesser to greater (surrounding tribes had to "obey" him, which means they had to "pay him tribute"), or express a temporal progression (Scyld "awaits," "grows" and then "prospers") with a measure of compact efficiency. By presenting and re-presenting an action, or naming and re-naming a character, an object is set before the hearer and examined, as it were, from several different angles. Like the elaboration of synonyms, variation contributes to the poem's austere but voluptuous *gravitas*, its stately and deliberate tone which is always full without being florid; it is also responsible for some lively effects of tone and scene, and meaningful juxtapositions of thought and theme. When Beowulf and his troop arrive at Heorot, the clangor and gleam of their armor fairly leaps off the page:

> The road was stone-paved, the path led
> the men together. Their mail coats shone
> hard, hand-linked, bright rings of iron

rang out on their gear, when right to the hall
they went trooping in their terrible armor.
Sea-weary, they set their broad shields,
wondrously-hard boards, against the building's wall;
they sat on a bench — their byrnies rang out,
their soldiers' war-gear; their spears stood,
the gear of the seamen all together,
a gray forest of ash. That iron troop
was worthy of its weapons. (320-31)

Though their arrival raises the hope of rescue, the Geatish warriors are potentially a threat to the demoralized Danes, and so
the poet dwells on the fact that they are armed, an emphasis
achieved through both repetition — the word *searo* (here translated "gear") appears three times — and variation: the men are
described in "mail coats" and "rings of iron," "in their gear" and
"in their...armor," with "broad shields" and "wondrously-hard
boards," in "byrnies" (shirts of linked mail) and "war-gear," with
"spears" and "gear" and "a forest of ash." Variation often works
in a subtle way to expand the meaning of a given passage or
even, at times, the whole poem: when Beowulf is set upon by
Grendel, the poet says that

he remembered his mighty strength,
the ample gifts which God had given him,
and trusted the Almighty for mercy,
favor and support (1270-73)

The hero's strength and God's grace are brought together, presented by the poet's variation as two aspects of the same thing.
    The formality of the poem's compositional principles,
including the formulaic expressions and scenes mentioned
above, dictates a different approach to reading the poem — a
reader must not expect headlong forward movement, bold new
language, breathless narrative advance, idiosyncratic turns of
phrase, and all the sorts of effects one might enjoy in a modern
novel, or (particularly) a modern poem. Most handbooks of
rhetoric and composition define "style" as the characteristics of
individual expression; this is not at all what the term implies in

Old English poetry. Like a kind of traditional jazz in which musicians express their individuality within the relatively narrow confines of a standard repertoire and technique, the aim of the Anglo-Saxon poet's art was apparently the capable crafting of a complex and solid story out of traditional materials, the re-making of an old tale in a new register. Recognizing this principle leads to a different kind of reading for a work like *Beowulf*; since a translation is nothing but a long and very explicit reading of a text, embracing it has entailed an adjustment of my own language as well.

The brute fact of translation is that it is a reading which sets out, after all its slow and passionate attention to the text, to replace its original inspiration. Perhaps all readings secretly do this. Like a commentary that obliterates what it explicates, a translation is, in the end, a gesture towards an empty space where a text used to be. In addition, any translation is a gesture from one place to another. The history of *Beowulf* translation (see Appendix E) shows how literary taste and linguistic knowledge have often shaped the translator's style far more powerfully than any primary responsibility to the poem itself; or rather, our primary responses to the poem occur only within a framework of expectation given to us by the literary world in which we live and move. The distance from Conybeare's Miltonic translation of 1826 to Raffel's vivid and free rendering in 1963 is not measured solely by the increase in knowledge of Old English language and literary form; each translator tries to satisfy the literary expectations of his or her own time. Each reads, in that sense, a different *Beowulf*. Any translator, then, hoping to rescue the poem from the obscurity of the past, risks plunging it into the obscurity of the present, and in the act of recovering the past we often lose what we set out to save. Yet one of the meanings of the Latin word *translatio* is "metaphor," a way of suggesting similarity through connections between dissimilar objects, a leap of imagination across a chasm of difference. This is how I have tried to imagine this translation: not as a substitute or simulacrum, nor a re-creation or a replacement, but a suggestion. Without trying to make Old English out of Modern English, I have tried to re-imagine some of what I have felt to be the effects of the language of the poem. But I know too well that my translation is only a sketch.

As with any translation certain effects are lost in the pursuit of others; placing fluency and precision at the top of my list of goals I have had to abandon any hope of a wholesale sound-for-sound equivalence. In the course of working on the translation I came to believe that this was not altogether a bad thing. Certain features that are structurally important in Old English verse – regular alliteration and a strongly-felt caesura – are only decorative in most English poetry since the Renaissance, and are so alien to the sound of Modern English that they tend to strike the ear too heavily, overwhelming all other sound-effects and distracting the listener from the larger patterns of the poetry such as sentences and verse-paragraphs. I have tried to write in a poetic idiom that is analogous to, not imitative of, the character of the original; the end result has been a translation which is somewhat quieter than most others. Each verse has four stresses, a medial pause, and alliteration, but these are by no means as marked as they are in the original, and on rare occasion are foregone altogether. I have allowed myself considerable license in the matter of stress; I have of necessity used far more unstressed syllables than an Anglo-Saxon poet could have tolerated, but each line, when read at a normal tempo, has four beats (occasionally rising to 4½ or even 5, just as certain types of OE lines had a secondary stress within the four-beat structure). At moments of great formality in the poem the lines resolve into decasyllables, though not into pentameter; this has no parallel in the original – apart from a few hypermetrical lines the poem is written in a single meter throughout – but seemed appropriate for certain passages of quotation or verse-within-the-verse. I have also taken liberties with alliteration, using it suggestively rather than structurally, and allowing alliteration on an unstressed syllable, on the last stress of a line, and in various other ways not found in Old English. I have tried to retain various effects of poetic diction – the metaphorical compounds (the sea is the "whale's riding," a sword a "battle-flame," and so on), the strongly nominal quality of the variations and repetitions, the proliferation of synonyms and compounds, the slightly contorted syntax, and the use of formulaic descriptions and narrative markers – but I have not tried to reproduce OE word order faithfully, and within sentences I have often rearranged a half-line or even two to make a smoother sentence.

I have assumed a level of complexity in the syntax of the poem which is not always found in other readings and translations. Old English used the same word, *þonne* or *þa*, as both conjunction "then" and adverb "when," and often used a pair of them to introduce consecutive clauses; it is not always easy to tell whether a pair of clauses containing these words ought to be translated paratactically as a sequence of independent clauses or hypotactically as a complex sentence with a subordinate clause. An example is found in lines 126-9:

> *When* in the dim twilight just before dawn
> Grendel's warfare was made known to men,
> *then* lamentation was lifted up after the feasting,
> a great morning-sound.

In Old English, the correlative *þa* is used twice, but I have translated the first "when" and the second "then," and throughout the translation I have probably erred on the side of subordination and syntactical complexity.

I have also avoided archaic language, except in a few inevitable cases like *byrnie* "mail coat" and *liege* (actually, of course, a French loanword which postdates the poem by a century or more) and the untranslatable OE word for fate, *wyrd*. Some words in Old English were confined to poetry; these must has struck the listener as "poetic" or "archaic," and some gesture towards this effect seemed reasonable. To mimic the formal diction of the poem I have used a slightly more multisyllabic vocabulary and Latinate syntax at certain points. Still, in all, despite my goal of making a relatively smooth but precise translation, I have tried to leave a bit of the difficulty and sharpness of the syntax and style of the original poem, however alien it may seem at times to a modern reader, in the conviction that such difficulty and sharpness was part of the effect of *Beowulf* even on its Old English audience.

A Note on the Text

In addition to the damage caused by the fire of 1731, the text of *Beowulf* presents many readings which are difficult for an editor; the poem's long history of emendation and supplementation is ably detailed by Birte Kelly. A number of lines are illegible, especially on folios 182 (lines 2207-50) and 201 (lines 3121-82); in many other places the scribes have apparently miscopied words, and modern editors have had to guess at what they meant to write. Elsewhere words and even lines are apparently omitted; in other places there are words which seem to have been copied correctly but whose meanings are unknown. For the most part I have followed the text of Klaeber, though I have ignored some of his emendations when I thought the manuscript reading or the suggestions of other scholars made better sense. I have adopted many though by no means all of the emendations and explanations for retained manuscript readings found in Bruce Mitchell and Fred C. Robinson's 1998 edition, which came to hand as this translation was being readied for the press, and have taken some advantage of their excellent notes and explanatory glosses. The paragraphing and to some extent the punctuation of the translation, however, tend to follow the lead of earlier editors. The frequent paragraph breaks and fairly full punctuation are meant as a convenience to the reader and part of the translator's license, and should not be taken too seriously; they are editorial, not authorial or even scribal. In the translation I have made rather more use of the dash than is commonly allowed in polite society; this is meant to accommodate the numerous parenthetical asides found in the Old English. In the manuscript punctuation is by a single dot, usually at the end of a verse, and has little relationship to the syntax and rhetorical structure of the poem's sentences; small capital letters mark the beginnings of paragraphs, nearly all of which are at major turning points in the narrative. This sparse punctuation, not at all unusual in Old English poetry, forces the audience to work out syntactical relationships for itself; in the translation I have done much of this work for the reader, but it ought to be remembered that it is the translator's opinion, not the author's.

London, British Library, MS Cotton Vitellius A.xv, fol. 129r
Beowulf, lines 1–21.

BEOWULF

PROLOGUE

Listen!
　　We have heard of the glory in bygone days
of the folk-kings of the spear-Danes,[1]
how those noble lords did lofty deeds.
　　Often Scyld Scefing[2] seized the mead-benches
from many tribes, troops of enemies,   5
struck fear into earls. Though he first was
found a waif, he awaited solace for that —
he grew under heaven and prospered in honor
until every one of the encircling nations
over the whale's-riding[3] had to obey him,   10
grant him tribute. That was a good king!
A boy was later born to him,
young in the courts, whom God sent
as a solace to the people — He saw their need,
the dire distress they had endured, lordless,   15
for such a long time. The Lord of Life,
Wielder of Glory, gave him worldly honor;
Beowulf,[4] the son of Scyld, was renowned,
his fame spread wide in Scandinavian lands.
Thus should a young man bring about good   20
with pious gifts from his father's possessions,
so that later in life loyal comrades
will stand beside him when war comes,
the people will support him — with praiseworthy deeds
a man will prosper among any people.   25
　　Scyld passed away at his appointed hour,
the mighty lord went into the Lord's keeping;

1　The Danes are described by many different epithets in the poem; see the *Glossary of Proper Names* for further instances.

2　The name means "Shield, Son of Sheaf (i.e., of grain)." The mysterious origins of Scyld, who seems to arrive providentially from nowhere and is returned to the sea after his death, have occasioned much critical speculation.

3　A condensed descriptive image of the sea – the riding-place of whales. Elsewhere the sea is the "gannet's bath" and the "swan's riding."

4　Not the monster-slaying hero of the title, but an early Danish king. Many scholars argue that the original name was *Beow.*

they bore him down to the brimming sea,
his dear comrades, as he himself had commanded
30   while the friend of the Scyldings[1] wielded speech —
that dear land-ruler had long held power.
In the harbor stood a ring-prowed ship,
icy, outbound, a nobleman's vessel;
there they laid down their dear lord,
35   dispenser of rings, in the bosom of the ship,
glorious, by the mast. There were many treasures
loaded there, adornments from distant lands;
I have never heard of a more lovely ship
bedecked with battle-weapons and war-gear,
40   blades and byrnies;[2] in its bosom lay
many treasures, which were to travel
far with him into the keeping of the flood.
With no fewer gifts did they furnish him there,
the wealth of nations, than those did who
45   at his beginning first sent him forth
alone over the waves while still a small child.[3]
Then they set a golden ensign
high over his head, and let the waves have him,
gave him to the Deep with grieving spirits,
50   mournful in mind. Men do not know
how to say truly — not trusted counselors,
nor heroes under the heavens — who received that cargo.

I

Then Beowulf Scylding, beloved king,
was famous in the strongholds of his folk
55   for a long while — his father having passed away,
a lord from earth — until after him arose
the great Healfdene, who held the glorious Scyldings

---

1   The Scyldings are the Danes, "sons of Scyld."
2   A "byrnie" is a coat of ring-mail.
3   Scyld was found destitute – this statement is an example of *litotes*, or ironic under-
    statement, not uncommon in Anglo-Saxon poetry.

all his life, ancient and fierce in battle.
Four children, all counted up,
were born to that bold leader of hosts: 60
Heorogar, Hrothgar, and Halga the Good,
I heard that ... was Onela's queen,[1]
dear bedfellow of the Battle-Scylfing.
        Then success in war was given to Hrothgar,
honor in battle, so that his beloved kinsmen   65
eagerly served him, until the young soldiers grew
into a mighty troop of men. It came to his mind
that he should order a hall-building,
have men make a great mead-house
which the sons of men should remember forever,[2]   70
and there inside he would share everything
with young and old that God had given him,
except for the common land and the lives of men.
Then the work, as I've heard, was widely proclaimed
to many nations throughout this middle-earth,   75
to come adorn the folk-stead. It came to pass
swiftly among men, and it was soon ready,
the greatest of halls; he gave it the name "Heorot",[3]
he who ruled widely with his words.
He remembered his boast; he gave out rings,   80
treasure at table. The hall towered
high and horn-gabled — it awaited hostile fires,
the surges of war; it was not yet long
before the sword-hate of sworn in-laws
should arise after ruthless violence.[4]   85
        A bold demon who waited in darkness

---

1   A name is missing from the manuscript here; it has been conjectured from parallel
    sources that it should be Yrse, or Ursula. The Swedish ("Scylfing") king Onela
    appears later in the story, causing much distress to Beowulf's nation.
2   Or "a greater meadhall / than the sons of men had ever heard of." The reading
    adopted here is that of Mitchell and Robinson.
3   "Hart." An object recovered from the burial-mound at Sutton Hoo, perhaps a royal
    insignia, is surmounted by the image of a hart.
4   The hall Heorot is apparently fated to be destroyed in a battle between Hrothgar
    and his son-in-law Ingeld the Heathobard, a conflict predicted by Beowulf in 2024–
    69. The battle itself happens outside the action of the poem.

wretchedly suffered all the while,
for every day he heard the joyful din
loud in the hall, with the harp's sound,
90 the clear song of the scop.[1] He said
who was able to tell of the origin of men
that the Almighty created the earth,
a bright and shining plain, by seas embraced,
and set, triumphantly, the sun and moon
95 to light their beams for those who dwell on land,
adorned the distant corners of the world
with leaves and branches, and made life also,
all manner of creatures that live and move.
— Thus this lordly people lived in joy,
100 blessedly, until one began
to work his foul crimes — a fiend from hell.
This grim spirit was called Grendel,
mighty stalker of the marches, who held
the moors and fens; this miserable man
105 lived for a time in the land of giants,
after the Creator had condemned him
among Cain's race — when he killed Abel
the eternal Lord avenged that death.[2]
No joy in that feud — the Maker forced him
110 far from mankind for his foul crime.
From thence arose all misbegotten things,
trolls and elves and the living dead,
and also the giants who strove against God
for a long while[3] — He gave them their reward for that.

---

1 A scop is a poet-singer. This is the first of several self-reflexive scenes of poetic entertainment in the poem.
2 The story of Cain and Abel is told in Genesis 4:1-16.
3 The poet lists a collection of Germanic, classical, and biblical horrors; all are ultimately traced to their biblical roots, though the characters in the poem are not aware of this.

II

When night descended he went to seek out   115
the high house, to see how the Ring-Danes
had bedded down after their beer-drinking.
He found therein a troop of nobles
asleep after the feast; they knew no sorrow
or human misery. The unholy creature,   120
grim and ravenous, was ready at once,
ruthless and cruel, and took from their rest
thirty thanes;[1] thence he went
rejoicing in his booty, back to his home,
to seek out his abode with his fill of slaughter.   125
When in the dim twilight just before dawn
Grendel's warfare was made known to men,
then lamentation was lifted up after the feasting,
a great morning-sound. Unhappy sat
the mighty lord, long-good nobleman,   130
suffered greatly, grieved for his thanes,
once they beheld that hostile one's tracks,
the accursed spirit; that strife was too strong,
loathsome and long.
                    It was not longer
than the next night until he committed   135
a greater murder, mourned not at all
for his feuds and sins — he was too fixed in them.
Then it was easy to find a thane
who sought his rest elsewhere, farther away,
a bed in the outbuildings,[2] when was pointed out —   140
truly announced with clear tokens —
that hall-thane's hate; he kept himself afterwards
farther and safer, who escaped the fiend.
So he ruled, and strove against right,

---

1   A "thane" is a retainer, one of the troop of companions surrounding a heroic king
    in Germanic literature.
2   Hrothgar's hall is apparently surrounded by smaller buildings, including the
    women's quarters (see lines 662-5, 920-4). Under normal circumstances the men
    sleep together in the hall, ready for battle (1239-50).

145 one against all, until empty stood
the best of houses. And so for a great while —
for twelve long winters the lord of the Scyldings
suffered his grief, every sort of woe,
great sorrow, for to the sons of men
150 it became known, and carried abroad
in sad tales, that Grendel strove
long with Hrothgar, bore his hatred,
sins and feuds, for many seasons,
perpetual conflict; he wanted no peace
155 with any man of the Danish army,
nor ceased his deadly hatred, nor settled with money,
nor did any of the counselors need to expect
bright compensation from the killer's hands,[1]
for the great ravager relentlessly stalked,
160 a dark death-shadow, lurked and struck
old and young alike, in perpetual night
held the misty moors. Men do not know
whither such whispering demons wander about.
        Thus the foe of mankind, fearsome and solitary,
165 often committed his many crimes,
cruel humiliations; he occupied Heorot,
the jewel-adorned hall, in the dark nights —
he saw no need to salute the throne,
he scorned the treasures; he did not know their love.[2]
170 That was deep misery to the lord of the Danes,
a breaking of spirit. Many a strong man sat
in secret counsel, considered advice,
what would be best for the brave at heart
to save themselves from the sudden attacks.
175 At times they offered honor to idols
at pagan temples, prayed aloud

---

1   Germanic and Anglo-Saxon law allowed that a murderer could make peace with
    the family of his victim by paying compensation, or *wergild*. The amount of com-
    pensation varied with the rank of the victim.
2   This is a much-disputed passage; my reading follows a suggestion made by Fred C.
    Robinson in "Why is Grendel's Not Greeting the *gifstol* a *wræc micel*?" and repeated
    in Mitchell and Robinson's *Beowulf*.

that the soul-slayer[1] might offer assistance
in the country's distress. Such was their custom,
the hope of heathens — they remembered hell
in their minds, they did not know the Maker,   180
the Judge of deeds, they did not know the Lord God,
or even how to praise the heavenly Protector,
Wielder of glory. Woe unto him
who must thrust his soul through wicked force
in the fire's embrace, expect no comfort,   185
no way to change at all! It shall be well for him
who can seek the Lord after his deathday
and find security in the Father's embrace.

III

With the sorrows of that time the son of Healfdene
seethed constantly; nor could the wise hero   190
turn aside his woe — too great was the strife,
long and loathsome, which befell that nation,
violent, grim, cruel, greatest of night-evils.
     Then from his home the thane of Hygelac,[2]
a good man among the Geats, heard of Grendel's deeds —   195
he was of mankind the strongest of might
in those days of this life,
noble and mighty. He commanded to be made
a good wave-crosser, said that that war-king
he would seek out over the swan's-riding,   200
the renowned prince, when he was in need of men.
Wise men did not dissuade him at all
from that journey, though he was dear to them;
they encouraged his bold spirit, inspected the omens.
From the Geatish nation that good man   205
had chosen the boldest champions, the best

---

1 The Devil. In the Middle Ages the gods of the pagans were often regarded as
   demons in disguise.
2 The hero is not named until more than a hundred lines later. Hygelac is his uncle
   and king.

he could find; one of fifteen,
he sought the sea-wood. A wise sailor
showed the way to the edge of the shore.
210 The time came — the craft was on the waves,
moored under the cliffs. Eager men
climbed on the prow — the currents eddied,
sea against sand — the soldiers bore
into the bosom of the ship their bright gear,
215 fine polished armor; the men pushed off
on their wished-for journey in that wooden vessel.
Over the billowing waves, urged by the wind,
the foamy-necked floater flew like a bird,
until in due time on the second day
220 the curved-prowed vessel had come so far
that the seafarers sighted land,
shining shore-cliffs, steep mountains,
wide headlands — then the waves were crossed,
the journey at an end. Thence up quickly
225 the people of the Weders¹ climbed onto the plain,
moored their ship, shook out their mail-shirts,
their battle-garments; they thanked God
that the sea-paths had been smooth for them.
        When from the wall the Scyldings' watchman,
230 whose duty it was to watch the sea-cliffs,
saw them bear down the gangplank bright shields,
ready battle-gear, he was bursting with curiosity
in his mind to know who these men were.
This thane of Hrothgar rode his horse
235 down to the shore, and shook mightily
his strong spear, and spoke a challenge:
"What are you, warriors in armor, wearing
coats of mail, who have come thus sailing
over the sea-road in a tall ship,
240 hither over the waves? Long have I been
the coast-warden, and kept sea-watch
so that no enemies with fleets and armies
should ever attack the land of the Danes.

---

1   The Weders are the Geats.

Never more openly have there ever come
shield-bearers here, nor have you heard   245
any word of leave from our warriors
or consent of kinsmen. I have never seen
a greater earl on earth than that one among you,
a man in war-gear; that is no mere courtier,
honored only in weapons — unless his looks belie him,   250
his noble appearance! Now I must know
your lineage, lest you go hence
as false spies, travel further
into Danish territory. Now, you sea-travelers
from a far-off land, listen to my   255
simple thought — the sooner the better,
you must make clear from whence you have come."

IV

The eldest one answered him,
leader of the troop, unlocked his word-hoard:
"We are men of the Geatish nation   260
and Hygelac's hearth-companions.
My father was well-known among men,
a noble commander named Ecgtheow;
he saw many winters before he passed away,
ancient, from the court; nearly everyone   265
throughout the world remembers him well.
With a friendly heart have we come
seeking your lord, the son of Healfdene,
guardian of his people; be of good counsel to us!
We have a great mission to that famous man,   270
ruler of the Danes; nor should any of it be
hidden, I think. You know, if things are
as we have truly heard tell,
that among the Scyldings some sort of enemy,
hidden evildoer, in the dark nights   275
manifests his terrible and mysterious violence,
shame and slaughter. With a generous spirit
I can counsel Hrothgar, advise him how,

wise old king, he may overcome this fiend —
280 if a change should ever come for him,
a remedy for the evil of his afflictions,
and his seething cares turn cooler;
or forever afterwards a time of anguish
he shall suffer, his sad necessity, while there stands
285 in its high place the best of houses."
                    The watchman spoke, as he sat on his horse,
a fearless officer: "A sharp shield-warrior
must be a judge of both things,
words and deeds, if he would think well.
290 I understand that to the Scylding lord
you are a friendly force. Go forth, and bear
weapons and armor — I shall guide your way;
and I will command my young companions
to guard honorably against all enemies
295 your ship, newly-tarred, upon the sand,
to watch it until the curved-necked wood
bears hence across the ocean-streams
a beloved man to the borders of the Weders —
and such of these good men as will be granted
300 that they survive the storm of battle."
They set off — their vessel stood still,
the roomy ship rested in its riggings,
fast at anchor. Boar-figures shone
over gold-plated cheek-guards,[1]
305 gleaming, fire-hardened; they guarded the lives
of the grim battle-minded. The men hastened,
marched together, until they could make out
the timbered hall, splendid and gold-adorned —
the most famous building among men
310 under the heavens — where the high king waited;
its light shone over many lands.

---

1   The boar was a sacred animal in Germanic mythology; in his *Germania* the Roman
     historian Tacitus mentions warriors wearing boar-images into battle (ch. 45).
     Images of boars may have been placed on helmets to protect the wearer from the
     "bite" of a sword, which was often quasi-personified as a serpent. Archaeologists
     have unearthed several Anglo-Saxon helmets with various kinds of boar-images on
     them.

Their brave guide showed them the bright court
of the mighty ones, so that they might go
straight to it; that fine soldier
wheeled his horse and spoke these words: 315
"Time for me to go. The almighty Father
guard you in his grace,
safe in your journeys! I must to the sea,
and hold my watch against hostile hordes."

V

    The road was stone-paved, the path led   320
the men together. Their mail coats shone
hard, hand-linked, bright rings of iron
rang out on their gear, when right to the hall
they went trooping in their terrible armor.
Sea-weary, they set their broad shields,   325
wondrously-hard boards, against the building's wall;
they sat on a bench — their byrnies rang out,
their soldiers' war-gear; their spears stood,
the gear of the seamen all together,
a gray forest of ash. That iron troop   330
was worthy of its weapons.
                Then a proud warrior[1]
asked those soldiers about their ancestry:
"From whence do you carry those covered shields,
gray coats of mail and grim helmets,
this troop of spears? I am herald and servant   335
to Hrothgar; never have I seen
so many foreign men so fearless and bold.
For your pride, I expect, not for exile,
and for greatness of heart you have sought out Hrothgar."
The courageous one answered him,   340
proud prince of the Weders, spoke words
hardy in his helmet: "We are Hygelac's
board-companions — Beowulf is my name.

---

1   Later identified as Wulfgar.

I wish to explain my errand
345 to the son of Healfdene, famous prince,
your lord, if he will allow us,
in his goodness, to greet him."
Wulfgar spoke — a prince of the Wendels,
his noble character was known to many,
350 his valor and wisdom: "I will convey
to the friend of the Danes, lord of the Scyldings,
giver of rings, what you have requested,
tell the famous prince of your travels,
and then quickly announce to you the answer
355 which that good man sees fit to give me."
　　　　　He hastily returned to where Hrothgar sat
old and gray-haired, with his band of earls;
he boldly went, stood by the shoulder
of the Danish king — he knew the noble custom.
360 Wulfgar spoke to his friend and lord:
"There have arrived here over the sea's expanse,
come from afar, men of the Geats;
the oldest among them, the fighting men
call Beowulf. They have requested
365 that they, my lord, might be allowed
to exchange words with you — do not refuse them
your reply, gracious Hrothgar!
In their war-trappings they seem worthy
of noble esteem; notable indeed is that chief
370 who has shown these soldiers the way hither."

VI

　　　　　Hrothgar spoke, protector of the Scyldings:
"I knew him when he was nothing but a boy —
his old father was called Ecgtheow,
to whom Hrethel the Geat[1] gave in marriage
375 his only daughter; now his daring son
has come here, sought a loyal friend.

1　Hrethel was the father of Hygelac and grandfather of Beowulf.

Seafarers, in truth, have said to me,
those who brought to the Geats gifts and money
as thanks, that he has thirty
men's strength, strong in battle,   380
in his handgrip. Holy God
in His grace has guided him to us,
to the West-Danes, as I would hope,
against Grendel's terror. To this good man
I shall offer treasures for his true daring.   385
Be hasty now, bid them enter
to see this troop of kinsmen all assembled;
and tell them in your words that they are welcome
to the Danish people."
                    He announced from within:[1]   390
"My conquering lord commands me to tell you,
ruler of the East-Danes, that he knows your ancestry,
and you are to him, hardy spirits,
welcome hither from across the rolling waves.
Now you may go in your war-gear   395
under your helmets to see Hrothgar,
but let your battle-shields and deadly spears
await here the result of your words."
                    The mighty one arose, and many a man with him,
powerful thanes; a few waited there,   400
guarded their battle-dress as the bold man bid them.
They hastened together as the man led them,
under Heorot's roof; [the warrior went][2]
hardy in his helmet, until he stood on the hearth.
Beowulf spoke — his byrnie gleamed on him,   405
war-net sewn by the skill of a smith — :
"Be well, Hrothgar! I am Hygelac's kinsman
and young retainer; in my youth I have done
many a glorious deed. This business with Grendel
was made known to me on my native soil;   410
seafarers say that this building stands,

---

1   There is no gap in the manuscript, but the two halves of the line do not alliterate,
    and something is probably missing from the text at this point. Most editors add two
    half-lines with the sense "Then Wulfgar went to the door."
2   A half-line is missing; the translation follows the most innocuous conjecture.

most excellent of halls, idle and useless
to every man, after evening's light
is hidden under heaven's gleaming dome.
415 Then my own people advised me,
the best warriors and the wisest men,
that I should, lord Hrothgar, seek you out,
because they knew the might of my strength;
they themselves had seen me, bloodstained from battle,
420 come from the fight, when I captured five,
slew a tribe of giants, and on the salt waves
fought sea-monsters by night, survived that tight spot,
avenged the Weder's affliction — they asked for trouble! —
and crushed those grim foes; and now with Grendel,
425 that monstrous beast, I shall by myself have
a word or two with that giant. From you now I wish,
ruler of the Bright-Danes, to request,
protector of the Scyldings, a single favor,
that you not refuse me, having come this far,
430 protector of warriors, noble friend to his people, —
that I might alone, o my own band of earls
and this hardy troop, cleanse Heorot.
I have also heard that this evil beast
in his wildness does not care for weapons,
435 so I too will scorn — so that Hygelac,
my liege-lord, may be glad of me —
to bear a sword or a broad shield,
a yellow battle-board, but with my grip
I shall grapple with the fiend and fight for life,
440 foe against foe. Let him put his faith
in the Lord's judgment, whom death takes!
I expect that he will, if he is allowed to win,
eat unafraid the folk of the Geats
in that war-hall, as he has often done,
445 the host of the Hrethmen. You'll have no need
to cover my head[1] — he will have done so,
gory, bloodstained, if death bears me away;

---

1 A burial custom. Beowulf grimly jokes that there will be no need to trouble with
   funeral expenses if Grendel wins this fight; he will have no head to bury.

he will take his kill, think to taste me,
will dine alone without remorse,
stain his lair in the moor; no need to linger 450
in sorrow over disposing of my body!
Send on to Hygelac, if battle should take me,
the best battledress, which my breast wears,
finest of garments; it is Hrethel's heirloom,
the work of Weland.[1] *Wyrd* always goes as it must!"[2] 455

VII

        Hrothgar spoke, protector of the Scyldings:
"For past favors, my friend Beowulf,
and for old deeds, you have sought us out.
Your father struck up the greatest of feuds,
when he killed Heatholaf by his own hand 460
among the Wylfings. When the Weder tribe
would not harbor him for fear of war,
thence he sought the South-Dane people
over the billowing seas, the Honor-Scyldings;
then I first ruled the Danish folk 465
and held in my youth this grand kingdom,
city of treasure and heroes — then Heorogar
was dead, my older brother unliving,
Healfdene's firstborn — he was better than I!
Later I settled that feud with fee-money; 470
I sent to the Wylfings over the crest of the waves
ancient treasures; he swore oaths to me.[3]
It is a sorrow to my very soul to say

---

1   Weland is the legendary blacksmith of the Norse gods. The antiquity of weapons
    and armor added to their value.

2   *Wyrd* is the Old English word for "fate"; it is sometimes quasi-personified, though
    apparently not to the extent that the goddess *Fortuna* was in Roman poetic
    mythology. The word survives, via Shakespeare's *Macbeth*, as the Modern English
    word "weird."

3   Hrothgar pays the *wergild* for the man Ecgtheow killed, and Ecgtheow swears an
    oath of loyalty and support. It is this oath, passed on to the next generation, that
    Beowulf is fulfilling (at least this is Hrothgar's public sentiment; his thoughts in the
    privacy of his council are somewhat different).

to any man what Grendel has done to me —
475 humiliated Heorot with his hateful thoughts,
his sudden attacks. My hall-troop,
my warriors, are decimated; *wyrd* has swept them away
into Grendel's terror. God might easily
put an end to the deeds of this mad enemy!
480 Often men have boasted, drunk with beer,
officers over their cups of ale,
that they would abide in the beerhall
Grendel's attack with a rush of sword-terror.
Then in the morning this meadhall,
485 lordly dwelling, was drenched with blood,
when daylight gleamed, the benches gory,
the hall spattered and befouled; I had fewer
dear warriors when death took them away.
Now sit down at my feast, drink mead in my hall,[1]
490 victorious man, as your mood urges."
　　　　Then a bench was cleared in the beerhall
for the men of the Geats all together;
the strong-minded men went to sit down,
proud in their strength. A thane did his service,
495 bore in his hands the gold-bright ale-cup,
poured the clear sweet drink. The scop sang
brightly in Heorot — there was the joy of heroes,
no small gathering of Danes and Geats.

VIII

　　　　Unferth[2] spoke, son of Ecglaf,
500 who sat at the feet of the Scylding lord,
unbound his battle-runes[3] — Beowulf's journey,
that brave seafarer, sorely vexed him,

---

1 The meaning of this line in Old English is disputed.
2 Unferth's name, which may be significant, means either "un-peace" or "un-reason." In the manuscript it is always spelled "Hunferth," though it alliterates with a vowel. His position at Hrothgar's feet appears to be one of honor.
3 Or "unleashed his hostile secret thoughts." *Run* in Old English often means "secret."

for he did not wish that any other man
on this middle-earth should care for glory
under the heavens, more than he himself: 505
"Are you the Beowulf who strove with Breca
in a swimming contest on the open sea,
where in your pride you tried the waves
and for a foolish boast risked your life
in the deep water? No man, whether   510
friend or foe, could dissuade you two
from that sad venture, when you swam in the sea;
there you seized in your arms the ocean-streams,
measured the sea-ways, flailed your hands
and glided over the waves — the water roiled,   515
wintry surges. In the keeping of the water
you toiled for seven nights, and he outswam you,
and had more strength. Then in the morning
the swells bore him to the Heathoream shore;
from thence he sought his own sweet land,   520
beloved by his people, the land of the Brondings,
the fair fortress, where he had his folk,
his castle and treasure. He truly fulfilled,
the son of Beanstan, his boast against you.
So I expect a worse outcome from you —   525
though you may have survived the storm of battle,
some grim combats — if for Grendel you dare
to lie in wait the whole night long."
        Beowulf spoke, son of Ecgtheow:
"What a great deal, Unferth my friend,   530
drunk with beer, you have said about Breca,
told his adventures! I will tell the truth —
I had greater strength on the sea,
more ordeals on the waves than any other man.
When we were just boys we two agreed   535
and boasted — we were both still
in our youth — that out on the great ocean
we would risk our lives, and we did just that.
We had bare swords, when we swam in the sea,
hard in our hands; we thought to protect   540
ourselves from whales. Not for anything

could he swim far from me on the sea-waves,
more swiftly on the water, nor would I go from him.
We two were together on the sea
545 for five nights, until the flood drove us apart,
surging waves, coldest of weathers,
darkening night, and a northern wind,
knife-sharp, pushed against us. The seas were choppy;
the fishes of the sea were stirred up by it.
550 There my coat of armor offered help,
hard, hand-locked, against those hostile ones,
my woven battle-dress lay on my breast
adorned with gold. Down to the ocean floor
a grisly foe dragged me, gripped me fast
555 in his grim grasp, yet it was given to me
to stab that monster with the point of my sword,
my war-blade; the storm of battle took away
that mighty sea-beast, through my own hand.

IX

Time and again those terrible enemies
560 sorely threatened me. I served them well
with my dear sword, as they deserved.
They got no joy from their gluttony,
those wicked maneaters, when they tasted me,
sat down to their feast on the ocean floor —
565 but in the morning, wounded by me,
they were washed ashore by the ocean waves,
dazed by sword-blows, and since that day
they never hindered the passage of any
sea-voyager. Light shone from the east,
570 God's bright beacon; the waves grew calm,
so that I could see the sea-cliffs,
the windswept capes. *Wyrd* often spares
an undoomed man, when his courage endures!
And so it came about that I was able to kill
575 nine of these sea-monsters. I have never heard
of a harder night-battle under heaven's vault,

nor a more wretched man on the water's stream;
yet I escaped alive from the clutches of my enemies,
weary from my journey. Then the sea washed me up,
the currents of the flood, in the land of the Finns,   580
the welling waters. I have never heard a word
about any such contest concerning you,
such sword-panic. In the play of battle
Breca has never — nor you either —
done a deed so bold and daring   585
with his decorated blade — I would never boast of it! —
though you became your brothers' killer,
your next of kin; for that you needs must suffer
punishment in hell, no matter how clever you are.[1]
I will say it truly, son of Ecglaf,   590
that never would Grendel have worked such terror,
that gruesome beast, against your lord,
or shames in Heorot, if your courage and spirit
were as fierce as you yourself fancy they are;
but he has found that he need fear no feud,   595
no storm of swords from the Victory-Scyldings,[2]
no resistance at all from your nation;
he takes his toll, spares no one
in the Danish nation, but indulges himself,
hacks and butchers and expects no battle   600
from the Spear-Danes. But I will show him
soon enough the strength and courage
of the Geats in war. Afterwards, let him who will
go bravely to mead, when the morning light
of a new day, the sun clothed in glory   605
shines from the south on the sons of men!"

---

1 Unferth's fratricide brings the general theme of kin-slaying, represented by Grendel's descent from Cain, inside Hrothgar's hall. In reality – at least in the reality of
   the heroic world depicted in poetry – it may not have been unthinkable for kinsmen to find themselves on opposite sides of a battle; loyalty to one's lord was supposed to outweigh the claims of blood-relation. The word "hell" is not in the
   manuscript, but it is attested by one of the early transcriptions. Mitchell and
   Robinson read *healle*, i.e., "hall."

2 Is this a nasty irony on Beowulf's part, or a conventional epithet used thoughtlessly
   by the poet?

Then the giver of treasure was greatly pleased,
gray-haired and battle-bold; the Bright-Danes' chief
had faith in his helper; that shepherd of his folk
610 recognized Beowulf's firm resolution.
There was man's laughter, lovely sounds
and winsome words. Wealhtheow went forth,
Hrothgar's queen, mindful of customs;
adorned with gold, she greeted the men in the hall,
615 then that courteous wife offered the full cup
first to the guardian of the East-Danes' kingdom,
bid him be merry at his beer-drinking,
beloved by his people; with pleasure he received
the feast and cup, victorious king.
620 The lady of the Helmings then went about
to young and old, gave each his portion
of the precious cup, until the moment came
when the ring-adorned queen, of excellent heart,
bore the mead-cup to Beowulf;
625 she greeted the Geatish prince, thanked God
with wise words that her wish had come to pass,
that she could rely on any earl for relief
from those crimes. He took the cup,
the fierce warrior, from Wealhtheow,
630 and then eager for battle he made his announcement.
Beowulf spoke, son of Ecgtheow:
"I resolved when I set out over the waves,
sat down in my ship with my troop of soldiers,
that I would entirely fulfill the wishes
635 of your people, or fall slain,
fast in the grip of my foe. I shall perform
a deed of manly courage, or in this meadhall
I will await the end of my days!"
These words well pleased that woman,
640 the boasting of the Geat; she went, the gold-adorned
and courteous folk-queen, to sit beside her lord.
Then, as before, there in that hall were
strong words spoken, the people happy,
the sounds of a victorious nation, until shortly

the son of Healfdene wished to seek   645
his evening rest; he knew that the wretched beast
had been planning to do battle in the high building
from the time they could first see the sunrise
until night fell darkening over all,
and creatures of shadow came creeping about   650
pale under the clouds. The company arose.
One warrior greeted another there,
Hrothgar to Beowulf, and wished him luck,
gave him control of the wine-hall in these words:
"I have never entrusted to any man,   655
ever since I could hold and hoist a shield,
the great hall of the Danes — except to you now.
Have it and hold it, protect this best of houses,
be mindful of glory, show your mighty valor,
watch for your enemies! You will have all you desire,   660
if you emerge from this brave undertaking alive."

X

Then Hrothgar and his troop of heroes,
protector of the Scyldings, departed from the hall;
the war-chief wished to seek Wealhtheow,
his queen's bedchamber. The glorious king[1]   665
had set against Grendel a hall-guardian
— as men had heard said — who did special service
for the king of the Danes, kept a giant-watch.
Surely the Geatish prince greatly trusted
his mighty strength, the Maker's favor,   670
when he took off his iron byrnie,
undid his helmet, and gave his decorated iron,
best of swords, to his servant
and bid him hold his battle-gear.
The good man, Beowulf the Geat,   675
spoke a few boasting words before he lay down:
"I consider myself no poorer in strength

---

1   Or "King of Glory," i.e., God?

and battle-deeds than Grendel does himself;
and so I will not kill him with a sword,
680 put an end to his life, though I easily might;
he knows no arts of war, no way to strike back,
hack at my shield-boss, though he be brave
in his wicked deeds; but tonight we two will
forego our swords, if he dare to seek out
685 a war without weapons — and then let the wise Lord
grant the judgment of glory, the holy God,
to whichever hand seems proper to Him."
　　　　　He lay down, battle-brave; the bolster took
the earl's cheek, and around him many
690 a bold seafarer sank to his hall-rest.
None of them thought that he should thence
ever again seek his own dear homeland,
his tribe or the town in which he was raised,
for they had heard it said that savage death
695 had swept away far too many of the Danish folk
in that wine-hall. But the Lord gave them
a web of victory, the people of the Weders,
comfort and support, so that they completely,
through one man's craft, overcame their enemy,
700 by his own might. It is a well-known truth
that mighty God has ruled mankind
always and forever.
　　　　　　　In the dark night he came
creeping, the shadow-goer. The bowmen slept
who were to hold that horned hall —
705 all but one. It was well-known to men
that the demon foe could not drag them under
the dark shadows if the Maker did not wish it;
but he, wakeful, keeping watch for his enemy,
awaited, enraged, the outcome of battle.

XI

Then from the moor, in a blanket of mist,   710
Grendel came stalking — he bore God's anger;
the evil marauder meant to ensnare
some of human-kind in that high hall.
Under the clouds he came until he clearly knew
he was near the wine-hall, men's golden house,   715
finely adorned. It was not the first time
he had sought out the home of Hrothgar,
but never in his life, early or late,
did he find harder luck or a hardier hall-thane.
To the hall came that warrior on his journey,   720
bereft of joys. The door burst open,
fast in its forged bands, when his fingers touched it;
bloody-minded, swollen with rage, he swung open
the hall's mouth, and immediately afterwards
the fiend strode across the paved floor,   725
went angrily; in his eyes stood
a light not fair, glowing like fire.
He saw in the hall many a soldier,
a peaceful troop sleeping all together,
a large company of thanes — and he laughed inside;   730
he meant to divide, before day came,
this loathsome creature, the life of each
man from his body, when there befell him
the hope of a feast. But it was not his fate
to taste any more of the race of mankind   735
after that night. The kinsman of Hygelac,
mighty one, beheld how that maneater
planned to proceed with his sudden assault.
Not that the monster[1] meant to delay —
he seized at once at his first pass   740

---

1   The OE word *æglæca*, which literally means "awesome one" or "terror," is elsewhere
applied to the dragon-slaying Sigemund (line 892, where it is translated "fierce
creature") and to Beowulf himself. Its translation here is admittedly tendentious.
The word appears elsewhere, variously translated, in lines 159, 433, 732, 556,
etc.

a sleeping man, slit him open suddenly,
bit into his joints, drank the blood from his veins,
gobbled his flesh in gobbets, and soon
had completely devoured that dead man,
745 feet and fingertips. He stepped further,
and took in his hands the strong-hearted
man in his bed; the monster reached out
towards him with his hands — he quickly grabbed him
with evil intent, and sat up against his arm.[1]
750 As soon as that shepherd of sins discovered
that he had never met on middle-earth,
in any region of the world, another man
with a greater handgrip, in his heart he was
afraid for his life, but none the sooner could he flee.
755 His mind was eager to escape to the darkness,
seek out a host of devils — his habit there
was nothing like he had ever met before.
The good kinsman of Hygelac remembered then
his evening speech, and stood upright
760 and seized him fast. His fingers burst;
the giant turned outward, the earl stepped inward.
The notorious one meant — if he might —
to turn away further and flee, away
to his lair in the fen; he knew his fingers
765 were held in a hostile grip. That was an unhappy journey
that the harm-doer took to Heorot!
The great hall resounded; to the Danes it seemed,
the city's inhabitants, and every brave earl,
like a wild ale-sharing.[2] Both were angry,
770 fierce house-wardens — the hall echoed.
It was a great wonder that the wine-hall

---

1 It is not entirely clear who grabs whom – apparently Grendel reaches out to
   Beowulf, who is lying down; the hero then grabs Grendel's arm and sits up against
   it.

2 The general sense of the OE word *ealuscerwen* is "panic" or "terror," but its precise
   meaning (probably "a dispensing of ale") is unclear: did the Danes think a wild
   party was going on? or were they dismayed by the loss of their mead-hall? or does
   OE *ealu* mean "luck"?

withstood their fighting and did not fall to the ground,
that fair building — but it was fastened
inside and out with iron bands,
forged with skill. From the floor there flew   775
many a mead-bench, as men have told me,
gold-adorned, where those grim foes fought.
The Scylding elders had never expected
that any man, by any ordinary means,
could break it apart, beautiful, bone-adorned,   780
or destroy it with guile, unless the embrace of fire
might swallow it in flames. The noise swelled
new and stark — among the North-Danes was
horrible terror, in each of them
who heard through the wall the wailing cry —   785
God's adversary shrieked a grisly song
of horror, defeated, the captive of Hell
bewailed his pain. He pinned him fast,
he who among men was the strongest of might
in those days of this life.   790

XII

That protector of earls would not for anything
let that murderous visitor escape alive —
he did not consider his days on earth
of any use at all. Many an earl
in Beowulf's troop drew his old blade,   795
longed to protect the life of his liege-lord,
the famous captain, however they could.
But they did not know as they entered the fight,
those stern-minded men of battle,
and thought to strike from all sides   800
and seek his soul, that no sword,
not the best iron anywhere in the world,
could even touch that evil sinner,
for he had worked a curse on weapons,
every sort of blade. His separation from the world   805

in those days of this life
would have to be miserable, and that alien spirit
would travel far into the keeping of fiends.
Then he discovered, who had done before
810 so much harm to the race of mankind,
so many crimes — he was marked by God —
that his body could bear it no longer,
but the courageous kinsman of Hygelac
had him in hand — hateful to each
815 was the life of the other. The loathsome creature felt
great bodily pain; a gaping wound opened
in his shoulder-joint, his sinews sprang apart,
his joints burst asunder. Beowulf was given
glory in battle — Grendel was forced
820 to flee, mortally wounded, into the fen-slopes,
seek a sorry abode; he knew quite surely
that the end of his life had arrived,
the sum of his days. The will of the Danes
was entirely fulfilled in that bloody onslaught!
825 He who had come from afar had cleansed,
wise and stout-hearted, the hall of Hrothgar,
warded off attack. He rejoiced in his night-work,
his great courage. That man of the Geats
had fulfilled his boast to the East-Danes,
830 and entirely remedied all their distress,
the insidious sorrows they had suffered
and had to endure from sad necessity,
no small affliction. It was a clear sign,
when the battle-brave one laid down the hand,
835 arm and shoulder — there all together
was Grendel's claw — under the curved roof.

XIII

Then in the morning was many a warrior,
as I have heard, around that gift-hall,
leaders of the folk came from far and near

throughout the wide land to see that wonder,   840
the loathsome one's tracks. His parting from life
hardly seemed sad to any man
who examined the trail of that inglorious one,
how he went on his weary way,
defeated by force, to a pool of sea-monsters,   845
doomed, put to flight, and left a fatal trail.
The water was welling with blood there —
the terrible swirling waves, all mingled together
with hot gore, heaved with the blood of battle,
concealed that doomed one when, deprived of joys,   850
he lay down his life in his lair in the fen,
his heathen soul — and hell took him.
          Then the old retainers returned from there,
and many a youth on the joyful journey,
bravely rode their horses back from the mere,   855
men on their white steeds. There they celebrated
Beowulf's glory: it was often said
that south or north, between the two seas,[1]
across the wide world, there was none
better under the sky's expanse   860
among shield-warriors, nor more worthy to rule—
though they found no fault with their own friendly lord,
gracious Hrothgar, but said he was a good king.
At times the proud warriors let their horses prance,
their fallow mares fare in a contest,   865
wherever the footpaths seemed fair to them,
the way tried and true. At times the king's thane,
full of grand stories, mindful of songs,
who remembered much, a great many
of the old tales, found other words   870
truly bound together; he began again
to recite with skill the adventure of Beowulf
adeptly tell an apt tale,
and weave his words. He said nearly all

---

1 A conventional expression like Modern English "coast to coast"; probably it
  originally referred to the North and Baltic seas.

875   that he had heard said of Sigemund's
       stirring deeds,[1] many strange things,
       the Volsung's strife, his distant voyages
       obscure, unknown to all the sons of men,
       his feuds and crimes — except for Fitela,
880   when of such things he wished to speak to him,
       uncle to nephew[2] — for always they were,
       in every combat, companions at need;
       a great many of the race of giants
       they slaughtered with their swords. For Sigemund
885   no small fame grew after his final day,
       after that hardened soldier, prince's son,
       had killed a dragon, keeper of a hoard;
       alone, he dared to go under gray stones,
       a bold deed — nor was Fitela by his side;
890   yet so it befell him that his sword pierced
       the wondrous serpent, stood fixed in the wall,
       the manly iron; the dragon met his death.
       That fierce creature had gone forth in courage
       so that he could possess that store of rings
895   and use them at his will; the son of Wæls
       loaded his sea-boat, bore the bright treasure
       to the ship's hold. The serpent melted in its own heat.

            He was the most famous of exiles, far and wide,
       among all people, protector of warriors,
900   for his noble deeds — he had prospered for them —
       since the struggles of Heremod had ceased,

---

1   Beowulf is praised indirectly, by being compared first to Sigemund, another famous
     monster-slayer (a different version of whose story is told in the Old Norse *Volsun-
     gasaga* and the Middle High German *Nibelungenlied*; there the dragon-slaying is
     attributed to Sigemund's son Siegfried), and then contrasted to Heremod, an earlier
     king of the Danes who descended into tyranny (it is sometimes assumed that the
     disastrous ending of Heremod's reign is the cause of the Danes' lordlessness and dis-
     tress mentioned at the beginning of the poem). The implication is that Beowulf's
     deeds place him in the ranks of other exemplary figures. The method of narration
     is allusive and indirect, as though the audience were expected to know the details
     of the story and appreciate an elliptical reference to them.
2   Fitela is actually Sigemund's son by his own sister – either the poet is being discreet,
     or his version of the story differs from the Norse.

his might and valor. Among the Eotens[1]
he was betrayed into his enemies' hands,
quickly dispatched. The surging of cares
had crippled him too long; he became a deadly burden   905
to his own people, to all noblemen;
for many a wise man had mourned
in earlier times over his headstrong ways
who had looked to him for relief from affliction,
hoped that that prince's son would prosper,   910
receive his father's rank, rule his people,
hoard and fortress, a kingdom of heroes,
the Scylding homeland. The kinsman of Hygelac
became to all of the race of mankind
a more pleasant friend; sin possessed him.[2]   915
    Sometimes, competing, the fallow paths
they measured on horseback. When morning's light
raced on and hastened away, many a retainer,
stout-hearted, went to see the high hall
to see the strange wonder; the king himself,   920
guard of the treasure-hoard, strode glorious
from the woman's chambers with a great entourage,
a chosen retinue, and his royal queen with him
measured the meadhall-path with a troop of maidens.

XIV

    Hrothgar spoke — he went to the hall,   925
stood on the steps, beheld the steep roof
plated with gold, and Grendel's hand:
"For this sight let us swiftly offer thanks
to the Almighty! Much have I endured
of dire grief from Grendel, but God may always   930
work, Shepherd of glory, wonder upon wonder.

---

1   Perhaps "Jutes." The word literally means "giants" and may be a tribal name, or an
    epithet, or may in fact refer to an actual race of giants.
2   Heremod.

It was not long ago that I did not expect
ever in my life to experience relief
from any of my woes, when, stained with blood,
935 this best of houses stood dripping, gory,
a widespread woe to all wise men
who did not expect that they might ever
defend the people's fortress from its foes,
devils and demons. Now a retainer has done
940 the very deed, through the might of God,
which we all could not contrive to do
with all our cleverness. Lo, that woman could say,
whosoever has borne such a son
into the race of men, if she still lives,
945 that the God of Old was good to her
in childbearing. Now I will cherish you,
Beowulf, best of men, like a son
in my heart; hold well henceforth
your new kinship. You shall have no lack
950 of the worldly goods which I can bestow.
Often have I offered rewards for less,
honored with gifts a humbler man,
weaker in battle. Now by yourself
you have done such deeds that your fame will endure
955 always and forever — may the Almighty
reward you with good, as He has already done!"
        Beowulf spoke, son of Ecgtheow:
"Freely and gladly have we fought this fight,
done this deed of courage, daringly faced
960 this unknown power. I would much prefer
that you might have seen the foe himself
decked in his finery,[1] fallen and exhausted!
With a hard grip I hoped to bind him
quickly and keenly on the killing floor,
965 so that for my handgrasp he would have to
lie squirming for life, unless he might slip away;

---

1 Literally "in his adornments," a peculiar phrase since Grendel is notoriously not
armed and unadorned. Perhaps Beowulf means "covered in a garment of blood"?

I could not — the Creator did not wish it —
hinder his going, no matter how hard I held
that deadly enemy; too overwhelming was
that fiend's flight. Yet he forfeited his hand,   970
his arm and shoulder, to save his life,
to guard his tracks — though he got thereby,
pathetic creature, little comfort;
the loathsome destroyer will live no longer,
rotten with sin, but pain has seized him,   975
grabbed him tightly in its fierce grip,
its baleful bonds — and there he shall abide,
guilty of his crimes, the greater judgment,
how the shining Maker wishes to sentence him."
        Then the son of Ecglaf[1] was more silent   980
in boasting words about his battle-works
after the noblemen, through the earl's skill,
looked on the hand over the high roof,
the enemy's fingers; at the end of each nail
was a sharp tip, most like steel,   985
heathen talons, the terrible spikes
of that awful warrior; each of them agreed
that not even the hardest of ancient and honorable
irons could touch him, or injure at all
the bloody battle-paw of that baleful creature.   990

XV

        Then it was quickly commanded that Heorot
be adorned by hands inside; many there,
men and women, prepared that wine-hall,
the guest-house. Gold-dyed tapestries
shone on the walls, many wonderful sights   995
to any man who might look on them.
That shining building was nearly shattered
inside, entirely, fast in its iron bands,

---

1   Unferth.

its hinges sprung; the roof alone survived
1000 unharmed, when that horrible creature,
stained with foul deeds, turned in his flight,
despairing of life. Death is not an easy
thing to escape — try it who will —
but compelled by necessity all must come
1005 to that place set aside for soul-bearers,
children of men, dwellers on earth,
where the body, fast on its bed of death,
sleeps after the feast.
                              Then was the set time
that the son of Healfdene went to the hall;
1010 the king himself wished to share in the feast.
I have never heard of a greater host
who bore themselves better before their treasure-giver.
Those men in their glory moved to their benches,
rejoiced in the feast; fairly those kinsmen
1015 took many a full mead-cup,
stouthearted in the high hall,
Hrothgar and Hrothulf. Heorot within was
filled with friends — no false treacheries
did the people of the Scyldings plot at that time.[1]
1020 He gave to Beowulf the blade of Healfdene,[2]
a golden war-standard as a reward for victory,
the bright banner, a helmet and byrnie,
a great treasure-sword — many saw them
borne before that man. Beowulf received
1025 the full cup in the hall, he felt no shame
at that gift-giving before his bowmen;
never have I heard tell of four treasures

---

1   Implicit in this statement is the idea that, at some later time, the people of the
    Scyldings did plot false treacheries; from other sources it is possible to infer that
    after the death of Hrothgar, his nephew Hrothulf ruled rather than Hrethric,
    Hrothgar's son. Many scholars assume that the story of some sort of treacherous
    usurpation was known to the audience; this gives a special urgency to much of
    what happens in these scenes of feasting, especially the speeches of Wealhtheow.
2   The translation follows the reading of Mitchell and Robinson, and see Bruce
    Mitchell, "Beowulf, line 1020b: *brand* or *bearn*?" The manuscript is usually emended
    to mean "The Son of Healfdene gave to Beowulf."

given more graciously, gold-adorned,
from one man to another on the ale-benches.
On the crown of the helmet as a head-protector   1030
a ridge, wound with wire, stood without,
so that the file-sharp swords might not terribly
harm him, shower-hard, when shield-fighters
had to go against hostile forces.
The protector of earls ordered eight horses   1035
with ornamented bridles led into the building,
in under the eaves; on one sat
a saddle, skillfully tooled, set with gemstones;
that was the warseat of the high-king
when the son of Healfdene sought to perform   1040
his swordplay — the widely-known warrior
never failed at the front, when the slain fell about him.
And the lord of the Ingwines[1] gave ownership
of both of them to Beowulf,
the horses and weapons, bid him use them well.   1045
So manfully did the mighty prince,
hoard-guard of warriors, reward the storm of battle
with steeds and treasures that none who will speak
the truth rightfully could ever reproach them.

XVI

Then the lord of earls, to each of those   1050
on the meadbenches who had made with Beowulf
a sea-journey, gave jeweled treasures,
antique heirlooms, and then ordered
that gold be paid for the man whom Grendel
had wickedly slain — he would have done more,   1055
if wise God and one man's courage
had not prevented that fate. The Maker ruled all
of the race of mankind, as He still does.
Therefore understanding is always best,

---

1   The "Ingwines" or "friends of Ing" are the Danes.

1060   spiritual foresight — he must face much,
both love and hate, who long here
endures this world in these days of strife.
      Noise and music mingled together
before the leader of Healfdene's forces,
1065   the harp was touched, tales often told,
when Hrothgar's scop was set to recite
among the mead-tables his hall-entertainment
about the sons of Finn, surprised in ambush,
when the hero of the Half-Danes, Hnæf the Scylding
1070   had to fall in a Frisian slaughter.[1]
      Hildeburh, indeed, had no need to praise
the good faith of the Jutes. Guiltless, she was
deprived of her dear ones in that shieldplay,
her sons and brothers — sent forth to their fate,
1075   dispatched by spears; she was a sad lady!
Not without cause did she mourn fate's decrees,
the daughter of Hoc, after daybreak came
and she could see the slaughter of her kin
under the very skies where once she held
1080   the greatest worldly joys. War took away
all of the thanes of Finn, except a few,
so that he could not continue at all
a fight with Hengest on the battlefield,
nor could that woeful remnant drive away
1085   the prince's thane — so they offered them[2] terms:
they would clear out another hall for them,
a house and high-seat, of which they should have

---

1   The story is obscure; the survival of a fragment of another poem telling the same
story (see Appendix A.5) helps clarify the action somewhat. Hnæf, prince of the
Danes, is visiting his sister Hildeburh at the home of her husband Finn, king of the
Frisians. While there, the Danish party is treacherously attacked (perhaps by a Jutish
contingent among Finn's troops, unless the "Jutes" and Frisians are one and the
same people); after five days of fighting Hnæf lies dead, along with many casualties
on either side. Hnæf's retainer Hengest is left to lead the remnant of Danish survivors.

2   The referent of this pronoun is not entirely clear – who offers what to whom?
The terms of the truce are unthinkable – no hero could honourably follow the
killer of his lord. In the following line "they" refers to the Frisians, "them" to the
Danes.

half the control with the sons of the Jutes,
and Folcwalda's son, with feasting and gifts,
should honor the Danes each and every day,   1090
gladden the troops of Hengest with gold rings
and ancient treasures, ornamented gold,
just as often as he would encourage
the hosts of the Frisians in the beerhall.
They swore their pledges then on either side,   1095
a firm compact of peace. With unfeigned zeal
Finn swore his oaths to Hengest, pledged that he,
with the consent of his counselors, would
support with honor those sad survivors,
and that none should break their pact in word or deed,   1100
nor through malice should ever make mention,
though they should serve their ring-giver's slayer,
without a lord, as they were led by need —
and if, provoking, any Frisian spoke
reminding them of all their murderous hate,   1105
then with the sword's edge they should settle it.
        The oath[1] was made ready, and ancient gold
was brought from the hoard; the Battle-Scyldings'
best fighting-man was ready for the fire.
It was easy to see upon that pyre   1110
the bloodstained battle-shirt, the gilded swine,
iron-hard boar-images, the noblemen
with fatal wounds — so many felled by war!
Then Hildeburh commanded at Hnæf's pyre
that her own son be consigned to the flames   1115
to be burnt, flesh and bone, placed on the pyre
at his uncle's shoulder; the lady sang
a sad lament. The warrior ascended;
to the clouds coiled the mighty funeral fire,
and roared before their mound; their heads melted,   1120
their gashes burst open and spurted blood,
the deadly body-bites. The flame devoured,
most greedy spirit, those whom war destroyed
of both peoples — their glory departed.

---

1   Some editors emend to *ad*, "pyre."

XVII

1125   The warriors left to seek their native lands,
bereft of friends, to behold Frisia,
their homes and high fortresses. Hengest still
stayed there with Finn that slaughter-stained winter,
unwilling, desolate. He dreamt of home,
1130 though on the frozen sea he could not[1] steer
his ring-prowed ship — the ocean raged with storms,
strove with the wind, and winter locked the waves
in icy bonds, until there came another
year to the courtyard — as it yet does,
1135 always observing its seasons and times,
bright glorious weather. Gone was the winter,
and fair the bosom of earth; the exile burned
to take leave of that court, yet more he thought
of stern vengeance than of sea-voyages,
1140 how he might arrange a hostile meeting,
remind the Jutish sons of his iron sword.
So he did not refuse the world's custom
when the son of Hunlaf[2] placed a glinting sword,
the best of battle-flames, upon his lap;
1145 its edge was not unknown among the Jutes.
And so, in turn, to the bold-minded Finn
befell cruel sword-evil in his own home,
when Guthlaf and Oslaf spoke of their grief,
the fierce attack after their sea voyage,
1150 and cursed their wretched lot — the restless heart
could not restrain itself. The hall was stained
with the lifeblood of foes, and Finn was slain,
the king among his host; the queen was seized.
The Scylding bowmen carried to their ships

---

1   OE *ne* "not" is not in the manuscript; most editors and translators add it to make better sense of the passage and of Hengest's character.

2   It is not clear who this is: perhaps Guthlaf or Oslaf (mentioned a few lines later), perhaps not; apparently some retainers remained with Hengest in Finn's hall, nursing their resentment throughout the winter. Some scholars take the OE word *hunlafing* as the name of a sword.

all the house property of that earth-king,
whatever they could find in Finn's homestead,
brooches and bright gems. On their sea journey
they bore that noble queen back to the Danes
and led her to her people.
                  The lay was sung,
the entertainer's song. Glad sounds rose again,
the bench-noise glittered, cupbearers gave
wine from wondrous vessels. Wealhtheow came forth
in her golden crown to where the good two
sat, nephew and uncle; their peace was still whole then,
each true to the other. Likewise Unferth, spokesman,[1]
sat at the foot of the Scylding lord; everyone trusted his spirit,
that he had great courage, though to his kinsmen he had
                                    not been
merciful in sword-play. Then the lady of the Scyldings spoke:
     "Take this cup, my noble courteous lord,
giver of treasure! Be truly joyful,
gold-friend of men, and speak to the Geats
in mild words, as a man should do!
Be gracious to the Geats, mindful of the gifts
which you now have from near and far.
I have been told that you would take this warrior
for your son. Heorot is cleansed,
the bright ring-hall — use your many rewards
while you can, and leave to your kinsmen
the folk and kingdom, when you must go forth
to face the Maker's decree. I know that my own
dear gracious Hrothulf will hold in honors
these youths, if you should give up the world
before him, friend of the Scyldings;
I expect that he would wish to repay
both our sons kindly, if he recalls all
the pleasures and honors that we have shown him,

---

1   The Old English word *thyle* has been variously interpreted, from "court jester" to
    "official speechmaker." The present translation grants Unferth a measure of dignity
    and position to which, perhaps, he is not entitled.

in our kindness, since he was a child."
She turned to the bench where her boys sat,
Hrethric and Hrothmund, and the hero's son,
1190   all the youths together; the good man,
Beowulf the Geat, sat between the brothers.

XVIII

The flagon was borne to him, a friendly greeting
conveyed with words, and wound gold
offered with good will, two armlets,
1195   garments and rings, and the greatest neck-collar
ever heard of anywhere on earth.
Under heaven I have not heard tell of a better
hoard-treasure of heroes, since Hama carried off
to the bright city the Brosinga necklace,
1200   the gem and its treasures; he fled the treachery
of Eormanric,[1] chose eternal counsel.
Hygelac the Geat on his last journey
had that neck-ring,[2] nephew of Swerting,
when under the banner he defended his booty,
1205   the spoils of slaughter. Fate struck him down
when in his pride he went looking for woe,
a feud with the Frisians. He wore that finery,
those precious stones, over the cup of the sea,
that powerful lord, and collapsed under his shield.
1210   Into Frankish hands came the life of that king,
his breast-garments, and the great collar too;
a lesser warrior looted the corpses
mown down in battle; Geatish men

---

1   The Brosinga necklace had apparently been worn by the Norse goddess Freya.
   Nothing much is known of Hama, who apparently stole the necklace from Eormanric, famous king of the Goths. The "bright city" and "eternal counsel" may
   refer to his retreat into a monastery and Christianity (a story told in the Old Norse
   Thidrekssaga), though this is not entirely certain.
2   The first of several mentions of Hygelac's ill-fated raid against the Frisians. Later we
   are told that Beowulf gives the necklace to Hygd, Hygelac's wife; she apparently let
   him borrow it when he went on his piratical raid.

held that killing field.
                    The hall swallowed the noise.
Wealhtheow stood before the company and spoke: 1215
"Beowulf, beloved warrior, wear this neck-ring
in good health, and enjoy this war-garment,
treasure of a people, and prosper well,
be bold and clever, and to these boys be
mild in counsel — I will remember you for that.   1220
You have made it so that men will praise you
far and near, forever and ever,
as wide as the seas, home of the winds,
surround the shores of earth. Be while you live
blessed, o nobleman! I wish you well   1225
with these bright treasures. Be to my sons
kind in your deeds, keeping them in joys!
Here each earl is true to the other,
mild in his heart, loyal to his liege-lord,
the thanes united, the nation alert,   1230
the troop, having drunk at my table, will do as I bid."
          She went to her seat. The best of feasts it was —
the men drank wine, and did not know *wyrd*,
the cruel fate which would come to pass
for many an earl once evening came,   1235
and Hrothgar departed to his own dwelling,
the mighty one to his rest. Countless men
guarded that hall, as they often had before.
They cleared away bench-planks, spread cushions
and bedding on the floor. One of those beer-drinkers   1240
lay down to his rest fated, ripe for death.
They set at their heads their round battle-shields,
bright boards; there on the bench was
easily seen over the noblemen
the high battle-helmet, the ringed byrnie,   1245
the mighty wooden spear. It was their custom
to be always ready, armed for battle,
at home or in the field, every one of them,
 on whatever occasion their overlord
had need of them; that was a good troop.   1250

XIX

They sank into sleep — one paid sorely
for his evening rest, as had often happened
when Grendel guarded that gold-hall,
committed his wrongs until he came to his end,
1255 died for his sins. It was clearly seen,
obvious to all men, that an avenger still
lived on after that enemy for a long time
after that grim battle — Grendel's mother,
monster-woman, remembered her misery,
1260 she who dwelt in those dreadful waters,
the cold streams, ever since Cain
killed with his blade his only brother,
his father's kin; he fled bloodstained,
marked for murder, left the joys of men,
1265 dwelled in the wasteland. From him awoke
many a fateful spirit — Grendel among them,
hateful accursed foe, who found at Heorot
a wakeful warrior waiting for battle.
There the great beast began to seize him,
1270 but he remembered his mighty strength,
the ample gifts which God had given him,
and trusted the Almighty for mercy,
favor and support; thus he overcame the fiend,
subdued the hellish spirit. He went away wretched,
1275 deprived of joy, to find his place of death,
mankind's foe. But his mother still
greedy, grim-minded, wanted to go
on her sorrowful journey to avenge her son's death.
She reached Heorot, where the Ring-Danes
1280 slept throughout the building; sudden turnabout
came to men, when Grendel's mother
broke into the hall. The horror was less
by as much as a maiden's strength,
a woman's warfare, is less than an armed man's
1285 when a bloodstained blade, its edges strong,
hammer-forged sword, slices through

the boar-image on a helmet opposite.[1]
Then in the hall was the hard edge drawn,
swords over seats, many a broad shield
raised in hands — none remembered his helmet   1290
or broad mail-shirt when that terror seized them.
She came in haste and meant to hurry out,
save her life, when she was surprised there,
but she had quickly seized, fast in her clutches,
one nobleman when she went to the fens.   1295
He was the dearest of heroes to Hrothgar
among his comrades between the two seas,
mighty shield-warrior, whom she snatched from his rest,
a glorious thane. Beowulf was not there,
but another place had been appointed   1300
for the famous Geat after the treasure-giving.
Heorot was in an uproar — she took the famous hand,
covered in gore; care was renewed,
come again to the dwellings. That was no good exchange,
that those on both sides should have to bargain   1305
with the lives of friends.
                Then the wise old king,
gray-bearded warrior, was grieved at heart
when he learned that he no longer lived —
the dearest of men, his chief thane, was dead.
Quickly Beowulf was fetched to the chambers,   1310
victory-blessed man. Just before dawn
that noble champion came with his companions,
went with his men to where the old king waited
wondering whether the Almighty would ever
work a change after his tidings of woe.   1315
Across the floor walked the worthy warrior
with his small troop — the hall-wood resounded —
and with his words he addressed the wise one,
lord of the Ingwines, asked him whether
the night had been agreeable, after his urgent summons.   1320

---

1   In fact Grendel's mother is a much more dangerous opponent for Beowulf; the
point of these lines is not clear.

XX

Hrothgar spoke, protector of the Scyldings:
"Ask not of joys! Sorrow is renewed
for the Danish people. Æschere is dead,
elder brother of Yrmenlaf,
1325 my confidant and my counselor
my shoulder-companion in every conflict
when we defended our heads when the footsoldiers clashed
and struck boar-helmets. As a nobleman should be,
always excellent, so Æschere was!
1330 In Heorot he was slain by the hand
of a restless death-spirit; I do not know
where that ghoul went, gloating with its carcass,
rejoicing in its feast. She avenged that feud
in which you killed Grendel yesterday evening
1335 in your violent way with a crushing vice-grip,
for he had diminished and destroyed my people
for far too long. He fell in battle,
it cost him his life, and now has come another
mighty evil marauder who means to avenge
1340 her kin, and too far has carried out her revenge,
as it may seem to many a thane
whose spirit groans for his treasure-giver,
a hard heart's distress — now that hand lies dead
which was wont to give you all good things.
1345   I have heard countrymen and hall-counselors
among my people report this:
they have seen two such creatures,
great march-stalkers holding the moors,
alien spirits. The second of them,
1350 as far as they could discern most clearly,
had the shape of a woman; the other, misshapen,
marched the exile's path in the form of a man,
except that he was larger than any other;
in bygone days he was called 'Grendel'
1355 by the local folk. They knew no father,
whether before him had been begotten

any more mysterious spirits. That murky land
they hold, wolf-haunted slopes, windy headlands,
awful fenpaths, where the upland torrents
plunge downward under the dark crags,   1360
the flood underground. It is not far hence
— measured in miles — that the mere stands;
over it hangs a grove hoar-frosted,
a firm-rooted wood looming over the water.
Every night one can see there an awesome wonder,   1365
fire on the water. There lives none so wise
or bold that he can fathom its abyss.
Though the heath-stepper beset by hounds,
the strong-horned hart, might seek the forest,
pursued from afar, he will sooner lose   1370
his life on the shore than save his head
and go in the lake — it is no good place!
The clashing waves climb up from there
dark to the clouds, when the wind drives
the violent storms, until the sky itself droops,   1375
the heavens groan. Now once again all help
depends on you alone. You do not yet know
this fearful place, where you might find
the sinful creature — seek it if you dare!
I will reward you with ancient riches   1380
for that feud, as I did before,
with twisted gold, if you return alive."

XXI

        Beowulf spoke, son of Ecgtheow:
       "Sorrow not, wise one! It is always better
1385 to avenge one's friend than to mourn overmuch.
       Each of us shall abide the end
       of this world's life; let him who can
       bring about fame before death — that is best
       for the unliving man after he is gone.
1390 Arise, kingdom's guard, let us quickly go
       and inspect the path of Grendel's kin.
       I promise you this: he[1] will find no protection —
       not in the belly of the earth nor the bottom of the sea,
       nor the mountain groves — let him go where he will!
1395 For today, you must endure patiently
       all your woes, as I expect you will."
       The old man leapt up, thanked the Lord,
       the mighty God, for that man's speech.
             Then for Hrothgar a horse was bridled
1400 with plaited mane. The wise prince
       rode in full array; footsoldiers marched
       with shields at the ready. The tracks were seen
       far and wide on the forest paths,
       a trail through the woods, where she went forth
1405 over the murky moor, bore the young man's
       lifeless body, the best of all those
       who had held watch over Hrothgar's home.
       The sons of nobles crossed over
       the steep stone cliffs, the constricted climb,
1410 a narrow solitary path, a course unknown,
       the towering headlands, home of sea-monsters.
       He went before with just a few
       wise men to see the way,
       until suddenly he saw mountain-trees,
1415 stunted and leaning over gray stone,

---

1   The hero does not note carefully enough the gender of Grendel's mother, or else
the pronoun *he* refers to OE *magan* "kinsman," a masculine noun.

a joyless wood; the water went under
turbid and dreary. To all the Danes,
the men of the Scyldings, many a thane,
it was a sore pain at heart to suffer,
a grief to every earl, when on the seacliff   1420
they came upon the head of Æschere.
The flood boiled with blood — the folk gazed on —
and hot gore. At times a horn sang
its eager war-song. The footsoldiers sat down.
They saw in the water many kinds of serpents,   1425
strange sea-creatures testing the currents,
and on the sloping shores lay such monsters
as often attend in early morning
a sorrowful journey on the sail-road,
dragons and wild beasts. They rushed away   1430
bitter, enraged; they heard the bright noise,
the sound of the battle-horn. A Geatish bowman
cut short the life of one of those swimmers
with a bow and arrow, so that in his body stood
the hard war-shaft; he was a slower swimmer   1435
on the waves, when death took him away.
At once in the water he was assailed
with the barbed hooks of boar-pikes,
violently attacked and dragged ashore,
the strange wave-roamer; the men inspected   1440
this grisly visitor.
                    Beowulf geared up
in his warrior's clothing, cared not for his life.
The broad war-shirt, woven by hand,
cunningly made, had to test the mere —
it knew well how to protect his bone-house   1445
so that a battle-grip might not hurt his breast
nor an angry malicious clutch touch his life.
The shining helmet protected his head,
set to stir up the sea's depths,
seek that troubled water, decorated with treasure,   1450
encircled with a splendid band, as a weapon-smith
in days of old had crafted it with wonders,

set boar-images, so that afterwards
no blade or battle-sword might ever bite it.
1455 Not the smallest of powerful supports was that
which Hrothgar's spokesman lent him at need;
that hilted sword was named Hrunting,
unique among ancient treasures —
its edge was iron, etched with poison-stripes,
1460 hardened with the blood of war; it had never failed
any man who grasped it in his hands in battle,
who dared to undertake a dreadful journey
into the very home of the foe — it was not the first time
that it had to perform a work of high courage.
1465 Truly, the son of Ecglaf, crafty in strength,
did not remember what he had said before,
drunk with wine, when he lent that weapon
to a better swordsman; he himself did not dare
to risk his life under the rushing waves,
1470 perform a lordly act; for that he lost honor,
his fame for courage. Not so with the other,
when he had geared himself up for battle.

XXII

Beowulf spoke, son of Ecgtheow:
"Consider now, famous kinsman of Healfdene,
1475 wise prince, now that I am eager to depart,
gold-friend to men, what we spoke of before:
if ever in your service I should
lose my life, that you would always be
in a father's place to me when I have passed away.
1480 Be a protector to my band of men,
my boon-companions, if battle should take me,
and send on to Hygelac, beloved Hrothgar,
the gifts of treasure which you have given me.
The lord of the Geats will understand by that gold,
1485 the son of Hrethel will see by that treasure,
that I found a ring-giver who was good

in ancient customs, and while I could, enjoyed it.
And let Unferth have that ancient heirloom,
that well-known man have my wave-patterned sword,
hard-edged, splendid; with Hrunting I shall   1490
win honor and fame, or death will take me!"
      After these words the Weder-Geat man
hastened boldly, by no means wished to
stay for an answer; the surging sea received
the brave soldier. It was the space of a day[1]   1495
before he could perceive the bottom.
Right away she who held that expanse of water,
bloodthirsty and fierce, for a hundred half-years,
grim and greedy, perceived that some man
was exploring from above that alien land.   1500
She snatched at him, seized the warrior
in her savage clutches, but none the sooner
injured his sound body — the ring-mail encircled him,
so that she could not pierce that war-dress,
the locked coat of mail, with her hostile claws.   1505
Then that she-wolf of the sea swam to the bottom,
and bore the prince of rings into her abode,
so that he might not — no matter how strong —
wield his weapons, but so many wonders
set upon him in the water, many a sea-beast   1510
with battle-tusks tearing at his war-shirt,
monsters pursuing him.[2]
               Then the earl perceived
that he was in some sort of battle-hall
where no water could harm him in any way,
and, for the hall's roof, he could not be reached   1515
by the flood's sudden rush — he saw a fire-light,
a glowing blaze shining brightly.
Then the worthy man saw that water-witch,
a great mere-wife; he gave a mighty blow
with his battle-sword — he did not temper that stroke —   1520

---

1   Or "it was daylight."
2   Or "attacked their adversary." The Old English word *æglæcan* may refer here to
    Beowulf or the sea-monsters.

so that the ring-etched blade rang out on her head
a greedy battle-song. The guest discovered then
that the battle-flame would not bite,
or wound her fatally — but the edge failed
1525 the man in his need; it had endured many
hand-to-hand meetings, often sheared through helmets,
fated war-garments. It was the first time
that the fame of that precious treasure had fallen.
      Again he was stalwart, not slow of zeal,
1530 mindful of glory, that kinsman of Hygelac —
the angry challenger threw away that etched blade,
wrapped and ornamented, so that it lay on the earth,
strong, steel-edged. He trusted his strength,
the might of his handgrip — as a man should do
1535 if by his warfare he thinks to win
long-lasting praise: he cares nothing for his life.
The man of the War-Geats grabbed by the shoulder
Grendel's mother — he had no regret for that feud;
battle-hardened, enraged, he swung her around,
1540 his deadly foe, so she fell to the ground.
Quickly she gave him requital for that
with a grim grasp, and grappled him to her —
weary, he stumbled, strongest of warriors,
of foot-soldiers, and took a fall.
1545 She set upon her hall-guest[1] and drew her knife,
broad, bright-edged; she would avenge her boy,
her only offspring. On his shoulders lay
the linked corselet; it defended his life,
prevented the entrance of point and blade.
1550 There the son of Ecgtheow would have ended his life
under the wide ground, the Geatish champion,
had not his armored shirt offered him help,
the hard battle-net, and holy God
brought about war-victory — the wise Lord,
1555 Ruler of the heavens, decided it rightly,
easily, once he stood up again.

---

1 Some translations read "sat down upon"; the meaning of OE *ofsæt* is disputed.

XXIII

He saw among the armor a victorious blade,
ancient giant-sword strong in its edges,
an honor in battle; it was the best of weapons,
except that it was greater than any other man   1560
might even bear into the play of battle,
good, adorned, the work of giants.[1]
The Scyldings' champion seized its linked hilt,
fierce and ferocious, drew the ring-marked sword
despairing of his life, struck in fury   1565
so that it caught her hard in the neck,
broke her bone-rings; the blade cut through
the doomed flesh — she fell to the floor,
the sword was bloody, the soldier rejoiced.
   The flames gleamed, a light glowed within   1570
even as from heaven clearly shines
the firmament's candle. He looked around the chamber,
passed by the wall, hefted the weapon
hard by its hilt, that thane of Hygelac,
angry and resolute — nor was the edge useless   1575
to that warrior, but he quickly wished
to pay back Grendel for the many battle-storms
which he had wrought on the West-Danes
much more often than on one occasion,
when Hrothgar's hall-companions   1580
he slew in their beds, devoured sleeping
fifteen men of the Danish folk,
and made off with as many more,
a loathsome booty. He paid him back for that,
the fierce champion, for on a couch he saw   1585
Grendel lying lifeless,
battle-weary from the wound he received
in the combat at Heorot. His corpse burst open
when he was dealt a blow after death,
a hard sword-stroke, and his head chopped off.   1590

---

1 Old, highly-praised weapons are often called "the work of giants"—whether this is
 meant to connect the sword to the giants "who fought against God" is not clear.

Soon the wise men saw it,
those who kept watch on the water with Hrothgar —
all turbid were the waves, and troubled,
the sea stained with blood. The graybearded
1595 elders spoke together about the good one,
said they did not expect that nobleman
would return, triumphant, to seek
the mighty prince; to many it seemed
that the sea-wolf had destroyed him.
1600 The ninth hour came; the noble Scyldings
abandoned the headland, and home went
the gold-friend of men. The guests[1] sat
sick at heart, and stared into the mere;
they wished, but did not hope, that they would
see their lord himself.
1605   Then the sword began,
that blade, to waste away into battle-icicles
from the war-blood; it was a great wonder
that it melted entirely, just like ice
when the Father loosens the frost's fetters,
1610 unwraps the water's bonds — He wields power
over times and seasons; that is the true Maker.
The man of the Geats took no more precious treasures
from that place — though he saw many there —
than the head, and the hilt as well,
1615 bright with gems; the blade had melted,
the ornamented sword burned up; so hot was the blood
of the poisonous alien spirit who died in there.
Soon he was swimming who had survived in battle
the downfall of his enemies, dove up through the water;
1620 the sea-currents were entirely cleansed,
the spacious regions, when that alien spirit
gave up life-days and this loaned world.
            The defender of seafarers came to land,
swam stout-hearted; he rejoiced in his sea-booty,
1625 the great burden which he brought with him.

---

1   The Geats who had come to Heorot with Beowulf.

That splendid troop of thanes went towards him,
thanked God, rejoiced in their prince,
that they might see him safe and sound.
Then from that bold man helmet and byrnie
were quickly unstrapped. Under the clouds   1630
the mere stewed, stained with gore.
They went forth, followed the trail,
rejoicing in their hearts; they marched along the road,
the familiar path; proud as kings
they carried the head from the sea-cliff   1635
with great trouble, even for two pairs
of stout-hearted men; four of them had to
bear, with some strain, on a battle-pole
Grendel's head to the gold-hall,
until presently fourteen proud   1640
and battle-hardy Geats came to the hall,
warriors marching; the lord of those men,
mighty in the throng, trod the meadhall-plain.
Then the ruler of thanes entered there,
daring in actions, honored in fame,   1645
battle-brave hero, to greet Hrothgar.
Then, where men were drinking, they dragged by its hair
Grendel's head across the hall-floor,
a grisly spectacle for the men and the queen.
Everyone stared at that amazing sight.   1650

XXIV

Beowulf spoke, son of Ecgtheow:
"Look! son of Healfdene, prince of the Scyldings,
we have brought you gladly these gifts from the sea
which you gaze on here, a token of glory.
Not easily did I escape with my life   1655
that undersea battle, did my brave deed
with difficulty — indeed, the battle would have been
over at once, if God had not guarded me.
Nor could I achieve anything at that battle

1660 with Hrunting, though that weapon is good;
but the Ruler of Men granted to me
that I might see on the wall a gigantic old sword,
hanging glittering — He has always guided
the friendless one — so I drew that weapon.
1665 In that conflict, when I had the chance, I slew
the shepherds of that house. Then that battle-sword
burned up with its ornaments, as the blood shot out,
hottest battle-sweat. I have brought the hilt
back from the enemy; I avenged the old deeds,
1670 the slaughter of Danes, as seemed only right.
Now you have my word that you may in Heorot
sleep without care with your company of men,
and every thane, young and old,
in your nation; you need fear nothing,
1675 prince of the Scyldings, from that side,
no deadly manslaughters, as you did before."
          Then the golden hilt was placed in the hand
of the gray-haired war-chief, wise old leader,
that old work of giants; it came to the keeping
1680 of the Danish lord after the fall of demons,
a work of wonder-smiths; and when that evil-hearted man,
God's adversary, gave up the world,
guilty of murders — and his mother too —
it passed to the possession of the best
1685 of world-kings between the two seas,
of all those that dealt out treasures in Danish lands.
          Hrothgar spoke — he studied the hilt
of the old heirloom, where was written[1] the origin
of ancient strife, when the flood slew,
1690 rushing seas, the race of giants —
they suffered awfully. That was a people alien
to the eternal Lord; a last reward
the Ruler gave them through the raging waters.
Also, on the sword-guard of bright gold

---

1   Or "carved." It is not clear whether the scene is visual or textual, depicted or writ-
    ten in (presumably runic) characters.

was rightly marked in rune-letters,   1695
set down and said for whom that sword,
best of irons, had first been made,
with scrollery and serpentine patterns. Then spoke
the wise son of Healfdene — all fell silent:
        "One may, indeed, say, if he acts in truth   1700
and right for the people, remembers all,
old guardian of his homeland, that this earl was
born a better man! My friend Beowulf,
your glory is exalted throughout the world,
over every people; you hold it all with patient care,   1705
and temper strength with wisdom. To you I shall fulfill
our friendship, as we have said. You shall become a comfort
everlasting to your own people,
and a help to heroes.
                Not so was Heremod
to the sons of Ecgwala, the Honor-Scyldings;   1710
he grew not for their delight, but for their destruction
and the murder of Danish men.
Enraged, he cut down his table-companions,
comrades-in-arms, until he turned away alone
from the pleasures of men, that famous prince;   1715
though mighty God exalted him in the joys
of strength and force, advanced him far
over all men, yet in his heart he nursed
a blood-ravenous breast-hoard. No rings did he give
to the Danes for their honor; he endured, joyless,   1720
to suffer the pains of that strife,
a long-lasting harm to his people. Learn from him,
understand virtue! For your sake I have told this,
in the wisdom of my winters.
                        It is a wonder to say
how mighty God in His great spirit   1725
allots wisdom, land and lordship
to mankind; He has control of everything.
At times He permits the thoughts of a man
in a mighty race to move in delights,
gives him to hold in his homeland   1730

the sweet joys of earth, a stronghold of men,
grants him such power over his portion of the world,
a great kingdom, that he himself cannot
imagine an end to it, in his folly.

1735 He dwells in plenty; in no way plague him
illness or old age, nor do evil thoughts
darken his spirit, nor any strife
or sword-hate shows itself, but all the world
turns to his will; he knows nothing worse.

XXV

1740   At last his portion of pride within him
grows and flourishes, while the guardian sleeps,
the soul's shepherd — that sleep is too sound,
bound with cares, the slayer too close
who, sinful and wicked, shoots from his bow.[1]

1745 Then he is struck in his heart, under his helmet
with a bitter dart — he knows no defense —
the strange, dark demands of evil spirits;
What he has long held seems too little,
angry and greedy, he gives no golden rings

1750 for vaunting boasts, and his final destiny
he neglects and forgets, since God, Ruler of glories,
has given him a portion of honors.
In the end it finally comes about
that the loaned life-dwelling starts to decay

1755 and falls, fated to die; another follows him
who doles out his riches without regret,
the earl's ancient treasure; he heeds no terror.
Defend yourself from wickedness, dear Beowulf,
best of men, and choose the better,

1760 eternal counsel; care not for pride,
great champion! The glory of your might
is but a little while; soon it will be

---

1   The slayer is sin or vice; the soul's guardian is reason, conscience or prudence.

that sickness or the sword will shatter your strength,
of the grip of fire, or the surging flood,
or the cut of a sword, or the flight of a spear,   1765
or terrible old age — or the light of your eyes
will fail and flicker out; in one fell swoop
death, o warrior, will overwhelm you.
      Thus, a hundred half-years I held the Ring-Danes
under the skies, and kept them safe from war   1770
from many tribes throughout this middle-earth,
from spears and swords, so that I considered none
under the expanse of heaven my enemy.
Look! Turnabout came in my own homeland,
grief after gladness, when Grendel became   1775
my invader, ancient adversary;
for that persecution I bore perpetually
the greatest heart-cares. Thanks be to the Creator,
eternal Lord, that I have lived long enough
to see that head, stained with blood,   1780
with my own eyes, after all this strife!
Go to your seat, enjoy the feast,
honored in battle; between us shall be shared
a great many treasures, when morning comes."
      Glad-hearted, the Geat went at once   1785
to take his seat, as the wise one told him.
Then again as before, a feast was prepared
for the brave ones who occupied the hall
on this new occasion. The dark helm of night
overshadowed the troop. The soldiers arose;   1790
the gray-haired ruler was ready for bed,
the aged Scylding. Immeasurably well
did rest please the Geat, proud shield-warrior;
at once a chamberlain led him forth,
weary from his adventure, come from afar,   1795
he who attended to all the needs
of that thane, for courtesy, as in those days
all battle-voyagers used to have.
      The great-hearted one rested; the hall towered
vaulted and gold-adorned; the guest slept within   1800

until the black[1] raven, blithe-hearted, announced
the joy of heaven. Then light came hurrying
[bright over shadows;] the soldiers hastened,
the noblemen were eager to travel
1805 back to their people; the bold-spirited visitor
wished to seek his far-off ship.
    The hardy one ordered Hrunting to be borne
to the son of Ecglaf,[2] bid him take his sword,
lordly iron; he thanked him for the loan,
1810 and said that he regarded it as a good war-friend,
skillful in battle, and the sword's edges
he did not disparage; he was a noble man.
And when the warriors were eager for their way,
equipped in their war-gear, the nobleman went,
1815 the Danes' honor, to the high seat where the other was:
the hero, brave in battle, saluted Hrothgar.

XXVI

    Beowulf spoke, son of Ecgtheow:
"Now we seafarers, come from afar,
wish to say that we desire
1820 to seek Hygelac. Here we were honorably
entertained with delights; you have treated us well.
If ever on earth I can do any thing
to earn more of your affection,
than the battle-deeds I have done already,
1825 ruler of men, I will be ready at once.
If ever I hear over the sea's expanse
that your neighbors threaten you with terror
as your enemies used to do,
I will bring you a thousand thanes,
1830 heroes to help you. I have faith in Hygelac —

---

1 Either OE *blac* "shining" or *blæc* "black"; the translation prefers the irony of the
image of the black raven, not otherwise known as a harbinger of joy, announcing
the surprising good news of a dawn without slaughter.
2 Unferth.

the lord of the Geats, though he be young,
shepherd of his people, will support me
with words and deeds, that I might honor you well
and bring to your side a forest of spears,
the support of my might, whenever you need men.   1835
If ever Hrethric decides, son of a prince,
to come to the Geatish court, he will find
many friends there; far-off lands
are better sought by one who is himself good."
        Hrothgar spoke in answer to him: 1840
"The wise Lord has sent those words
into your heart; I have never heard
a shrewder speech from such a young man.
You are strong in might, and sound in mind,
prudent in speech! I expect it is likely   1845
that if it should ever happen that the spear
or the horrors of war take Hrethel's son,[1]
or sickness or sword strike the shepherd of his people,
your lord, and you still live,
that the sea-Geats could not select   1850
a better choice anywhere for king,
hoard-guard of heroes, if you will hold
the realm of your kinsmen. Your character pleases me
better and better, beloved Beowulf.
You have brought it about that between our peoples,   1855
the Geatish nation and the spear-Danes,
there shall be peace, and strife shall rest,
the malicious deeds that they endured before,
as long as I shall rule this wide realm,
and treasures together; many shall greet   1860
another with gifts across the gannet's bath;
the ring-necked ship shall bring over the sea
tribute and tokens of love. I know these nations
will be made fast against friend and foe,
blameless in everything, in the old way."   1865
        The protector of heroes, kinsman of Healfdene,

---

1   Hygelac.

gave him twelve great treasures in the hall;
bid him seek his own dear people in safety
with those gifts, and quickly come again.
1870 Then the good king, of noble kin, kissed
that best of thanes and embraced his neck,
the Scylding prince; tears were shed
by that gray-haired man. He was of two minds —
but in his old wisdom knew it was more likely
1875 that never again would they see one another,
brave in their meeting-place. The man was so dear to him
that he could not hold back the flood in his breast,
but in his heart, fast in the bonds of his thought,
a deep-felt longing for the dear man
1880 burned in his blood. Beowulf from thence,
gold-proud warrior, trod the grassy lawn,
exulting in treasure; the sea-goer awaited
its lord and owner, where it rode at anchor.
As they were going, the gift of Hrothgar
1885 was often praised; that king was peerless,
blameless in everything, until old age took from him
— it has injured so many— the joy of his strength.

XXVII

Those men of high courage then came to the sea,
that troop of young retainers, bore their ring-mail,
1890 locked shirts of armor. The coast-guard observed
the return of those earls, as he had once before;
he did not greet those guests with insults
on the clifftop, but he rode towards them,
said that the warriors in their shining armor
1895 would be welcome in their ships to the people of the Weders.
The sea-curved prow, the ring-necked ship,
as it lay on the sand was laden with war-gear,
with horses and treasures; the mast towered high
over Hrothgar's hoard-gifts.

To the ship's guardian he[1] gave a sword,   1900
bound with gold, so that on the mead-benches
he was afterwards more honored by that heirloom,
that old treasure. Onward they went, the ship
sliced through deep water, gave up the Danish coast.
The sail by the mast was rigged fast with ropes,   1905
a great sea-cloth; the timbers creaked,
the wind over the sea did not hinder at all
the wave-floater on its way; the sea-goer sped on,
floated foamy-necked, forth upon the waves,
the bound prow over the briny streams,   1910
until they could make out the cliffs of Geatland,
familiar capes; the keel drove forward
thrust by the wind, and came to rest on land.
Right away the harbor-guard was ready at the shore,
who for a long time had gazed far   1915
over the currents, eager for the beloved men;
he moored the broad-beamed ship on the beach
fast with anchor-ropes, lest the force of the waves
should drive away the handsome wooden vessel.
He bade that the nobleman's wealth be borne ashore,   1920
armor and plated gold; they had not far to go
to seek their dispenser of treasure,
Hygelac son of Hrethel, where he dwelt at home
with his companions, near the sea-wall.
          The building was splendid, the king quite bold,   1925
high in his hall, Hygd[2] very young,
wise, well-mannered, though few winters
had the daughter of Hæreth passed within
the palace walls — yet not poor for that,
nor stingy of gifts to the Geatish people,   1930
of great treasures. She considered Thryth's pride,[3]

---

1   Beowulf.
2   Hygelac's queen.
3   These lines are difficult. Some editions and translations read the name as
    "Modthryth"; the reading adopted here smoothes out a transition that is otherwise
    abrupt even by the standards of this poem. This "digression" on the character of a
    queen, with some elements of a folktale, is the counterpart to the story of Heremod
    in earlier sections.

famous folk-queen, and her terrible crimes;
no man so bold among her own retainers
dared to approach her, except as her prince,[1]
1935 or dared to look into her eyes by day;
for he knew that deadly bonds, braided by hand,
were waiting for him — first the hand-grip,
and quickly after a blade appointed,
so that a patterned sword had to settle things,
1940 proclaim the execution. That is no queenly custom
for a lady to perform — no matter how lovely —
that a peace-weaver[2] should deprive of life
a friendly man after a pretended affront.
The kinsman of Hemming[3] put a halt to that:
1945 then ale-drinkers told another tale,
said she caused less calamity to the people,
less malicious evil, after she was
given gold-adorned to the young champion,
fair to that nobleman, when to Offa's floor
1950 she sought a journey over the fallow sea
at her father's wish, where she afterwards
on the throne, famous for good things,
used well her life while she had it,
held high love with that chief of heroes,
1955 of all mankind, as men have told me,
the best between the two seas,
of all the races of men; therefore Offa,
in gifts and battle, spear-bold man,
was widely honored, and held in wisdom
1960 his own homeland. From him arose Eomer
as a help to heroes, kinsman of Hemming,
grandson of Garmund, skilled in violence.

---

1   I.e., as a husband; or else the line means "except the prince himself," i.e. her father.
2   This epithet reflects the common practice, whose sometimes-tragic consequences
    are explored at length elsewhere in the poem, of settling intertribal feuds with a
    marriage between the daughter of one lord and the son of another.
3   Offa I, fourth-century king of the continental Angles, not Offa II, the eighth-cen-
    tury king of Mercia. The elaborate praise offered to Offa I has been taken to sug-
    gest that the poem may have been written or circulated in the court of Offa II, but
    there is otherwise no evidence for this.

XXVIII

The hardy man[1] with his hand-picked troop
went across the sand, trod the sea-plain,
the wide shore. The world's candle shone,   1965
hastening from the south. They had survived their journey,
went boldly to where they knew
the protector of earls, slayer of Ongentheow,[2]
good young battle-king, gave out rings
in his fortress. To Hygelac   1970
the arrival of Beowulf was quickly reported,
that to the enclosures his battle-companion,
protector of warriors, came walking alive
back to his court, safe from his battle-play.
Quickly, as the powerful one commanded,   1975
the hall was cleared out inside for the foot-guests.
        He sat down with him, who had survived the fight,
kinsmen together, after he greeted
his friend and liege-lord with a formal speech,
with courteous words and cups of mead.   1980
The daughter of Hæreth passed through the hall,
cared for the people, bore the cup
to the hand of the hero.[3] Hygelac began
the question his companion courteously
in the high hall — curiosity pressed him   1985
to know how the sea-Geats' adventures were:
        "How did you fare, beloved Beowulf,
in your journey, when you suddenly resolved
to seek a far-off strife over the salt sea,
a battle in Heorot? Did you better at all   1990
the well-known woe of Hrothgar,
the famous prince? For that I seethed
with heart-care and distress, mistrusted the adventure

---

1 Beowulf.
2 Hygelac. The death of the Swedish king Ongentheow (at the hands of Wulf and
   Eofor, retainers of Hygelac) is told below, section XL.
3 The manuscript reads "to the hands of heathens," which makes sense, but is usually
   emended. The "daughter of Hæreth" is Hygd.

of my beloved man; long I implored
1995　that you not seek that slaughter-spirit at all,
let the south-Danes themselves make
war against Grendel. I say thanks to God
that I might see you again safe and sound."
　　　　Beowulf spoke, son of Ecgtheow:
2000　"It is no mystery to many men,
my lord Hygelac — the great meeting,
what a time of great struggle Grendel and I
had in that place where he made so many
sorrows for the victory-Scyldings,
2005　life-long misery — I avenged them all,
so that none of Grendel's tribe needs to boast
anywhere on earth of that uproar at dawn,
whoever lives longest of that loathsome kind,
enveloped in foul evil. First I came there
2010　to the ring-hall to greet Hrothgar;
quickly the famous kinsman of Healfdene,
once he knew of my intentions,
assigned me a seat with his own sons.
That troop was in delight; never in my life
2015　have I seen among hall-sitters, under heaven's vault,
a more joyous feast. At times the famous queen,
bond of peace to nations, passed through the hall,
urged on her young sons; often she gave
twisted rings before she took her seat.
2020　At times before the hall-thanes the daughter of Hrothgar
bore the ale-cup to the earls in the back —
Freawaru, I heard the men in the hall
call her, when the studded treasure-cup
was passed among them. She is promised,
2025　young, gold-adorned, to the gracious son of Froda;[1]
the ruler of the Scyldings has arranged this,
the kingdom's shepherd, and approves the counsel

1　Ingeld, prince of the Heathobards. His attack on the Danes, alluded to earlier in the
poem (80-5), was apparently unsuccessful; another Old English poem, *Widsith* (see
Appendix A.6) reports that "Hrothulf and Hrothgar...humbled Ingeld's battle-
array."

that he should settle his share of feud and slaughter
with this young woman. But seldom anywhere
after the death of a prince does the deadly spear rest   2030
for even a brief while, though the bride be good!
      It may, perhaps, displease the Heathobards' prince,
and every retainer among his tribe,
when across the floor, following that woman, goes
a noble son of the Danes, received with honors;   2035
on him glitters an ancestral heirloom,
hard, ring-adorned, once a Heathobard treasure
as long as they were able to wield their weapons.

XXIX

And then in that deadly shield-play they undid
their beloved comrades and their own lives.   2040
Then an old spear-bearer[1] speaks over his beer,
who sees that ring-hilt and remembers all
the spear-deaths of men — his spirit is grim —
begins, sad-minded, to test the mettle
of a young thane with his innermost thoughts,   2045
to awaken war, and says these words:
      "Can you, my friend, recognize that sword,
which your father bore into battle
in his final adventure beneath the helmet,
that dear iron, when the Danes struck him,   2050
ruled the field of slaughter after the rout of heroes,
when Withergyld[2] fell — those valiant Scyldings?
Now here some son or other of his slayer
walks across this floor, struts in his finery,
brags of the murder and bears that treasure   2055
which ought, by right, to belong to you."

---

1   of the Heathobards, outraged by the presence of his former enemies, the Danes. In
    heroic poetry when a warrior falls, his killer is often awarded his armor; the sword
    is a vivid reminder of the fate of its former owner and the duty of revenge which is
    passed on to the next generation.
2   Apparently a famous Heathobard warrior.

He urges and reminds him on every occasion
with cruel words, until the time comes
that Freawaru's thane, for his father's deeds,
2060 sleeps, bloodstained from the bite of a sword,
forfeits his life; from there the other
escapes alive, for he knows the land well.
Then on both sides the sworn oaths of earls
will be broken, once bitter violent hate
2065 wells up in Ingeld, and his wife-love
grows cooler after his surging cares.
Thus I expect that the Heathobards' part
in the Danish alliance is not without deceit,
nor their friendship fast.

                I will speak further
2070 concerning Grendel, so that you might certainly know,
giver of treasure, how it turned out,
the heroic wrestling-match. When heaven's gem
slipped under the ground, the angry spirit came,
horrible, evening-grim, sought us out
2075 where, unharmed, we guarded the hall.
The attack came first against Hondscio[1] there,
deadly to that doomed man — he fell first,
a girded champion; Grendel was
that famous young retainer's devourer,
2080 gobbled up the body of that beloved man.
None the sooner did that slayer, blood in his teeth,
mindful of misery, mean to leave
that gold-hall empty-handed,
but in his mighty strength he tested me,
2085 grabbed with a ready hand. A glove[2] hung
huge, grotesque, fast with cunning clasps;

---

1   We finally learn the name of the retainer killed in section XI. The name, as in
modern German (Handschuh), means "glove."

2   It is not clear what this is; apparently a pouch of some kind. It is characteristic of a
troll in Norse legend. In any case it does not figure in the narrator's own description of Grendel's attack, and is but one of several discrepancies between the two
tellings of the story. Is Beowulf embellishing his tale? Or do such inconsistencies
matter in a story like this?

it was all embroidered with evil skill,
with the devil's craft and dragons' skins.
Inside there, though I was innocent,
that proud evil-doer wanted to put me,   2090
one of many; but it was not to be,
once I angrily stood upright.

XXX[1]

It is too long to tell how I handed back payment
to the people's enemy for all his evils —
there, my prince, I did honor to your people   2095
with my actions. He escaped away,
enjoyed his life a little while longer;
yet behind him, guarding his path, was his right
hand in Heorot, and wretched, he went hence,
sad at heart, and sank to the sea-floor.   2100
          For that bloody onslaught the friend of the Scyldings
repaid me greatly with plated gold,
many treasures, when morning came,
and we had gathered together to the feast again.
There was song and joy; the aged Scylding,[2]   2105
widely learned, told of far-off times;
at times the brave warrior touched the song-wood,
delight of the harp, at times made lays
both true and sad, at times strange stories
he recounted rightly. That great-hearted king,   2110
gray-bearded old warrior wrapped in his years,
at times began to speak of his youth again,
his battle-strength; his heart surged within him
when, old in winters, he remembered so much.
And so there inside we took our ease   2115

---

1 The placement of this section is conjectural; the sectional divisions of the manuscript are confused at this point.
2 It is not clear whether this is Hrothgar or not, or how many storytellers and singers
   are at this banquet.

all day long, until night descended
again upon men. There, quickly ready
with revenge for her griefs, Grendel's mother
journeyed sorrowful; death took her son,
2120   the war-hate of the Weders. That monstrous woman
avenged her son, killed a soldier
boldly at once — there the life of Æschere,
wise old counselor, came to its end.
And when morning came the men of the Danes
2125   were not able to burn his body, death-weary,
with flames, nor place him on a funeral pyre,
beloved man; she bore away his corpse
in her evil embrace under the upland streams.
That, to Hrothgar, was the most wrenching distress
2130   of all those that had befallen that folk-leader.
Then the prince — by your life — implored me,
his mind wracked, that in the roaring waves
I should do a noble deed, put my life in danger,
perform glorious things — he promised me reward.
2135   In the waves I found, as is widely known,
a grim, horrible guardian of the abyss.
There for a while, we fought hand-to-hand;
the sea foamed with blood, and I severed the head
of Grendel's mother with a mighty sword
2140   in that [battle-]hall;[1] I barely managed
to get away with my life — I wasn't doomed yet —
and the protector of earls once again gave me
many treasures, that kinsman of Healfdene.

XXXI

So that nation's king followed good customs;
2145   in no wise have I lost those rewards,
the prize for my strength, but the son of Healfdene

---

1   A word is missing; other editors and translators supply different words, such as *grund*
or "earth."

offered me treasures at my own choice,
which I wish to bring to you, o war-king,
to show good will. Still all my joys
are fixed on you alone; I have few   2150
close kinsmen, my Hygelac, except for you."
      He ordered to be borne in the boar standard,
the helmet towering in battle, the gray byrnie,
the decorated sword, and told this story:
"Hrothgar gave me this battle-gear,   2155
wise prince, and commanded particularly
that first I should tell you the story of his gift —
he said that Heorogar[1] the king first had it,
lord of the Scyldings, for a long while;
none the sooner would he give to his own son,   2160
the valiant Heoroward — loyal though he was —
that breast-armor. Use all well!"
Then, as I've heard, four swift horses,
fallow as apples, well-matched, followed
that war-gear; he gave him as a gift   2165
the horses and harness — as kinsman should behave,
never knitting a net of malice for another
with secret plots, preparing death
for his hand-picked comrades. Hygelac's nephew
was loyal to him, hardy in the fight,   2170
and each man to the other mindful of benefits. —
I heard that he gave the necklace to Hygd,
the wondrous ornamented treasure which Wealhtheow
                                 had given him,
to that lord's daughter, along with three horses
graceful and saddle-bright; her breast was adorned   2175
the more graciously after that ring-giving.
      So the son of Ecgtheow showed himself brave,
renowned for battles and noble deeds,
pursued honor, by no means slew, drunken,
his hearth-companions; he had no savage heart,   2180
but the great gift which God had given him,

---

1   Eldest brother of Hrothgar.

the greatest might of all mankind, he held,
brave in battle. He had been long despised,[1]
as the sons of the Geats considered him no good,
2185 nor did the lord of the Weders wish to bestow
many good things upon him on the meadbenches,
for they assumed that he was slothful,
a cowardly nobleman. Reversal came
to the glorious man for all his griefs.
2190   The protector of earls, battle-proud king,
ordered the heirloom of Hrethel[2] brought in,
adorned with gold; among the Geats there was
no finer treasure in the form of a sword.
He laid the sword in Beowulf's lap,
2195 and gave him seven thousand hides of land,[3]
a hall and a princely throne. Both of them held
inherited land in that nation, a home
and native rights, but the wider rule
was reserved to the one who was higher in rank.
2200   Then it came to pass[4] amid the crash of battle
in later days, after Hygelac lay dead,
and for Heardred[5] the swords of battle held
deadly slaughter under the shield-wall,
when the Battle-Scylfings sought him out,
2205 those hardy soldiers, and savagely struck down
the nephew of Hereric in his victorious nation —
then came the broad kingdom
into Beowulf's hands; he held it well
for fifty winters — he was then a wise king,
2210 old guardian of his homeland — until
in the dark nights a dragon began his reign,

---

1   The reasons for ascribing to the hero an unpromising youth, elsewhere not men-
    tioned, are not clear.
2   Father of Hygelac.
3   The "hide" is a unit of land, originally the amount of land which could support a
    peasant and his family; its actual size varied from one region to another. Seven
    thousand hides is by any measure a very generous area.
4   This section is easier to follow if the reader refers to the *Genealogies* in the Appen-
    dix. The stories are told in greater detail later in the poem.
5   Son of Hygelac.

who guarded his hoard in the high heaths
and the steep stone barrows; the path below
lay unknown to men. Some sort of man
went inside there, found his way to   2215
the heathen hoard — his hand ...
inlaid with jewels.[1] He[2] got no profit there,
though he had been trapped in his sleep
by a thief's trickery: the whole nation knew,
and all the people around them, that he was enraged.   2220

XXXII

Not for his own sake did he who sorely harmed him
break into that worm-hoard, or by his own will,
but in sad desperation some sort of slave[3]
of a warrior's son fled the savage lash,
the servitude of a house, and slipped in there,   2225
a man beset by sins. Soon he gazed around
and felt the terror from that evil spirit;
yet ...
          ...made...
                    ... when the terror seized him   2230
he snatched a jeweled cup.[4]
                              There were many such
antique riches in that earth-hall,
for in ancient days an unknown man
had thought to hide them carefully there,
the rich legacy of a noble race,   2235
precious treasures. In earlier times
death had seized them all, and he who still survived
alone from that nation's army lingered there,

---

1 The manuscript is damaged here and some text is unreadable. Among many conjectural restorations one thing is clear – a cup is taken from the dragon's hoard.
2 The thief; "he" in the following line refers to the dragon. These lines are nearly
   illegible and other readings have been proposed.
3 The word is illegible in the manuscript; the translation follows most editions.
4 The manuscript is unreadable at this point.

a mournful sentry, expected the same,
2240 that he might enjoy those ancient treasures
for just a little while. A waiting barrow
stood in an open field near the ocean waves,
new on the cape, safe with crafty narrow entrances;
he bore within the noble wealth,
2245 the plated gold, that guardian of rings,
a share worthy of a hoard, and spoke few words:
          "Hold now, o thou earth, for heroes cannot,
the wealth of men — Lo, from you long ago
those good ones first obtained it! Death in war,
2250 and awful deadly harm have swept away
all of my people who have passed from life,
and left the joyful hall. Now have I none
to bear the sword or burnish the bright cup,
the precious vessel — all that host has fled.
2255 Now must the hardened helm of hammered gold
be stripped of all its trim; the stewards sleep
who should have tended to this battle-mask.
So too this warrior's coat, which waited once
the bite of iron over the crack of boards,
2260 molders like its owner. The coat of mail
cannot travel widely with the war-chief,
beside the heroes. Harp-joy have I none,
no happy song; nor does the well-schooled hawk
soar high throughout the hall, nor the swift horse
2265 stamp in the courtyards. Savage butchery
has sent forth many of the race of men!"
          So, grieving, he mourned his sorrow,
alone after all. Unhappy sped
both days and nights, until the flood of death
2270 broke upon his heart. An old beast of the dawn
found that shining horde standing open —
he who, burning, seeks the barrows,
a fierce and naked dragon, who flies by night
in a pillar of fire; people on earth
2275 fear him greatly. It is his nature to find
a hoard in the earth, where, ancient and proud,

he guards heathen gold, though it does him no good.[1]
Three hundred winters that threat to the people
held in the ground his great treasury,
wondrously powerful, until one man   2280
made him boil with fury; he[2] bore to his liege-lord
the plated cup, begged for peace
from his lord. Then the hoard was looted,
the hoard of rings fewer, a favor was granted
the forlorn man; for the first time   2285
his lord looked on that ancient work of men.
When the dragon stirred, strife was renewed;
he slithered along the stones, stark-hearted he found
his enemy's footprint — he had stepped too far
in his stealthy skill, too close to the serpent's head.   2290
Thus can an undoomed man easily survive
wrack and ruin, if he holds to the Ruler's
grace and protection![3] The hoard-guardian
searched along the ground, greedy to find
the man who had sorely harmed him while he slept;   2295
hot, half-mad, he kept circling his cave
all around the outside, but no one was there
in that wilderness to welcome his warfare
and the business of battle. Soon he returned to his barrow,
sought his treasure; he soon discovered   2300
that some man had disturbed his gold,
his great wealth. The hoard-guardian waited
impatiently until evening came;
the barrow's shepherd was swollen with rage,
the loathsome foe would repay with fire   2305
his precious drinking-cup. Then day was departed
to the delight of that worm; he did not linger
on the barrow wall, but took off burning
in a burst of flames. The beginning was terror
to the people on land, and to their ring-giving lord   2310
the ending soon would be sore indeed.

---

1   The association of dragons and hoarded treasure is ancient and proverbial.
2   The thief.
3   This is the narrator's version of Beowulf's comment at lines 572-3.

XXXIII

Then that strange visitor began to spew flames
and burn the bright courts; his burning gleams
struck horror in men. That hostile flier
2315 would leave nothing alive.
The worm's warfare was widely seen,
his ferocious hostility, near and far,
how the destroyer hated and harmed
the Geatish people, then hastened to his hoard,
2320 his dark and hidden hall, before the break of day.
He had surrounded the people of that region with fire,
flames and cinders; he took shelter in his barrow,
his walls and warfare — but that trust failed him.
To Beowulf the news was quickly brought
2325 of that horror — that his own home,
best of buildings, had burned in waves of fire,
the gift-throne of the Geats. To the good man that was
painful in spirit, greatest of sorrows;
the wise one believed he had bitterly offended
2330 the Ruler of all, the eternal Lord,
against the old law; his breast within groaned
with dark thoughts — that was not his custom.
The fire-dragon had found the stronghold of that folk,
that fortress, and had razed it with flames
2335 entirely and from without; for that the war-king,
prince of the Weders, devised revenge.
Then the lord of men bade them make,
protector of warriors, a wondrous war-shield,
all covered with iron; he understood well
2340 that wood from the forest would not help him,
linden against flames. The long-good nobleman
had to endure the end of his loaned days,
this world's life — and so did the worm,
though he had held for so long his hoarded wealth.
2345 Then that prince of rings scorned to seek out
the far-flung flier with his full force of men,
a large army; he did not dread that attack,

nor did he worry much about the dragon's warfare,
his strength or valor, because he had survived
many battles, barely escaping alive   2350
in the crash of war, after he had cleansed,
triumphant hero, the hall of Hrothgar,
and at battle crushed Grendel and his kin,
that loathsome race.
      It was not the least
of hand-to-hand combats when Hygelac was slain,   2355
when the king of the Geats, in the chaos of battle,
the lord of his people, in the land of the Frisians,
the son of Hrethel, died sword-drunk,
beaten by blades. Beowulf escaped from there
through his own strength, took a long swim;   2360
he had in his arms the battle-armor
of thirty men, when he climbed to the cliffs.
By no means did the Hetware[1] need to exult
in that fight, when they marched on foot to him,
bore their linden shields; few came back   2365
from that brave soldier to seek their homes.
The son of Ecgtheow crossed the vast sea,
wretched, solitary, returned to his people,
where Hygd offered him the hoard and kingdom,
rings and royal throne; she did not trust   2370
that her son could hold the ancestral seat
against foreign hosts, now that Hygelac was dead.
But despite their misery, by no means
could they prevail upon that prince at all
that he should become lord over Heardred,   2375
or choose to rule the kingdom.
Yet he upheld him[2] in the folk with friendly counsel,
good will and honors, until he was older,
and ruled the Weder-Geats.
       Wretched exiles,
the sons of Ohthere,[3] sought him out across the seas;   2380

---

1 A Frankish tribe apparently on the side of the Frisians.
2 Beowulf upheld Heardred, as champion and in effect a kind of regent.
3 Eanmund and Eadgils.

they had rebelled against the Scylfings' ruler,[1]
the best of all the sea-kings
who dispensed treasure in the Swedish lands,
a famous king. That cost him[2] his life:
2385 for his hospitality he took a mortal hurt
with the stroke of a sword, that son of Hygelac;
and the son of Ongentheow afterwards went
to seek out his home, once Heardred lay dead,
and let Beowulf hold the high throne
2390 and rule the Geats — that was a good king.

XXXIV

In later days he[3] did not forget
that prince's fall, and befriended Eadgils
the wretched exile; across the open sea
he gave support to the son of Ohthere
2395 with warriors and weapons. He[4] wreaked his revenge
with cold sad journeys, and took the king's life.
        And so the son of Ecgtheow had survived
every struggle, every terrible onslaught,
with brave deeds, until that one day
2400 when he had to take his stand against the serpent.
Grim and enraged, the lord of the Geats
took a dozen men[5] to seek out the dragon;
he had found out by then how the feud arose,
the baleful violence; the precious vessel

---

1 Onela, son of Ongentheow. Ohthere had succeeded his father Ongentheow, but
   after his death his brother Onela apparently seized the throne and drove the two
   young men Eanmund and Eadgils into exile. They take refuge at the Geatish court,
   for which Heardred is attacked and killed by Onela. Later Eanmund is killed by
   Weohstan (see section XXXVI below) but Eadgils, with the help of Beowulf,
   becomes king (section XXXIV).
2 Heardred.
3 Beowulf, whose revenge for the death of his lord Heardred takes a curiously indi-
   rect form – he supports Eadgils' return to Sweden, where Onela is killed.
4 Eadgils.
5 Literally "one of twelve" – Beowulf, Wiglaf, and ten others. The thief who leads
   the way is the thirteenth man.

had come to him through the thief's hands.   2405
He was the thirteenth man among that troop,
who had brought about the beginning of that strife,
a sad-minded captive — wretched and despised
he led the way to that plain. He went against his will
to where he alone knew the earth-hall stood,   2410
an underground cave near the crashing waves,
the surging sea; inside it was full
of gems and metal bands. A monstrous guardian,
eager for combat, kept his gold treasures
ancient under the ground; getting them   2415
was no easy bargain for any man.
          The battle-hardened king sat down on the cape,
then wished good health to his hearth-companions,
the gold-friend of the Geats. His heart was grieving,
restless and ripe for death — the doom was immeasurably near   2420
that was coming to meet that old man,
seek his soul's treasure, split asunder
his life and his body; not for long was
the spirit of that noble king enclosed in its flesh.
          Beowulf spoke, the son of Ecgtheow: 2425
"In my youth I survived many storms of battle,
times of strife — I still remember them all.
I was seven years old when the prince of treasures,
friend to his people, took me from my father;[1]
Hrethel the king held me and kept me,   2430
gave me gems and feasts, remembered our kinship.
I was no more hated to him while he lived
— a man in his stronghold — than any of his sons,
Herebeald and Hæthcyn and my own Hygelac.
For the eldest,[2] undeservedly,   2435
a death-bed was made by the deeds of a kinsman,
after Hæthcyn with his horn bow
struck down his own dear lord with an arrow —
he missed his mark and murdered his kinsman,
one brother to the other with a bloody shaft.   2440

---

1   Beowulf was brought up as a noble foster-child in the royal court.
2   Herebeald.

That was a fight beyond settling, a sinful crime,
shattering the heart; yet it had to be
that a nobleman lost his life unavenged.
      So it is sad for an old man
2445 to live to see his young son
ride on the gallows[1] — then let him recount a story,
a sorry song, when his son hangs
of comfort only to the ravens, and he cannot,
though old and wise, offer him any help.
2450 Each and every morning calls to mind
his son's passing away; he will not care
to wait for any other heir or offspring
in his fortress, when the first one has
tasted evil deeds and fell death.
2455 He looks sorrowfully on his son's dwelling,
the deserted wine-hall, the windswept home,
bereft of joy — the riders sleep,
heroes in their graves; there is no harp-music,
no laughter in the court, as there had been long before.

XXXV

2460 He takes to his couch and keens a lament
all alone for his lost one; all too vast to him
seem the fields and townships.
              So the protector of the Weders[2]
bore surging in his breast heartfelt sorrows
for Herebeald. He could not in any way
2465 make amends for the feud with his murderer,
but neither could he hate that warrior

---

1   It is usually suggested that this is a kind of epic simile, comparing Hrethel's grief
over his son's death – a death beyond the scope of vengeance – to the grief of a
criminal's father, who cannot claim compensation for the execution of his son.
Mitchell and Robinson suggest that this is rather a reference to a pagan practice,
part of the cult of Odin, in which the body of a man who did not die in battle was
ritually hanged on a gallows. If this interpretation is correct, the "old man" is
Hrethel himself.
2   Hrethel.

for his hostile deeds, though he was not dear to him.
Then with the sorrow which befell him too sorely,
he gave up man's joys, chose God's light;[1]
he left to his children his land and strongholds   2470
— as a blessed man does — when he departed this life.
        Then there was strife between Swedes and Geats,[2]
a quarrel in common across the wide water,
hard hostility after Hrethel died,
until the sons of Ongentheow[3]   2475
were bold and warlike, wanted no peace
over the sea, but around the Hill of Sorrows[4]
they carried out a terrible and devious campaign.
My friends and kinsmen got revenge for those
feuds and evils[5] — as it is said —   2480
although one of them paid for it with his own life,
a hard bargain; that battle was fatal
for Hæthcyn, king of the Geats.
Then, I've heard, the next morning, one kinsman
avenged the other with the sword's edge,[6]   2485
when Ongentheow attacked Eofor;
his battle-helm slipped, the old Scylfing
staggered, corpse-pale; Eofor's hand recalled
his fill of feuds, and did not withhold the fatal blow.
        I have paid in battle for the precious treasures   2490
he[7] gave me, as was granted to me,
with a gleaming sword; he gave me land,
a joyous home. He had no need
to have to go seeking among the Gifthas
or the Spear-Danes or the Swedes   2495

---

1   I.e., he died.
2   This refers to a time a generation before the conflicts of Heardred, Eanmund and
    Eadgils; the Swedish-Geatish feud is longstanding.
3   Ohthere and Onela.
4   A hill in Geatland, in OE *Hreosnabeorh*.
5   The scene of this revenge is apparently Sweden, in a place called "Ravenswood";
    this battle is described again in sections XL and XLI.
6   Hygelac avenged the death of Hæthcyn on his slayer Ongentheow – not directly
    but through his man Eofor.
7   Hygelac.

for a worse warrior, or buy one with his wealth;
always on foot I would go before him,
alone in the front line — and all my life
I will wage war, while this sword endures,
2500 which before and since has served me well,
since I slew Dæghrefn, champion of the Hugas,[1]
with my bare hands in front of the whole army.
He could not carry off to the Frisian king
that battle-armor and that breast-adornment,[2]
2505 but there in the field the standard-bearer fell,
a nobleman in his strength; no blade was his slayer,
but my warlike grip broke his beating heart,
cracked his bone-house. Now the blade's edge,
hand and hard sword, shall fight for the hoard."
2510   Beowulf spoke, said boasting words
for the very last time: "I have survived
many battles in my youth; I will yet
seek out, an old folk-guardian, a feud
and do a glorious deed, if only that evildoer
2515 will come out to me from his earth-hall."
Then for the last time he saluted
each of the soldiers, his own dear comrades,
brave in their helmets: "I would not bear a sword
or weapon to this serpent, if I knew any other way
2520 I could grapple with this great beast[3]
after my boast, as I once did with Grendel;
but I expect the heat of battle-flames there,
steam and venom; therefore shield and byrnie
will I have on me. From the hoard's warden
2525 I will not flee a single foot, but for us
it shall be at the wall as *wyrd* decrees,
the Ruler of every man. My mind is firm—
I will forego boasting against this flying foe.
Wait on the barrow, protected in your byrnies,

---

1   The Hugas, like the Hetware, are Frankish tribes allied to the Frisians; the battle in
    question may be the same as Hygelac's fatal raid.
2   Possibly the same as the necklace described in 1195-1214.
3   The OE word *æglæcan* is here used of the dragon.

men in war-gear, to see which of the two of us
after the bloody onslaught can better
bear his wounds. It is not your way,
nor proper for any man except me alone,
that he should match his strength against this monster,
do heroic deeds. With daring I shall
get that gold — or grim death
and fatal battle will bear away your lord!"
     Then that brave challenger stood up by his shield,
stern under his helmet, bore his battle-shirt
under the stone-cliffs, trusted the strength
of a single man — such is not the coward's way.
He saw then by the wall — he who had survived
a great many conflicts, good in manly virtues,
the crash of battles when footsoldiers clashed —
stone arches standing, and a stream
shooting forth from the barrow; its surge
was hot with deadly flames, and near the hoard
he could not survive for very long
unburnt, for the dragon's flaming breath.
Enraged, the ruler of the Weder-Geats
let a word burst forth from his breast,
shouted starkly; the sound entered
and resounded battle-clear under the gray stone.
Hate was stirred up — the hoard-warden recognized
the voice of a man; there was no more time
to sue for peace. First there issued
the steam of that great creature out of the stone,
hot battle-sweat; the earth bellowed.
The warrior in the barrow turned his shield-board
against the grisly stranger, lord of the Geats,
when the writhing beast's heart was roused
to seek combat. The good war-king
had drawn his sword, its edges undulled,
an ancient heirloom; each of the two
hostile ones was horrified by the other.
He stood stouthearted behind his steep shield,
that friend and commander, when the worm coiled itself

swiftly together — he waited in his war-gear.
Then coiled, burning, slithering he came,
2570 rushing to his fate. The shield defended well
the life and limb of the famous lord
for less time than he might have liked;
there on that day for the first time
he faced the outcome,[1] and *wyrd* did not
2575 grant victory in battle. The lord of the Geats
raised his hand, struck that mottled horror
with his ancient sword, so that that edge failed
bright against the bony scales, bit less strongly
that the king of that nation needed it to do,
2580 hard-pressed in battle. Then the barrow-warden
was more savage after that battle-stroke,
and spit out gruesome fire; wide sprang
the battle-flames. The gold-friend of the Geats
did not boast of his glorious victories; his bare sword
2585 failed at need, as it should never have done,
that ancient good iron. It was no easy journey
for the famous son of Ecgtheow to agree
to give up his ground in that place;
he was forced, against his will, to find
2590 a place of rest elsewhere — just as every one of us
must give up these loaned days.
                              It was not long
until those two great creatures[2] came together again.
The hoard-guard took heart, his breast swelled with breath
once again; he[3] suffered anguish,
2595 trapped by flames, he who had once ruled his folk.
His comrades, hand-chosen, sons of noblemen,
did not take their stand in a troop around him,
with warlike valor — they fled to the woods
and saved their lives. The spirit rose up in sorrow
2600 in the heart of one of them; nothing can overrule
kinship at all, in one who thinks well.

---

1 Or "if he could have controlled the outcome for the first time."
2 OE *æglæcan* again, here referring to Beowulf and the dragon together.
3 Beowulf.

XXXVI

He was called Wiglaf, Weohstan's son,
a worthy shield-warrior, a prince of the Scylfings,[1]
kinsman of Ælfhere. He saw his liege-lord
suffer heat under his war-helmet;   2605
he recalled the honors he had received from him,
the wealthy homestead of the Waegmundings,
every folk-right that his father had possessed;
he could not hold back — his hand seized
the pale linden shield, and he drew his old sword.   2610
It was known among men as the heirloom of Eanmund,
son of Ohthere; that friendless exile
was slain in battle with the edge of a sword
by Weohstan, who brought to his kinsman
the burnished helmet, the ringed byrnie   2615
the old giant-work sword; Onela gave to him
the war-equipment of his young kinsman,
the shining armor — he never spoke of a feud,
though he had slain his brother's son.[2]
He[3] kept that war-gear for a great many years,   2620
the blade and byrnie, until his boy could
perform brave deeds like his father before him;
he gave him among the Geats that battle-gear,
every piece of it, when, old, he departed this life
and went forth. That was the first time   2625
that the young warrior had to weather
the storm of battle beside his noble lord.
His courage did not melt, nor did his kinsman's legacy
weaken in war; the worm discovered that,
when they began to meet together.   2630
        Wiglaf spoke, said to his companions

---

1 Wiglaf's nationality is in question – he is both a Swede and a Wægmunding (like
   Beowulf; see lines 2813-4). His father fought on the Swedish side in their feuds
   with the Geats. Tribal allegiance is more fluid than modern nationality.
2 Onela never spoke of a feud, though Weohstan had killed Onela's brother's son, for
   he wished him dead. As elsewhere in the poem, a sword is the reminder of both
   victory and vengeance.
3 Weohstan.

many true words — he was mournful at heart —
"I remember the time that we took mead together,
when we made promises to our prince
2635 in the beer-hall — he gave us these rings —
that we would pay him back for this battle-gear,
these helmets and hard swords, if such a need
as this ever befell him. For this he chose us from the army
for this adventure by his own will,
2640 thought us worthy of glory, and gave me these treasures —
for this he considered us good spear-warriors,
proud helmet-wearers, even though our prince,
shepherd of his people, intended to perform
this act of courage all alone,
2645 because he has gained the most glory among men,
reckless heroic deeds. Now the day has come
that our noble lord has need of the support
of good warriors; let us go to it,
help our warlord, despite the heat,
2650 grim fire-terror. God knows for my part
that I would much prefer that the flames should enfold
my body alongside my gold-giving lord.
It seems wrong to me that we should bear shields
back to our land, unless we first might
2655 finish off this foe, defend the life
of the prince of the Weders. I know full well
that he does not deserve to suffer
this torment all alone among the Geatish troop,
or fall in the struggle; now sword and helmet,
2660 byrnie and battle-dress, shall be ours together!"
        He hurried through the deadly fumes, bore his helmet
to the aid of his lord, spoke little:
"Dear Beowulf, do all well,
as in your youth you said you would,
2665 that you would never let in your whole life
your fame decline; now firm in deeds,
single-minded nobleman, with all your strength
you must protect your life — I will support you."
After these words the worm came angrily,

terrible vicious creature, a second time,   2670
scorched with surging flames, seeking out his enemies,
the hated men. The hot flames rolled in waves,
burned the shield to its rim; the byrnie was not
of any use to the young soldier,
but he showed his courage under his kinsman's shield,   2675
the young warrior, when his own was
charred to cinders. Still the battle-king
remembered his glory, and with his mighty strength
swung his warblade with savage force,
so that it stuck in the skull. Nægling shattered —   2680
the sword of Beowulf weakened at battle,
ancient and gray. It was not granted to him
that iron-edged weapons might ever
help him in battle; his hand was too strong,
he who, I am told, overtaxed every blade   2685
with his mighty blows, when he bore to battle
a wound-hardened[1] weapon — it was no help to him at all.
      Then that threat to the people for a third time,
fierce fire-dragon, remembering his feud,
rushed on the brave man, hot and bloodthirsty,   2690
when he saw the chance, seized him by the neck
in his bitter jaws; he was bloodied
by his mortal wounds — blood gushed in waves.

XXXVII

Then, I have heard, in his king's hour of need
the earl[2] beside him showed his bravery,   2695
the noble skill which was his nature.
He did not heed that head when he helped his kinsman;
that brave man's hand was burned, so that
he struck that savage foe a little lower down,
the soldier in armor, so that his sword plunged in   2700
bejeweled and bloody, so that the fire began

---

1   Or "wondrously hard"; the OE text is unclear.
2   Wiglaf.

to subside afterwards. The king himself
still had his wits, drew the war-dagger,
bitter and battle-sharp, that he wore in his byrnie;
2705 the protector of the Weders carved through the worm's midsection.
They felled their foe — their force took his life —
and they both together had brought him down,
the two noble kinsmen; a thane at need,
as a man should be! But that, for the prince, was
2710 his last work of victory, by his own will,
of worldly adventures.
                        When the wound
which the earth-dragon had worked on him
began to burn and swell, he soon realized
that in his breast, with an evil force,
2715 a poison welled; then the nobleman went,
still wise in thought, so that he sat
on a seat by the wall. On that work of giants he gazed,
saw how stone arches and sturdy pillars
held up the inside of that ancient earth-hall.
2720 Then with his hands the thane, immeasurably good,
bathed with water his beloved lord,
the great prince, spattered with gore,
sated with battle, and unstrapped his helmet.
Beowulf spoke — despite his wound,
2725 that deadly cut; he knew clearly
that his allotted life had run out,
and his joys in the earth; all gone
was his portion of days, death immeasurably near:
        "Now I should wish to give my war-gear
2730 to my son, if there had been such,
flesh of my flesh, if fate had granted me
any heir. I held this people
fifty winters; there was no folk-king,
not any of the neighboring tribes,
2735 who dared to face me with hostile forces
or threaten fear. The decrees of fate
I awaited on earth, held well what was mine,

I sought no intrigues, nor swore many
false or wrongful oaths. For all that I may
have joy, though sick with mortal wounds,   2740
because the Ruler of men need not reproach me
with the murder of kinsmen, when my life
quits my body. Now go quickly
to look at the hoard under the hoary stone,
dear Wiglaf, now that the worm lies dead,   2745
sleeps with his wounds, stripped of his treasure.
Hurry, so I might witness that ancient wealth,
those golden goods, might eagerly gaze on
the bright precious gems, and I might more gently,
for that great wealth, give up my   2750
life and lordship, which I have held so long."

XXXVIII

Then swiftly, I have heard, the son of Weohstan
after these words obeyed his lord,
sick with wounds, wore his ring-net,
the woven battle-shirt, under the barrow's roof.   2755
As he went by the seat he saw there, triumphant,
the brave young warrior, many bright jewels,
glittering gold scattered on the ground,
wonders on the walls, and the lair of that worm,
the old dawn-flier — flagons standing,   2760
ancient serving-vessels without a steward,
their trappings all moldered; there was many a helmet
old and rusty, a number of arm-bands
with twisted ornaments. — Treasure may easily,
gold in the ground, give the slip   2765
to any one of us: let him hide it who will![1] —
Likewise he saw an ensign, all golden,
hanging high over the hoard, greatest hand-work,
linked together with skill; light gleamed from it

---

1   Or "can get the better of any man – heed [these words] who will!" The OE is
    uncertain; the translation follows Mitchell and Robinson.

2770 so that he could see the cave's floor,
survey those strange artifacts. There was no sign
of the serpent there — a sword had finished him off.
Then the hoard in that barrow, as I've heard, was looted,
ancient work of giants, by one man alone;
2775 he piled in his arms cups and plates,
whatever he wanted; he took the ensign too,
brightest of beacons. His aged lord's blade
—its edge was iron— had earlier harmed
the one who was protector of those treasures
2780 for such a long time, who bore his fiery terror
flaming before the hoard, seething fiercely
in the darkest night, until he died a bloody death.
        The messenger rushed out, eager to return,
burdened with treasures; he was burning to know
2785 whether, stout-hearted, he would find still alive
the prince of the Weders, weakened by wounds,
in the place where he had left him on that plain.
Then with the treasures he found the famous prince,
his own lord, his life at an end,
2790 all bloody; he began once more
to sprinkle water on him, until the point of a word
escaped from his breast.[1]
Old, full of grief, he looked on the gold:
        "For all these treasures, I offer thanks
2795 with these words to the eternal Lord,
King of Glory, for what I gaze upon here,
that I was able to acquire such wealth
for my people before my death-day.
Now that I have sold my old lifespan
2800 for this hoard of treasures, they will attend[2]
to the needs of the people; I can stay no longer.
The brave in battle will bid a tomb be built
shining over my pyre on the cliffs by the sea;

---

1   Half a line (or more?) is missing from the manuscript at this point.
2   Usually translated "you [Wiglaf] will attend..."; the OE verb may be indicative or
    imperative, but it is unambiguously plural, and the imperative plural is not used
    elsewhere in the poem to address a single person.

it will be as a monument to my people
and tower high on Whale's Head,
so that seafarers afterwards shall call it
'Beowulf's Barrow', when their broad ships
drive from afar over the darkness of the flood."
          The boldminded nobleman took from his neck
a golden circlet, and gave it to the thane,   2810
the young spear-carrier, and the gold-covered helmet,
ring and byrnie, bid him use them well:
"You are the last survivor of our lineage,
the Waegmundings; fate has swept away
all of my kinsmen, earls in their courage,   2815
to their final destiny; I must follow them."
That was the last word of the old warrior,
his final thought before he chose the fire,
the hot surging flames — from his breast flew
his soul to seek the judgment of the righteous.[1]   2820

XXXIX

          Then it came to pass with piercing sorrow
that the young warrior had to watch
his most precious lord fare so pitifully,
his life at an end. Likewise his slayer lay dead,
the awesome earth-dragon deprived of his life,   2825
overcome by force. The coiled serpent
could no longer rule his hoard of rings —
edges of iron did away with him,
the hard, battle-scarred shards of the smithy,
so that the wide-flier, stilled by his wounds,   2830
toppled to the ground near his treasure-house.
No more soaring about in the skies
at midnight, preening in his precious treasures,

---

1   Literally "the *dom* (fame) of the truth-fast," an ambiguous pronouncement. It is not
    clear whether this is a means that Beowulf's soul will receive the sort of judgment
    that a righteous soul ought to receive (and so go to Heaven), or that it would be
    judged by those "fast in truth" (and so go to Hell as an unbaptized pagan).

showing his face — he fell to earth
2835 through that war-commander's handiwork.
Indeed, few men on earth, no matter how strong,
could succeed at that, as I have heard tell,
though he were daring in every deed,
could rush against the reek of that venomous foe,
2840 or rifle through that ring-hall with his hands,
if he should find a waking warden
waiting in that barrow. Beowulf's share
of that royal treasure was repaid by his death —
each of them had journeyed to the end
of this loaned life.
2845   It was not long before
the men late for battle left the woods,
ten of those weak traitors all together
who had not dared to hoist their spears
when their lord of men needed them most;
2850 now shamefaced, they carried their shields
and battledress to where the old man lay dead,
to stare at Wiglaf. He sat exhausted,
a foot-soldier at his lord's shoulder,
tried to rouse him with water — but it was no use.
2855 He could not, no matter how much he wanted,
keep the life in the body of his captain,
nor change any bit of the Ruler's decree;
the judgment of God would guide the deeds
of every man, as it still does today.
2860 Then it was easy to get a grim answer
from that youth to those who gave up courage.
Wiglaf spoke, son of Weohstan,
looked, sad-hearted, on those unloved:
         "He can say — o yes — who would speak the truth
2865 that the liege-lord who gave you those gifts of treasures,
the military gear that you stand in there,
when on the ale-benches he often handed out
helmets and byrnies to the hall-sitters,
a lord to his followers, whatever he could find
2870 finest anywhere, far or near —

that all that battle-dress he absolutely
and entirely threw away, when war beset him.
Our nation's king had no need to boast
of his comrades-in-arms! But the Ruler of victories
allowed that he, alone with his blade,   2875
might avenge himself when he needed your valor.
Only a little life-protection could I offer
him in battle, but began nevertheless
to support my kinsman beyond my own strength;
ever the worse was the deadly enemy   2880
when I struck with my sword, a fire less severe
surging from his head. Too few supporters
thronged around our prince in his great peril.
Now the getting of treasure, the giving of swords,
and all the happy joys of your homeland,   2885
shall end for your race; empty-handed
will go every man among your tribe,
deprived of his land-rights, when noblemen learn
far and wide of your flight,
your inglorious deed. Death is better   2890
for any earl than a life of dishonor!"

XL

        He bade that the battle-work be announced to the camp
up by the cliff's edge, where that troop of earls,
shield-bearers, sat sad-minded
all the long morning, expecting either   2895
the final day of their dear lord
or his homecoming. He who rode up to the cape
was not at all silent with his new tidings,
but he spoke truly in the hearing of all:
        "Now is the joy-giver of the Geatish people,   2900
the lord of the Weders, laid on his deathbed,
holding a place of slaughter by the serpent's deeds;
beside him lies his life-enemy,
sick with knife-slashes; he could not with his sword

2905 make in the monstrous beast
any kind of wound. Wiglaf sits,
Weohstan's offspring, over Beowulf,
one earl over the other, now dead;
he holds with desperate heart the watch
over friend and foe.
2910   Now this folk may expect
a time of trouble, when this is manifest
to the Franks and Frisians, and the fall of our king
becomes widespread news. The strife was begun
hard with the Hugas, after Hygelac came
2915 travelling with his ships to the shores of Frisia,
where the Hetware attacked him in war,
advanced with valor and a vaster force,
so that the warrior in his byrnie had to bow down,
and fell amid the infantry; not at all did that lord
2920 give treasure to his troops. Ever after that
the Merovingians have not shown mercy to us.
                Nor do I expect any peace or truce
from the Swedish nation, but it has been well-known
that Ongentheow ended the life
2925 of Haethcyn, son of Hrethel, in Ravenswood,[1]
when in their arrogant pride the Geatish people
first sought out the Battle-Scylfings.
Immediately the ancient father of Ohthere,
old and terrifying, returned the attack —
2930 the old warrior cut down the sea-captain,[2]
rescued his wife, bereft of her gold,
Onela's mother and Ohthere's;
and then hunted down his deadly enemies
until they escaped, with some difficulty,
2935 bereft of their lord, into Ravenswood.
With his standing army he besieged those sword-leavings,
weary, wounded; he kept threatening woe

---

1   See XXXV above. The allusive complexity of the narration of human feuds and
    battles is in striking contrast to the straightforward telling of the hero's battles
    against non-human opponents.
2   Ongentheow killed Hæthcyn. Hygelac is not present at this battle, but arrives later.

to that wretched troop the whole night through —
in the morning, he said, with the edge of his sword
he would gut them, and leave some on the gallows-tree   2940
as sport for birds.[1] But for those sad-hearted men
solace came along with the sunrise,
after they heard Hygelac's horn and trumpet
sounding the charge, when the good man came
following the trail of that people's troop.   2945

XLI

The bloody swath of the Swedes and Geats,
the slaughter of men, was easily seen,
how the folk had stirred up feud between them.
That good man[2] then departed, old, desperate,
with a small band of kinsmen, sought his stronghold,   2950
the earl Ongentheow turned farther away;
he had heard of proud Hygelac's prowess in battle,
his war-skill; he did not trust the resistance
he might muster against the seafarers' might
to defend from the wave-borne warriors his treasure,   2955
his women and children; he ran away from there,
old, into his fortress. Then the pursuit was offered
to the Swedish people, the standard of Hygelac
overran the place of refuge,
after the Hrethlings thronged the enclosure.   2960
There with the edge of a sword was Ongentheow,
old graybeard, brought to bay,
so that the king of that nation had to yield
to Eofor's will. Angrily he struck;
Wulf the son of Wonred lashed at him with his weapon,   2965
so that with his blow the blood sprang in streams
from under his hair. Yet the ancient Scylfing

---

1   Ongentheow may be threatening to sacrifice the corpses of his defeated enemies to
    a pagan god of war.
2   Ongentheow, whose vicious hostility towards the Geats does not earn him the nar-
    rator's censure.

was undaunted, and dealt back quickly
a worse exchange for that savage stroke,
2970 once the ruler of that people turned around.
The ready son of Wonred could not
give a stroke in return to the old soldier,
for he had cut through the helmet right on his head
so that he collapsed, covered in blood,
2975 fell to the ground — he was not yet fated to die,
but he recovered, though the cut hurt him.
The hardy thane of Hygelac[1] then let
his broad blade, as his brother lay there,
his ancient giant-made sword, shatter that gigantic helmet
2980 over the shield-wall; then the king stumbled,
shepherd of his people, mortally stricken.
     There were many there who bandaged his kinsman,[2]
quickly raised him up, when a way was clear for them,
so that they had control of that killing field.
2985 Then one warrior plundered another,[3]
took from Ongentheow the iron byrnie,
his hard hilted sword and his helmet too,
and carried the old man's armor to Hygelac.
He[4] took that war-gear and promised him gifts
2990 among his people — and he kept that promise;
the king of the Geats repaid that carnage,
the offspring of Hrethel, when he made it home,
gave to Eofor and Wulf extravagant treasures,
gave them each lands and locked rings,
2995 worth a hundred thousand.[5] Not a man in this world could
reproach those rewards, since they had won them
                              with their deeds;
and to Eofor he gave his only daughter,
the pride of his home, as a pledge of his friendship.
     That is the feud and the fierce enmity,

---

1   Eofor, Wulf's brother.
2   His = Eofor's.
3   Eofor plundered Ongentheow.
4   Hygelac.
5   A monetary unit, though it is not clear which one.

savage hatred among men, that I expect now,
when the Swedish people seek us out
after they have learned that our lord
has perished, who had once protected
his hoard and kingdom against all hostility,
after the fall of heroes, the valiant Scyldings,[1]
worked for the people's good, and what is more,
performed noble deeds. Now we must hurry
and look upon our people's king,
and go with him who gave us rings
on the way to the pyre. No small part
of the hoard shall burn with that brave man,
but countless gold treasures, grimly purchased,
and rings, here at last with his own life
paid for; then the flames shall devour,
the fire enfold — let no warrior wear
treasures for remembrance, nor no fair maiden
have a ring-ornament around her neck,
but sad in mind, stripped of gold, she must
walk a foreign path, not once but often,
now that leader of our troop has laid aside laughter,
his mirth and joy. Thus many a cold morning
shall the spear be grasped in frozen fingers,
hefted by hands, nor shall the sound of the harp
rouse the warriors, but the dark raven,
greedy for carrion, shall speak a great deal,
ask the eagle how he fared at his feast
when he plundered corpses with the wolf."[2]
     Thus that brave speaker was speaking
a most unlovely truth; he did not lie much
in words or facts. The troop of warriors arose;
they went, unhappy, to the Cape of Eagles,

---

1   The manuscript reading ("Scyldings" is a further object of "protected") is often
emended to *Scylfingas*, i.e., Swedes, or *scildwigan*, "shield-warriors"; the present reading is that of Mitchell and Robinson. As it stands in the manuscript the Geatish
herald is referring to Beowulf's earlier adventures against Grendel and his mother.
2   The eagle, wolf, and raven, the "beasts of battle," are a recurring motif in Old English poetry.

with welling tears to look at that wonder.
There on the sand they found the soulless body
of the one who gave them rings in earlier times
3035 laid out to rest; the last day
had come for the good man, when the war-king,
prince of the Weders, died a wondrous death.
But first they saw an even stranger creature,
a loathsome serpent lying on the plain
3040 directly across from him; grim with his colors
the fire-dragon was, and scorched with his flames.
He was fifty feet long, lying there
stretched out; once he had joy in the air
in the dark night, and then down he would go
3045 to seek his den, but now he was fast in death;
he had come to the end of his cave-dwelling.
Cups and vessels stood beside him,
plates lay there and precious swords,
eaten through with rust, as if in the bosom of the earth
3050 they had lain for a thousand winters;
all that inheritance was deeply enchanted,
the gold of the ancients was gripped in a spell
so that no man in the world would be able to touch
that ring-hall, unless God himself,
3055 the true King of Victories, Protector of men,
granted to whomever He wished to open the hoard,
to whatever person seemed proper to Him.[1]

---

1 The power of the pagan spell can be overruled by the will of the true God.

XLII

Then it was plain that the journey did not profit
the one[1] who had wrongfully hidden under a wall
that great treasure. The guardian had slain   3060
that one and few others;[2] then that feud was
swiftly avenged. It is a wonder to say
where a valiant earl should meet the end
of his span of life, when he may no longer
dwell in the meadhall, a man with his kinsmen.   3065
So it was with Beowulf, when he sought the barrow's guardian
and a hostile fight; even he did not know
how his parting from life should come to pass,
since until doomsday mighty princes had deeply
pronounced, when they placed it there,   3070
that the man who plundered that place would be
harried by hostile demons, fast in hellish bonds,
grievously tortured, guilty of sins,
unless the Owner's grace had earlier
more readily favored the one eager for gold.[3]   3075
        Wiglaf spoke, son of Weohstan:
"Often many earls must suffer misery
through the will of one man, as we have now seen.
We could not persuade our dear prince,
shepherd of a kingdom, with any counsel,   3080
that he should not greet that gold-guardian,
let him lie there where he long had been,
inhabit the dwellings until the end of the world:
he held to his high destiny. The hoard is opened,
grimly gotten; that fate was too great   3085
which impelled the king of our people thither.
I was in there, and looked over it all,

---

1 The dragon.
2 Or "that one of a few," i.e., "a unique man" or "a man of rare greatness."
3 The OE text is corrupt and the precise meaning of this passage is not certain; the
   present translation tries to incorporate several suggested interpretations. The general sense seems to be clear enough – the gold was cursed, and only God's special
   grace would enable anyone to remove it. What this implies about Beowulf's failure,
   and his moral status, is less clear.

the hall's ornaments, when a way was open to me;
by no means gently was a journey allowed
3090 in under that earth-wall. In eager haste I seized
in my hands a great mighty burden
of hoard-treasure, and bore it out hither
to my king. He was still conscious then,
thoughtful and alert; he spoke of many things,
3095 an old man in his sorrow, and ordered that I greet you;
he asked that you build a great high barrow
for your prince's deeds, in the place of his pyre,
mighty and glorious, since he was of men
the most worthy warrior throughout the wide world,
3100 while he could enjoy the wealth of a hall.
Let us now make haste for one more time
to see and seek out that store of cunning gems,
the wonder under the wall; I will direct you
so that you can inspect them up close,
3105 abundant rings and broad gold. Let the bier be ready,
quickly prepared, when we come out,
then let us bear our beloved lord,
that dear man, to where he must long
rest in the keeping of the Ruler."
3110   Then the son of Weohstan, brave battle-warrior,
let it be made known to many heroes
and householders, that they should bring from afar
the wood for the pyre to that good one,[1]
the leader of his folk: "Now the flames must devour,
3115 the black blaze rise over the ruler of warriors,
who often awaited the showers of iron
when the storm of arrows hurled from bow-strings
shot over the wall, the shafts did their duty
swift on feather-wings, sent on the arrow-heads."
3120   Lo, then the wise son of Weohstan
summoned from that host some of the best
of the king's thanes, seven altogether;
he went, one of eight, under that evil roof;

---

1   The dead Beowulf.

one of the brave warriors bore in his hands
a flaming torch, and went before them.   3125
It was not chosen by lots who should loot that hoard,[1]
once the men saw it sitting in the hall,
every part of it unprotected,
lying there wasting; there was little lament
that they should have to hurry out with   3130
the precious treasures. They also pushed the dragon,
the worm over the cliff-wall, let the waves take him,
the flood embrace the guard of that finery;
then the twisted gold, an uncountable treasure,
was loaded in a wagon, and the noble one was carried,   3135
the Gray-haired warrior, to the Cape of Whales.

XLIII

The people of the Geats then prepared for him
a splendid pyre upon the earth,
hung with battle-shields and helmets
and bright byrnies, as he had bidden;   3140
there in the middle they laid the mighty prince,
the heroes lamenting their dear lord.
Then the warriors kindled there on the cliff
the greatest of funeral pyres; dark over the flames
the woodsmoke rose, the roaring fire   3145
mingled with weeping — the wind lay still —
until it had broken that bone-house
hot at the heart. With heavy spirits
they mourned their despair, the death of their lord;
and a sorrowful song sang the Geatish woman,[2]   3150
with hair bound up, for Beowulf the king,
with sad cares, earnestly said

---

1   I.e., everybody had a share; there was enough for all.
2   The manuscript is damaged throughout this section and the readings in this passage
    are conjectural; it is not clear who the "Geatish woman" is, though her advanced
    age is indicated by her bound-up hair. Typically, in Germanic poetry, it is women
    (and poets) who mourn.

that she dreaded the hard days ahead,
the times of slaughter, the host's terror,
3155 harm and captivity. Heaven swallowed the smoke.
      Then the Weder people wrought for him
a barrow on the headland; it was high and broad,
visible from afar to sea-voyagers,
and in ten days they built the beacon
3160 of that battle-brave one; the ashes of the flames
they enclosed with a wall, as worthily
as the most clever of men could devise it.
In the barrow they placed rings and bright jewels,
all the trappings that those reckless men
3165 had seized from the hoard before,
let the earth hold the treasures of earls,
gold in the ground, where it yet remains,
just as useless to men as it was before.
Then round the mound rode the battle-brave men,
3170 offspring of noblemen, twelve in all,
they wished to voice their cares and mourn their king,
utter sad songs and speak of that man;
they praised his lordship and his proud deeds
judged well his prowess. As it is proper
3175 that one should praise his lord with words,
should love him in his heart when the fatal hour comes,
when he must from his body be led forth,
so the men of the Geats lamented
the fall of their prince, those hearth-companions;
3180 they said that he was of all the kings of the world
the mildest of men and the most gentle,
the kindest to his folk and the most eager for fame.

Glossary of Proper Names

Abel	slain by his brother **Cain**; the story is told in Genesis 4:1–16
Ælfhere	kinsman of **Wiglaf**
Æschere	a prominent Dane, advisor to **Hrothgar**; slain by Grendel's mother
Battle-Scylding	see **Scyldings**
Battle-Scylfing	see **Scylfings**
Beanstan	father of **Breca**
Beowulf	(prologue) Danish king, son of **Scyld**
Breca	engaged in a youthful swimming contest with Beowulf
Bright-Danes	see **Danes**
Brondings	the people of **Breca**
Brosinga	makers of the magical necklace of Freya in Norse myth, to which a necklace in the story is compared
Cain	slayer of **Abel** in Genesis 4:1–16; father of the race of monsters
Dæghrefn	a warrior of the **Hugas** slain by Beowulf in hand-to-hand combat during **Hygelac**'s ill-fated raid on **Frisia**
Danes	**Hrothgar**'s people; the **Scyldings**; also called Bright-, Half-, Ring-, Spear-, East-, West-, North-, and South-Danes.
Eadgils	son of **Ohthere**, brother of **Eanmund**
Eanmund	son of **Ohthere**, brother of **Eadgils**; slain by **Weohstan**
East-Danes	see **Danes**
Ecglaf	father of **Unferth**
Ecgtheow	father of Beowulf
Ecgwala	a Danish king; the 'sons of Ecgwala' are the **Danes**
Eofor	a warrior of the **Geats**; brother of **Wulf**; slayer of **Ongentheow**
Eomer	son of **Offa**

Eormanric	king of the Ostrogoths
Eotens	unclear: perhaps the **Jutes**, perhaps the **Frisians**, perhaps 'giants' (the literal meaning of the word) as a nickname for one group or the other
Finn	king of the **Frisians**, husband of **Hildeburh**; killed by **Hengest**
Finns	the people of Finland; the Lapps
Fitela	legendary companion, nephew (and son) of **Sigemund**
Folcwalda	father of **Finn**
Franks	a Germanic tribe; see **Hetware**, **Hugas**, **Merovingians**
Freawaru	daughter of **Hrothgar** betrothed to **Ingeld**
Frisians	a Germanic tribe; **Finn**'s people
Froda	chief of the **Heathobards**, father of **Ingeld**
Garmund	father of **Offa**
Geats	**Hygelac**'s people and Beowulf 's; a Germanic tribe; also called War-Geats, Hrethmen, Hrethlings, Weders
Gifthas	an East-Germanic tribe
Grendel	descendent of **Cain**; monstrous marauder of the **Danes**
Guthlaf	a Danish warrior, companion of **Hengest**
Hæreth	father of **Hygd**
Hæthcyn	Geatish prince, second son of **Hrethel**
Half-Danes	see **Danes**
Halga	Danish prince, younger brother of **Hrothgar**
Hama	legendary Goth; stole **Brosinga** necklace
Healfdene	king of the **Danes**, father of **Hrothgar**
Heardred	king of the **Geats**, son of **Hygelac**
Heathobards	**Ingeld**'s people; a Germanic tribe
Heatholaf	a **Wylfing** slain by **Ecgtheow**
Heathoream	a Scandinavian tribe: Norwegians, more or less

Helmings	the family of **Wealhtheow**
Hemming	kinsman of **Offa** and **Eomer**
Hengest	leader of the **Danes**; killed **Finn** in **Frisia**
Heorogar	Dane, eldest brother of **Hrothgar**
Heorot	the great hall of **Hrothgar**
Heoroward	Dane; son of **Heorogar**
Herebeald	Geatish prince, eldest son of **Hrethel**; killed by his brother **Hæthcyn**
Heremod	king of the **Danes** in the poem's distant past, before the Scylding dynasty
Hereric	brother of **Hygd**, uncle of **Heardred**
Hetware	a Frankish tribe, allied with the **Frisians**; fought against **Hygelac**
Hildeburh	sister of the Danish **Hnæf**, wife of the Frisian **Finn**
Hnæf	chief of the **Half-Danes**, brother of **Hildeburh**; killed by **Finn**
Hoc	Dane, father of **Hildeburh** and **Hnæf**
Hondscio	Geatish warrior, comrade of Beowulf; slain by **Grendel**
Honor-Scyldings	see **Scyldings**
Hrethel	king of the **Geats**, father of **Hygelac**, grandfather of Beowulf
Hrethlings	sons of **Hrethel**, i.e., the **Geats**
Hrethmen	the **Geats**
Hrethric	Dane, son of **Hrothgar**
Hrothgar	aged king of the **Danes** beset by **Grendel**; helped by Beowulf
Hrothmund	Dane, son of **Hrothgar**
Hrothulf	Dane, son of **Halga**, nephew of **Hrothgar**; not to be trusted
Hrunting	the sword of **Unferth**
Hugas	the **Franks**, allies of the **Frisians**
Hunlaf	father of one of the warriors in **Hengest**'s troop
Hygd	queen of the **Geats**, wife of **Hygelac**, daughter of **Hæreth**

Hygelac	king of the **Geats**, uncle of Beowulf
Ingeld	prince of the **Heathobards**, son of **Froda**, betrothed to **Freawaru**; after the events narrated in the poem he burns down the great hall of **Heorot**
Ingwines	the 'friends of Ing': the **Danes**
Jutes	allies of the **Frisians**; see **Eotens**
Merovingians	the **Franks**
Nægling	Beowulf's sword
North-Danes	see **Danes**
Offa	king of the Angles, husband of **Thryth**
Ohthere	Swede, son of **Ongentheow**
Onela	Swede, son of **Ongentheow**; usurped throne
Ongentheow	Swedish king; killed by **Wulf** and **Eofer**
Oslaf	a Danish warrior, companion of **Hengest**
Ring-Danes	see **Danes**
Scyld Scefing	legendary founder of the Danish royal family
Scyldings	the Danes; also called Battle-, Honor-, Victory-Scylding
Scylfings	the Swedes
Sigemund	legendary Germanic hero, son of **Wæls**
South-Danes	see **Danes**
Spear-Danes	see **Danes**
Swerting	uncle of **Hygelac**
Thryth	(often construed as **Modthryth**) wife of **Offa**
Unferth	Danish spokesman ('thyle') and courtier of **Hrothgar**
Victory-Scyldings	see **Scyldings**
Volsung	another name for **Sigemund**, son of **Wæls**
Waegmundings	the family of **Weohstan**, **Wiglaf**, and Beowulf
Wæls	father of **Sigemund**
War-Geats	see **Geats**
Wealhtheow	Danish queen, wife of **Hrothgar**

Weders	the **Geats**
Weland	legendary Germanic smith
Wendels	a Germanic tribe; perhaps the Vandals, perhaps not
Weohstan	father of **Wiglaf**; killed **Eanmund**
West-Danes	see **Danes**
Wiglaf	son of **Weohstan**, young retainer of Beowulf
Withergyld	a dead **Heathobard**
Wonred	a **Geat**, father of **Wulf** and **Eofor**
Wulf	a warrior of the **Geats**, brother of **Eofor**; assisted in killing **Ongentheow**
Wulfgar	a warrior of the **Danes**; herald at the court of **Hrothgar**
Wylfings	a Germanic tribe of which **Heatholaf** was a member, until **Ecgtheow** killed him
Yrmenlaf	a Dane, younger brother of **Æschere**

Genealogies

1. The Danes (Scyldings)

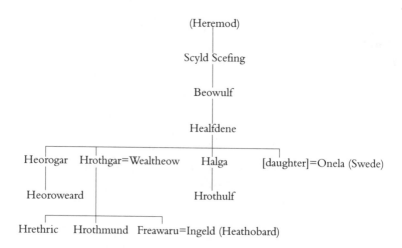

(Heremod)

Scyld Scefing

Beowulf

Healfdene

Heorogar   Hrothgar=Wealtheow   Halga   [daughter]=Onela (Swede)

Heoroweard   Hrothulf

Hrethric   Hrothmund   Freawaru=Ingeld (Heathobard)

2. The Geats

Hrethel

Herebeald   Haethcyn   Hygelac   [daughter]=Ecgtheow

Beowulf

Eofor=[daughter]   Heardred

3. The Swedes (Scylfings)

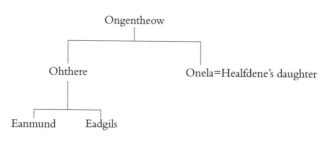

Ongentheow

Ohthere   Onela=Healfdene's daughter

Eanmund   Eadgils

The Geatish-Swedish Wars

When the story of Beowulf's fight with the dragon begins, the narrator leaps over fifty years in one brief passage. It is a tumultuous condensation of a complex chain of events (2200-08):

Then it came to pass amid the crash of battle
in later days, after Hygelac lay dead,
and for Heardred the swords of battle held
deadly slaughter under the shield-wall,
when the Battle-Scylfings sought him out,
those hardy soldiers, and savagely struck down
the nephew of Hereric in his victorious nation —
then came the broad kingdom
into Beowulf's hands...

These events are referred to throughout the last thousand lines of the poem, but they are not told in a straightforward way or in chronological order. The fortunes of the Geatish royal house may be reconstructed as follows:

1. Haethcyn accidentally kills his brother Herebeald; their father Hrethel dies of grief (2432-71). Haethcyn becomes king.

2. After the death of Hrethel Ohthere and Onela, the sons of the Swedish king Ongentheow, attack the Geats (2472-78).

3. In retaliation, Haethcyn attacks Ongentheow in Sweden (2479-84); at first he is successful, but is killed at Ravenswood (2922-41). Hygelac's men Wulf and Eofor kill Ongentheow, and Hygelac (Hæthcyn's brother) is victorious (2484-89, 2942-99). Ohthere becomes king of the Swedes.

4. Hygelac is killed in Frisia; his son Heardred becomes king (2354-78).

5. Ohthere's brother Onela seizes the Swedish throne and drives out the sons of Ohthere, Eanmund and Eadgils (2379-84). Heardred takes in these exiles, and Onela attacks Heardred for this hospitality and kills him. Onela allows Beowulf to rule the Geats (2385-90).

6. Around this time Weohstan, father of Wiglaf, kills Eanmund on behalf of Onela (2611-19).

7. Eadgils escapes later to kill Onela in Sweden, with help sent by Beowulf (2391-96); he presumably becomes king of the Swedes.

8. During Beowulf's fifty-year reign, the death of Eanmund is unavenged. After Beowulf's death, Eanmund's brother Eadgils will probably seek vengeance against Wiglaf, son of Weohstan (2999-3005).

Appendix A: Characters mentioned in Beowulf

I. Gregory of Tours,[1] *History of the Franks* III.3.

After this, the Danes and their king, whose name was Chlochi-laicus, attacked the Franks by ship from the sea. When they came ashore they devastated one district of the kingdom of Theuderic [king of the Franks] and took prisoners; after loading their ships with these prisoners and the rest of their plunder, they sought to return to their own land. But their king stayed on the shore while the ships were taking to the deep sea, for he was going to follow a short time after. When the news had been brought to Theudericus that one of his districts had been plundered by foreigners, he sent his son Theudebertus to those parts with a great army and a large stock of weapons. After killing the king, he set upon the enemy in a battle at sea and conquered them, and restored all the plunder to his own land.

[Source: Latin text in Klaeber, *Beowulf*, p.268. Translation RML.]

2. The *Liber Monstrorum*[2] I.2.

There are also monsters of amazing size, like King Higlacus, who ruled the Getae and was slain by the Franks. When he was only twelve years old no horse could carry him. His bones are preserved on an island in the Rhine, where it empties into the ocean, and are shown as a wonder to people who come from afar.

[Source: The Latin text of the *Liber Monstrorum* and an English

---

1   Gregory of Tours (539-594), Frankish historian and Bishop of Tours. In his *History* he mentions that the Danes plundered the coastal regions of the Franks; the event is also mentioned in the anonymous eight-century *Liber Historiae Francorum*, ch. 19. Gregory's *Chlochilaicus* is Beowulf's uncle Hygelac.

2   Anonymous eighth-century (?) Anglo-Latin catalogue of monstrosities, surviving in five ninth- and tenth-century manuscripts.

translation are found in Andrew Orchard, *Pride and Prodigies: Studies in the Monsters of the Beowulf-Manuscript* (Cambridge: D. S. Brewer, 1995), pp. 254-317 (at p. 258). Translation RML.]

3. Alcuin,[1] *Letter to 'Speratus'* (797).

Let the Word of God be read at the clergy's meals. There it is proper to hear the reader, not the harpist; the sermons of the Fathers, not the songs of the heathens. What has Ingeld to do with Christ? The house is narrow, it cannot hold them both. The King of heaven will have no fellowship with so-called kings who are pagan and damned, for the Eternal King reigns in Heaven, while the pagan is damned and laments in Hell. The voices of readers should be heard in your houses, not the crowd of revelers in the streets.

[Source: Latin text in Dümmler, *Alcuini Epistolae*, p. 183; translation RML.]

4. West-Saxon Royal Genealogies.

i. Asser,[2] *Life of King Alfred* (893), ch. 1.

---

1 Alcuin of York (735-804), head of the cathedral school at York and after 782 head of Charlemagne's palace school at Aachen. The recipient of this letter, 'Speratus', was formerly identified as Hygebald, Bishop of Lindisfarne (797), but is now thought to be a Mercian bishop. Alcuin's rhetorical question is a Christian commonplace, deriving ultimately from St. Paul (2 Corinthians 6:15) by way of Tertullian and Jerome. Ingeld is also mentioned in *Widsith* 45-9 (see below, appendix A.6). See further Levine, "Ingeld and Christ," and Bullough, "What has Ingeld to do with Lindisfarne?"

2 Asser, Monk, Bishop, and biographer of Alfred, King of Wessex. His work begins with the genealogy of the West-Saxon royal house, a list which includes a number of names familiar from Beowulf. A modern English version of Asser's life may be found in *Alfred the Great: Asser's Life of King Alfred and other contemporary sources*, tr. and ed. By Simon Keynes and Michael Lapidge (Hammondsworth: Penguin, 1983). The *Anglo-Saxon Chronicle*, a record of English history begun in the latter decades of the ninth century, contains a similar genealogy in its entry for the year 855. The genealogy suggests not only an interest in blending the Danish and English past, but the conflation of Germanic and biblical stories in the creation of royal authority.

In the year of our Lord's incarnation 849 Alfred, king of the Anglo-Saxons, was born at the royal village called Wantage in the region which is named Berkshire, a region whose name derives from Berroc Wood, where the box-tree grows most plentifully. His genealogy is traced in this order: King Alfred was the son of king Æthelwulf, who was the son of Egbert, who was the son of Ealhmund, who was the son of Eafa, who was the son of Eoppa, who was the son of Ingild. Ingild and Ine, that famous king of the West Saxons, were two brothers; Ine traveled to Rome, and there ending this present life honorably he entered the heavenly kingdom, to reign with Christ. Ingild and Ina were the sons of Cenred, who was the son of Ceolwald, who was the son of Cutha, who was the son of Cuthwin, who was the son of Ceawlin, who was the son of Cynric, who was the son of Creoda, who was the son of Cerdic, who was the son of Elesa, who was the son of Gewis (from whom the Britons call all that nation Gewisse), who was the son of Brand, who was the son of Bældæg, who was the son of Woden, who was the son of Frithowald, who was the son of Frealaf, who was the son of Frithuwulf, who was the son of Finn [who was the son] of Godwulf, who was the son of Geat, whom the pagans long worshipped as a god. The poet Sedulius makes mention of him in his metrical *Carmen Paschale,* saying thus:

When heathen poets have tried to puff up their fictions in a high-sounding style, or in the moans of tragedy, or with the ridiculous comic Geta,[1] or by any kind of verse strive to retell sordid deeds of violent crimes and sing of monumental wickedness, and with a schoolmaster's zeal commit these many lies to paper, why should I, used to singing the Psalms of David in the measure of the harp and standing in the holy choir and singing heavenly melodies in pleasing phrases, say nothing of the miracles of Christ who brought salvation?

---

1 This 'Geta' is in reality a comic character in the plays of Terence, and has nothing to do with any tribe in *Beowulf.* Since Sedulius was fairly well-known to the Anglo-Saxons, it is not clear why Asser would have made this mistake.

Geat was the son of Taetwa, who was the son of Beaw, who was the son of Sceldwa, who was the son of Heremod, who was the son of Itermon, who was the son of Hathra, who was the son of Hwala, who was the son of Bedwig, who was the son of [Shem], who was the son of Noah, who was the son of Lamech, who was the son of Methuselah, who was the son of Enoch, [who was the son of Iared,] who was the son of Mahalaleel, who was the son of Cainan, who was the son of Enos, who was the son of Seth, who was the son of Adam.

[Source: *Asser's Life of King Alfred, together with the Annals of Saint Neots*, ed. W.H. Stevenson (Oxford, 1904); rpt. with introduction by Dorothy Whitelock, 1959. Translation RML.]

ii. Æthelweard (d. c. 1000),[1] Chronicle, III.3.

...Godwulf, son of Geat, son of Tatwa, son of Beow, son of Scyld, son of Sceaf. This Sceaf, surrounded by weapons, was driven ashore in a ship on an island in the ocean which is called Scani; and he was a very young boy and unknown to the inhabitants of that land. However, he was taken in by them, and they looked after him with tender care as one of their own household, and later chose him as their king. From his line King Æthelwulf traces his descent.

[Source: A. Campbell, ed., *The Chronicle of Æthelweard* (London, 1962), p. 33; translation RML.]

---

1 Æthelweard, Anglo-Saxon nobleman, descendant of Alfred the Great and Latin historian. His genealogy is largely derived from Asser but contains additional information; the story he tells of Sceaf is told of his son Scyld in *Beowulf*. For more information on Anglo-Saxon royal genealogy, see Sisam, "Anglo-Saxon Royal Genealogies," Dumville, "Anglian Collection" and "Kingship, Genealogies and Regnal Lists," Moisl, "Anglo-Saxon Royal Genealogies," and Murray, "*Beowulf*, the Danish Invasions, and Royal Genealogy."

5. The Fight at Finnsburh[1]

       ... are burning."
Then Hnæf spoke, the battle-young king:
"This is not the eastern dawn; no dragon flies here,
nor are the gables of this hall aflame,
But they bear forth here...
       ...birds are singing,   5
the gray-coated one howls, the war-wood resounds,
shield echoes to shaft. Now this moon shines
wandering under the clouds; now woeful deeds arise
which will make enemies for our people.
But awake now, my warriors!   10
take up your shields, think of valor,
fight in the vanguard, and be resolute!"
Then many a gold-laden thane arose, girded his sword;
then to the door went the noble warriors
Sigeferth and Eaha, drew their swords,   15
and at the other door Ordlaf and Guthlaf,
and Hengest himself was at their heels.
— Meanwhile Garulf exhorted Guthere
that he should not risk so precious a life
at the first attack on the hall-door,   20
since a hardy warrior wished to take it away,
but he asked over all, openly,
the bold-minded hero, who held the door.
"Sigeferth is my name," said he, "I am a prince of the Secgan,
a well-known exile; I have survived many woes,   25
hard battles, and here there is appointed to you
whatever fate you wish to seek from me."
   Then in the hall was the sound of slaughter:

---

1 Anonymous and undated Old English poem. The only record of this poem is a
transcription in George Hickes' 1705 *Thesaurus*. Hickes reports that he found the
poem on a single leaf in the Archbishop of Canterbury's library at Lambeth Palace,
London, but the leaf has never been found. Hickes' transcript is probably not
entirely accurate, and the language of the poem is somewhat difficult, but the poem
appears to recount an episode in the battle between Finn and Hengest alluded to in
Beowulf 1063-1162. See further Fry, *Finnsburh*, Tolkien, *Finn and Hengest*, and
Stanley, "Heroic Lay."

the hollow shield, the body's guard, was to shatter
30 in the hands of the brave; the rafters rattled,
until in the battle Garulf fell,
the foremost of all the men of that country,
the son of Guthlaf, and around him a host of good men,
the corpses of the brave. The raven wheeled,
35 dark and dusky. The gleam of swords shone
as if all Finnesburh were on fire.
I have never heard of sixty more worthy warriors
bearing themselves better in the clash of foes;
nor ever was the sweet mead better repaid
40 than those young companions paid to Hnæf.[1]
They fought five days, so that none fell
among those retainers, but they held the door.
    Then a wounded hero took himself away,
said that his mail-coat was broken,
45 his armor useless and his helmet pierced;
then the ruler of the people quickly asked him
how those other warriors endured their wounds,
or which of the two young men...

[Source: text in F. Klaeber, *Beowulf*, pp. 245-9. Translation RML.]

6. Widsith[2]

Widsith spoke, unlocked his word-hoard,
he who had wandered most widely over the earth
among the races of men; often he had received
precious treasures in the hall. His noble blood
5 sprang from the Myrgings. He was with Ealhilde,

---

1 The meaning of these lines is disputed and the text corrupt. They seem to refer to the idea that warriors who drank at their lord's table incurred an obligation to repay his generosity with their loyalty in battle. The mead is sweet, the repayment bitter.

2 Anonymous and undated Old English poem found in the 'Exeter Book' of Old English poetry, a manuscript written c. 975 and kept since that time in the Cathedral Library in Exeter. The Exeter Book is a miscellaneous collection — it begins with a group of Advent lyrics and ends with a collection of sometimes obscene

beloved peace-weaver, on his first journey,
when she sought the country of the victorious king
Ermanric, east among the Angles,
the scourge of traitors.[1] He began to speak of many things:
    "Much have I heard of men who wield power!   10
Every prince must practice virtue,
each nobleman guide his land like others,
if he wishes his princely throne to prosper.
    For a time Hwala was the best of these,
and Alexander the most powerful of all   15
the race of men, and he prospered the most
of all those I've heard of on the face of the earth.
Attila ruled the Huns, Ermanric the Goths,
Becca the Banings and the Burgundians Gifica.
Caesar ruled the Greeks and Caelic the Finns,   20
Hagen the Holmrygs and Henden the Glomman.
Witta ruled the Swaefe, Wada the Halsings,
Meaca the Myrgings, Mearchealf the Hundings.
Theodric ruled the Franks, Thyle the Rondings,
Breca the Brondings, Billing the Werns.   25
Oswine ruled the Eow and Gefwulf the Jutes,
Finn Folcwalding the race of the Frisians.
Sighere for a long time ruled the Sea-Danes,
Hnæf the Hocings, Helm the Wulfings,
Wald the Woings, Wod the Thuringians,   30
Sæferth the Sycges, the Swedes Ongentheow.
Sceafthere the Ymbers, Sceafa the Langobards,
Hun the Hætwera and Holen the Wrosns.

---

riddles — and the various origins of its various pieces are unknown. This poem
tells of a *scop* or poet named Widsith (whose name means 'far-traveler') who boasts
of the many lands he has seen and the generous kings he has entertained. His fabulous journeys include some tribes and rulers who are no more than names today,
and may not have been much more than that to the poem's original audience, but
his catalogue also mentions a number of characters found in *Beowulf.* See Malone,
Widsith, for further discussion of the obscurer personages in the poem, and Joyce
Hill, "*Widsið* and the Tenth Century" (*Neuphilologische Mitteilungen* 85 (1984), 305–
15); still useful is R.W. Chambers, *Widsith: A Study in Old English Heroic Legend*
(Cambridge: Cambridge UP, 1912).

1 Or 'the cruel oath-breaker', an allusion to Eormanric's future slaying of his wife.
The reading here is that of Malone.

Hringweald was called the king of the War-farers,

35 Offa ruled the Angles, Alewih the Danes;
he was the bravest of all these men,
yet he did not surpass the valor of Offa,
for Offa won, while still a boy
in his first manly fight, the greatest of kingdoms.

40 No one in his day could equal him in valor
on the field of battle. With a single sword
he redrew the map of the Myrgings
around Fifeldore; afterwards the Angles
and Swedes held their land just as Offa had won it.

45 Hrothulf and Hrothgar held peace together
for a long time, uncle and nephew,
after they had driven off the race of vikings
and humbled Ingeld's battle-array,
hacked down at Heorot the pride of the Heathobards.

50 Since I have sojourned in many strange lands
across the wide world, where I have come to know
good and evil, cut off from my home,
wandered wide, far away from my kinsmen,
therefore I can sing and tell a tale,

55 make known before the crowd in the mead-hall
how my noble patrons chose to reward me.
I was with the Huns and with the Hreth-Goths,
with the Swedes and the Geats and the South-Danes.
With the Wendels I was, and the Wærns and the vikings,

60 with the Gifthas I was, and the Wineda and the Gefflegas,
With the Angles I was, and the Swedes and the Ænenas,
with the Saxons I was, and the Sycges and the Swordsmen.
With the Hrones I was, and the Deans and the Heathoreams,
With the Thuringians I was and the Throwends,

65 and with the Burgundians, where I received a ring;
Guth-here gave me a gracious treasure there
as a reward for my song — that was no miserly king!
With the Franks I was, and the Frisians and the Frumtings,
with the Rugians I was, and the Glomman and the Romans.

70 I was also in Italy with Ælfwine,
who had, to my knowledge, the readiest hand

of any man for earning praise,
the most generous heart for giving our rings,
bright circlets, the son of Eadwine.

    With the Sercings I was and with the Serings, 75
with the Greeks I was, and the Finns and with Caesar,
who had possession of the cities of wine,
riches and beauty and the realms of the Walas.
I was with the Scots and the Picts and the Scride-finns,
with the Lid-vikings and the Leons and the Langobards, 80
with heathens and heroes and Hundings.
I was with the Israelites and the Assyrians,
the Hebrews and Hindus and Egyptians;
I was with the Medes and the Persians and the Myrgings,
and the Ongen-Myrgings and the Mofdings, 85
and with the Amothings. With the East-Thuringians I was
and with the Eols and the Ists and the Idumings.
And I was with Eormanric all the while,
where the king of the Goths did good for me;
he gave me a ring, that prince of city-dwellers, 90
whose worth was reckoned at six hundred smæts
of brightest gold, counted out in shillings;
I gave it over to Eadgils,
my lord and protector, when I came to my home,
a reward for the dear one because he gave me land, 95
the lord of the Myrgings, my father's homeland.
And then Ealhhild gave me another,
noble queen, daughter of Eadwin.
Her praise spread far and wide in many lands,
when I could tell in my songs 100
where I knew under the skies the best
gold-laden queen for giving of gifts,
when Scilling and I raised up a song
with a clear voice for our victorious lord,
loud with the harp the joyful noise rang, 105
when many men, proud of heart,
said in words what they knew well,
that they had never heard a better song.

    Afterwards I passed through all the land of the Goths,

110 always seeking the best companions:
such was the household of Eormanric.
I sought Hehca and Beadeca and the Herelings,
I sought Emerca and Frindla and East-Goth,
the wise and good father of Unwen.
115 I sought Secca and Becca, Seafola and Theodric,
Heathoric and Sifeca, Hlitha and Incgentheow;
I sought Eadwin and Elsa, Ægelmund and Hungar,
and the proud troop of the With-Myrgings.
I sought Wulfhere and Wyrmhere, where war seldom ceased,
120 when the army of Hræd with hard swords
had to defend around Vistula-wood
the old ancestral home from the people of Attila.
I sought Rædhere and Rondere, Rumstan and Gislhere,
Withergild and Frederic, Wudga and Hama;
125 that band of comrades was by no means the worst,
though I must name them last in my song.
Often from that throng flew hissing
the singing spear among an angry people;
those exiles, Wudga and Hama, there commanded
130 the twisted gold of men and women.
Thus I have always found in my journeys
that he is most beloved to land-dwellers
to whom God gives power over men
into his hands while he lives here."
135   And so, wandering as their fate unfolds,
the bards of men among many lands,
speaking of necessity, saying words of thanks,
always south or north they meet one
wise in songs, not stingy with gifts,
140 who would raise up his fame in the presence of his men,
do noble deeds until it all fades away,
light and life together; he earns glory,
and had towering fame under the heavens.

[Source: Kemp Malone, *Widsith* (revised ed. Copenhagen, 1962); translation RML.]

Appendix B: Analogues to Themes and Events *in* Beowulf

I. Grettissaga[1] (c. 1300).

i. The Fight in the Hall, ch. 32-5.

[A farmer named Thorhall hires a strong man named Glam to work as a shepherd on his haunted farmstead. Glam is killed on Christmas day (after mocking the Christian customs of the holiday); his body, too foul and heavy to move, is buried under a cairn.]

It was not long before men became aware that Glam was not easy in his grave. Many men suffered severe injuries; some who saw him were struck senseless and some lost their wits. Soon after the festival was over, men began to think they saw him about their houses. The panic was great and many left the neighborhood. Next he began to ride on the house-tops by night, and nearly broke them to pieces. Almost night and day he walked, and people would scarcely venture up the valley, however pressing their business. The district was in a grievous condition.

[The situation grows worse over time; eventually the hero Grettir learns of Glam's predations, and resolves to see things for himself.]

Grettir rode to Thorhallsstad where he was welcomed by the bondi [farmer]. He asked Grettir whither he was bound, and Grettir said he wished to spend the night there if the bondi permitted. Thorhall said he would indeed be thankful to him for staying there.

---

1   Anonymous Norse prose saga. Parallels between *Beowulf* and *Grettir's Saga* were noted as early as 1878 (Guðbrandur Vigfússon, 'Prolegomena.' *Sturlunga saga.* 2 vols. Oxford, 1878), though scholars disagreed over which work had influenced the other. *Grettir's Saga* is a long tale, and only the episodes which are parallel to episodes of *Beowulf* are presented here. See further Chambers, *Beowulf*; Benson, "Originality of *Beowulf*"; Turville-Petre, Liberman, Scowcroft, and Stitt.

"Few," he said, "think it a gain to stay here for any time. You must have heard tell of the trouble that is here, and I do not want you to be inconvenienced on my account. Even if you escape unhurt yourself, I know for certain that you will lose your horse, for no one can keep his beast in safety who comes here."

Grettir said there were plenty more horses to be had if anything happened to this one.

Thorhall was delighted at Grettir's wishing to remain, and received him with both hands. Grettir's horse was placed securely under lock and key and they both went to bed. The night passed without Glam showing himself.

"Your being here has already done some good," said Thorhall. "Glam has always been in the habit of riding on the roof or breaking open the doors every night, as you can see from the marks."

"Then," Grettir said, "either he will not keep quiet much longer, or he will remain so more than one night. I will stay another night and see what happens."

Then they went to Grettir's horse and found it had not been touched. The bondi thought that all pointed to the same thing. Grettir stayed a second night and again the thrall did not appear. The bondi became hopeful and went to see the horse. There he found the stable broken open, the horse dragged outside and every bone in his body broken. Thorhall told Grettir what had occurred and advised him to look to himself, for he was a dead man if he waited for Glam.

Grettir answered: "I must not have less for my horse than a sight of the thrall."

The bondi said there was no pleasure to be had from seeing him: "He is not like any man. I count every hour a gain that you are here."

The day passed, and when the hour came for going to bed Grettir said he would not take off his clothes, and lay down on a seat opposite to Thorkell's sleeping apartment. He had a shaggy cloak covering him with one end of it fastened under his feet and the other drawn over his head so that he could see through the neck-hole. He set his feet against a strong bench which was in front of him. The frame-work of the outer door had been all broken away and some bits of wood had been rigged up roughly in its place. The partition which had once divided the hall from the entrance passage was all broken, both above the cross-beam and below, and all the bedding had been upset. The place looked rather desolate. There was a light burning in the hall by night.

When about a third part of the night had passed Grettir heard a loud noise. Something was going up on to the building, riding above the hall and kicking with its heels until the timbers cracked again. This went on for some time, and then it came down towards the door. The door opened and Grettir saw the thrall stretching in an enormously big and ugly head. Glam moved slowly in, and on passing the door stood upright, reaching to the roof. He turned to the hall, resting his arms on the cross-beam and peering along the hall. The bondi uttered no sound, having heard quite enough of what had gone on outside. Grettir lay quite still and did not move. Glam saw a heap of something in the seat, came farther into the hall and seized the cloak tightly with his hand. Grettir pressed his foot against the plank and the cloak held firm. Glam tugged at it again still more violently, but it did not give way. A third time be pulled, this time with both hands and with such force that he pulled Grettir up out of the seat, and between them the cloak was torn in two. Glam looked at the bit which he held in his hand and wondered much who could pull like that against him. Suddenly Grettir sprang under his arms, seized him round the waist and squeezed his back with all his might, intending in that way to bring him down, but the thrall wrenched his arms till he staggered from the violence. Then Grettir fell back to another bench. The benches flew about and everything was shattered around them. Glam wanted to get out, but Grettir tried to prevent him by stemming his foot against anything he could find. Nevertheless Glam succeeded in getting him outside the hall. Then a terrific struggle began, the thrall trying to drag him out of the house, and Grettir saw that however hard he was to deal with in the house, he would be worse outside, so he strove with all his might to keep him from getting out.

Then Glam made a desperate effort and gripped Grettir tightly towards him, forcing him to the porch. Grettir saw that he could not put up any resistance, and with a sudden movement he dashed into the thrall's arms and set both his feet against a stone which was fastened in the ground at the door. For that Glam was not prepared, since he had been tugging to drag Grettir towards him; he reeled backwards and tumbled hind-foremost out of the door, tearing away the lintel with his shoulder and shattering the roof, the rafters and the frozen thatch. Head over heels he fell out of the house and Grettir fell on top of him. The moon was shining very brightly outside, with light clouds passing over it and hiding it now and again. At the moment when Glam fell the moon shone forth, and Glam turned his eyes up towards it. Grettir himself has related that that sight was the only one which ever made him tremble. What with fatigue and all else that he had endured, when he saw the horrible rolling of Glam's eyes his heart sank so utterly that he had not strength to draw his sword, but lay there well-nigh betwixt life and death. Glam possessed more malignant power than most fiends, for he now spoke in this wise:

"You have expended much energy, Grettir, in your search for me. Nor is that to be wondered at, if you should have little joy thereof. And now I tell you that you shall possess only half the strength and firmness of heart that were decreed to you if you had not striven with me. The might which was yours till now I am not able to take away, but it is in my power to ordain that never shall you grow stronger than you are now. Nevertheless your might is sufficient, as many shall find to their cost. Hitherto you have earned fame through your deeds, but henceforward there shall fall upon you exile and battle; your deeds shall turn to evil and your guardian-spirit shall forsake you. You will be outlawed and your lot shall be to dwell ever alone. And this I lay upon you, that these eyes of mine shall be ever before your vision. You will find it hard to live alone, and at last it shall drag you to death."

When the thrall had spoken the faintness which had come over Grettir left him. He drew his short sword, cut off Glam's head and laid it between his thighs. Then the bondi came out, having put on his clothes while Glam was speaking, but he did not venture to come near until he was dead. Thorhall praised God and thanked Grettir warmly for having laid this unclean spirit. Then they set to work and burned Glam to cold cinders, bound the ashes in a skin and buried them in a place far away from the haunts of man or beast. Then they went home, the day having nearly broken. Grettir was very stiff and lay down to rest. Thorhall sent for some men from the next farms and let them know how things had fared. They all realized the importance of Grettir's deed when they heard of it; all agreed that in the whole country side for strength and courage and enterprise there was not the equal of Grettir the son of Asmund.

Thorhall bade a kindly farewell to Grettir and dismissed him with a present of a fine horse and proper clothes, for all that he had been wearing were torn to pieces. They parted in friendship. Grettir rode to Ass in Vatnsdal and was welcomed by Thorvald, who asked him all about his encounter with Glam. Grettir told him everything and said that never had his strength been put to trial as it had been in their long struggle. Thorvald told him to conduct himself discreetly; if he did so he might prosper, but otherwise he would surely come to disaster. Grettir said that his temper had not improved, that he had even less discretion than before, and was more impatient of being crossed. In one thing a great change had come over him; he had become so frightened of the dark that he dared not go anywhere alone at night. Apparitions of every kind came before him. It has since passed into an expression, and men speak of "Glam's eyes" or "Glam visions" when things appear otherwise than as they are.

Having accomplished his undertaking Grettir rode back to Bjarg and spent the winter at home.

ii. The Fight at the Falls, ch. 64–6.

[Grettir, now an outlaw travelling in disguise under the name of Gest, comes to the aid of a woman named Steinvor, mistress of a farmstead at Sandhaugar which is haunted by trolls. Twice at the Yule celebration the farm has been raided by some creature, and a man has disappeared. Grettir hears of this problem and offers his help:]

When he had eaten something he told the servants to go to the other end of the hall. Then he got some boards and loose logs and laid them across the hall to make a great barricade so that none of the servants could get across. No one dared to oppose him or to object to anything. The entrance was in the side wall of the hall under the back gable, and near it was a cross bench upon which Grettir laid himself, keeping on his clothes, with a light burning in the room. So he lay till into the night....

Towards midnight he heard a loud noise outside, and very soon there walked a huge troll-wife into the room. She carried a trough in one hand and a rather large cutlass in the other. She looked round the room as she entered, and on seeing Gest lying there she rushed at him; he started up and attacked her furiously. They fought long together; she was the stronger but he evaded her skillfully. Everything near them and the paneling of the back wall were broken to pieces. She dragged him through the hall door out to the porch, where he resisted vigorously. She wanted to drag him out of the house, but before that was done they had broken up all the fittings of the outer door and borne them away on their shoulders. Then she strove to get to the river and among the rocks. Gest was terribly fatigued, but there was no choice but either to brace himself or be dragged down to the rocks. All night long they struggled together, and he thought he had never met with such a monster for strength. She gripped him so tightly to herself that he could do nothing with either hand but cling to her waist. When at last they reached a rock by the river he swung the monster round and got his right hand loose. Then he quickly seized the short sword which he was wearing, drew it and struck at the troll's right shoulder, cutting off her right arm and releasing himself. She sprang among the rocks and disappeared in the waterfall. Gest, very stiff and tired, lay long by the rock. At daylight he went home and lay down on his bed, blue and swollen all over.

When the lady of the house came home she found the place rather in disorder. She went to Gest and asked him what had happened, and why everything was broken to pieces. He told her everything just as it had happened. She thought it a matter of great moment and asked him who he was. He told her the truth, said that he wished to see a priest and asked her to send for one. She did so; Steinn came to Sandhaugar and soon learnt that it was Grettir the son of Asmund who had come there under the name of Gest. The priest asked him what he thought had become of the men who had disappeared; Grettir said he thought that they must have gone among the rocks. The priest said he could not believe his word unless he gave some evidence of it. Grettir said that later it would be known, and the priest went home. Grettir lay many days in his bed and the lady did all she could for him; thus Yule-tide passed. Grettir himself declared that the trollwoman sprang among the rocks when she was wounded, but the men of Bardardal say that the day dawned upon her while they were wrestling; that when he cut off her arm she broke, and that she is still standing there on the mountain in the likeness of a woman. The dwellers in the valley kept Grettir there in hiding.

One day that winter after Yule Grettir went to Eyjardalsa and met the priest, to whom he said: "I see, priest, that you have little belief in what I say. Now I wish you to come with me to the river and to see what probability there is in it."

The priest did so. When they reached the falls they saw a cave up under the rock. The cliff was there so abrupt that no one could climb it, and nearly ten fathoms down to the water. They had a rope with them. The priest said: "It is quite impossible for any one to get down to that."

Grettir answered: "It is certainly possible; and men of high mettle are those who would feel themselves happiest there. I want to see what there is in the fall. Do you mind the rope."

The priest said he could do so if he chose. He drove a stake into the ground and laid stones against it.

Grettir now fastened a stone in a loop at the end of the rope, and lowered it from above into the water.

"Which way do you mean to go?" asked the priest.

"I don't mean to be bound when I come into the fall," Grettir said. "So my mind tells me."

Then he prepared to go; he had few clothes on and only a

short sword; no other arms. He jumped from a rock and got down to the fall. The priest saw the soles of his feet but after that did not know what had become of him. Grettir dived beneath the fall. It was very difficult swimming because of the currents, and he had to dive to the bottom to get behind the fall. There was a rock where he came up, and a great cave under the fall in front of which the water poured. He went into the cave, where there was a large fire burning and a horrible great giant most fearful to behold sitting before it. On Grettir entering the giant sprang up, seized a pike and struck at him, for he could both strike and thrust with it. It had a wooden shaft and was of the kind called "heptisax." Grettir struck back with his sword and cut through the shaft. Then the giant tried to reach up backwards to a sword which was hanging in the cave, and at that moment Grettir struck at him and cut open his lower breast and stomach so that all his entrails fell out into the river and floated down the stream. The priest who was sitting by the rope saw some debris being carried down all covered with blood and lost his head, making sure that Grettir was killed. He left the rope and ran off home, where he arrived in the evening and told them for certain that Grettir was dead, and said it was a great misfortune to them to have lost such a man.

Grettir struck few more blows at the giant before he was dead. He then entered the cave, kindled a light and explored. It is not told how much treasure he found there, but there is supposed to have been some. He stayed there till late into the night and found the bones of two men, which he carried away in a skin. Then he came out of the cave, swam to the rope and shook it, thinking the priest was there; finding him gone he had to swarm up the rope and so reached the top. He went home to Eyjardalsa and carried the skin with the bones in it into the vestibule of the church together with a rune-staff, upon which were most beautifully carved the following lines:

> "Into the fall of the torrent I went;
> dank its maw towards me gaped.
> The floods before the ogress' den
> Mighty against my shoulder played";

and then:

> "Hideous the friend of troll-wife came.
> Hard were the blows I dealt upon him.
> The shaft of Heptisax was severed.
> My sword has pierced the monster's breast."

There too it was told how Grettir had brought the bones from the cave. The priest when he came to the church on the next morning found the staff and all that was with it and read the runes. Grettir had then returned home to Sandhaugar.

[Source: The translation is that of G. A. Hight, first published in 1913; it is reprinted in *The Saga of Grettir the Strong*, ed. Peter Foote (London: J. R. Dent, 1965).]

2. Saxo Grammaticus,[1] *Gesta Danorum* (II.1.1-3).

[Frothi son of Hadingus, king of Denmark, in search of adventures and the funds to pay for them, overhears the song of a countryman:]

> "Near here, rising in gentle slopes, lies an island
> whose hills conceal a rich hoard of treasure.
> The guardian of the mount keeps the choice pile,
> a dragon intricately twined and curled in multiple
> spirals, dragging the sinuous folds of its tail,
> lashing its manifold coils and vomiting poison.
> To overcome it, stretch the skins of bulls
> over your shield and cover your body with oxhides,
> so that you do not expose your naked flesh

---

1 Saxo Grammaticus, late twelfth-century Danish churchman and historian. His *Gesta Danorum* records the early history of Denmark from its legendary founder Dan through a host of fabulous heroes and kings. Its style has not attracted many modern readers, but it is a treasury of legendary history and strange stories, including an early version of the revenge-tale that would become Shakespeare's *Hamlet*. A number of characters in *Beowulf* appear in Saxo's work, though they are often hard to recognize; some scenes in Saxo, like the one presented here, offer analogues to the action in *Beowulf.*

to the biting venom and be burnt by the slaver it spews.
Though its flickering triple tongue leaps from its gaping
mouth and its grim fangs threaten hideous wounds,
be fearless, nor let the spikes of its teeth, nor its starkness,
nor the virulence shot from its darting jaws dismay you.
Its tough scales scoff at man's weapons, but know there's a place
far beneath its belly to plunge in your blade;
seek this with your sword-point and probe its snaky guts.
Safely then go to the mountain and with a mattock
rake out the hollows; soon you will drench your purse
in treasure, and sail your gold-laden ship to shore."

Frothi believed him and crossed over alone to the island with
no more company to attack the monster than when champions
fight a duel. The dragon was returning to its cave after quench-
ing its thirst as Frothi's weapon struck, but its hard prickly exte-
rior made light of it. His next attempt was foiled when he
launched javelins, which only rebounded idly. When its back
proved impenetrably hard he found on closer inspection that
the softness of its stomach gave access to his sword. It tried to
bite him in retaliation, but its sharp-pointed teeth only fastened
on his shield, and with many quick little jabs of its tongue it
gasped away its life and poison at the same time.

Enriched by his treasure-trove the king was able to equip
himself with a fleet and sail into the area of the Kurlanders.

[Source: Saxo Grammaticus, *The History of the Danes.* 2 vols. Tr.
Peter Fisher, Ed. H. Ellis Davidson (Cambridge: D. S. Brewer,
1979).]

3. Snorri Sturluson,[1] *Heimskringla* (c. 1223-35), *Ynglinga saga*

[from ch. 8] Odin ... established by law that all dead men should be burned, and their belongings laid with them upon the pile, and the ashes be cast into the sea or buried in the earth. Thus, said he, every one will come to Valhalla with the riches he had with him upon the pile; and he would also enjoy whatever he himself had buried in the earth. For men of consequence a mound should be raised to their memory, and for all other warriors who had been distinguished for manhood a standing stone; which custom remained long after Odin's time.

[from ch. 10] It is said that ... at his [Odin's] pile there was great splendor. It was their [the Swedes'] faith that the higher the smoke arose in the air, the higher he would be raised whose pile it was; and the richer he would be, the more property that was consumed with him.

[from ch. 27] King Hake [of Sweden] had been so grievously wounded that he saw his days could not be long; so he ordered a warship which he had to be loaded with his dead men and their weapons, and to be taken out to the sea; the tiller to be shipped, and the sails hoisted. Then he set fire to some tarwood, and ordered a pile to be made over it in the ship. Hake was almost if not quite dead, when he was laid upon this pile of his. The wind was blowing off the land — the ship flew, burning in clear flame, out between the islets, and into the ocean. Great was the fame of this deed in after times.

[Source: The English translation is by Samuel Laing (London,

---

1 Snorri Sturluson (1179-1241), Icelandic poet, chronicler, and law-speaker of Iceland, roughly the 'president' of the Althing or legislature. He is the author of the *Prose Edda* (or *Younger Edda*), a handbook for poets that is also a compendium of Scandinavian mythological lore. His other major work is the *Heimskringla*, a collection of sagas forming a history of the various rulers of Norway from from legendary times to 1177 CE. The first saga Snorri includes is *Ynglinga saga* (The Story of the Yngling Family from Odin to Halfdan the Black); it tells among many other things of Odin's institution of cremation customs. Odin in Snorri is a lawgiver and founder of customs; the funeral rites described in Snorri are similar to those practiced in *Beowulf*. See further Lee M. Hollander, *Heimskringla* (Austin, TX, 1964).

1844). The text is found in *Heimskringla*, ed. Bjarni Athalb-jarnarson, vol. I-III (Reykjavik, 1946-51).]

4. The Life of Saint Gildas[1]

[When the saint is about to die, he says to his companions and disciples:] "I charge you by Christ, my sons, not to quarrel over the remains of my corpse, but as soon as I have sent forth my spirit, carry me down and lay me on a ship, placing under my shoulders the stone on which I used to lie down. Let none of you remain with me in the ship, but push it into the sea and let it go where God wishes. The Lord will provide a place for my burial where it will please Him."

[Source: *Gildae de Excidio Britanniae, Fragmenta, Liber de Paenitentia*, ed. Hugh Williams (Cymmrodorion Record Series 3. London, 1899), p. 366. Translation RML.]

5. *Blicking Homily*[2] 17, lines 237ff.

[The Archangel Michael is giving St. Paul a tour of the under-world:] As Saint Paul was looking toward the northern part of this world, where all waters descend, he also saw over the waters a gray stone. And north of the stone had grown very frosty groves, and there were gloomy mists, and under the stone was the dwelling-place of sea-monsters and evil spirits. And he saw that on the cliff many black souls were hanging in the icy groves, bound by their hands, and devils in the shape of sea-monsters were clutching at them like greedy wolves. And the water was black under the cliff below, and from the cliff to the

---

1 Anonymous Breton saint's life. The date of composition of this work is not known; its presentation of what is a fairly common motif in the lives of the Celtic saints — the revealing of God's will by the drifting of a rudderless boat — is reminiscent of the funeral of Scyld Scefing in *Beowulf*. See further Angus Cameron, "Saint Gildas and Scyld Scefing," and Meaney, "Scyld Scefing" 29.

2 A collection of anonymous early tenth-century homilies preserved in Princeton University Library, W. H. Scheide Collection 71. The occasion of the sermon is the dedication of St Michael's church; its sources are of questionable orthodoxy but undoubted popularity. See further Malone, "Grendel and His Abode."

water was about twelve miles. And when the boughs broke, the souls that hung on the twigs fell down, and the sea-monsters seized them. These were the souls of those who had sinned here in this world, and would not cease from it before their life's end. But let us now eagerly ask St Michael that he lead our souls to bliss, where they might rejoice without end in eternity.

[Source: R. Morris, *The Blickling Homilies of the Tenth Century* (Early English Text Society os 58, 63, 73. Oxford, 1874-80); translation RML.]

Appendix C: Christians and Pagans

1. Gregory the Great[1] (c. 540-604), letter to Abbot Mellitus (601).

Since the departure of our congregation, which is with you, we have been in a state of great suspense from having heard nothing of the success of your journey. But when Almighty God shall have brought you to our most reverend brother the Bishop Augustine, tell him that I have long been considering with myself about the case of the Angli; to wit, that the temples of idols in that nation should not be destroyed, but that the idols themselves that are in them should be. Let blessed water be prepared, and sprinkled in these temples, and altars constructed, and relics deposited, since, if these same temples are well built, it is needful that they should be transferred from the worship of idols to the service of the true God; that, when the people themselves see that these temples are not destroyed, they may put away error from their heart, and, knowing and adoring the true God, may have recourse with the more familiarity to the places they have been accustomed to. And, since they are wont to kill many oxen in sacrifice to demons, they should have also some solemnity of this kind in a changed form, so that on the day of dedication, or on the anniversaries of the holy martyrs whose relics are deposited there, they may make for themselves tents of the branches of trees around these temples that have been changed into churches, and celebrate the solemnity with religious feasts. Nor let them any longer sacrifice animals to the devil, but slay animals to the praise of God for their own eating, and return thanks to the Giver of all for their fullness, so that, while some joys are reserved to them outwardly, they may be

---

1 Gregory the Great, Pope from 590 to 604, is regarded as the last of the great Fathers of the Church. His works, well-known to the Anglo-Saxons, include the *Pastoral Care* (instructions for bishops), the *Dialogues* (lives of St Benedict and other Italian saints), and a commentary on the biblical book of Job. His long interest in converting the English culminated in his sending of Augustine and a number of monks as missionaries there in 597. This letter is addressed to a French abbot (later bishop) on his way to England.

able the more easily to incline their minds to inward joys. For it is undoubtedly impossible to cut away everything at once from hard hearts, since one who strives to ascend to the highest place must needs rise by steps or paces, and not by leaps. Thus to the people of Israel in Egypt the Lord did indeed make Himself known; but still He reserved to them in His own worship the use of the sacrifices which they were accustomed to offer to the devil, enjoining them to immolate animals in sacrifice to Himself; to the end that, their hearts being changed, they should omit some things in the sacrifice and retain others, so that, though the animals were the same as what they had been accustomed to offer, nevertheless, as they immolated them to God and not to idols, they should be no longer the same sacrifices. This then it is necessary for Your Love to say to our aforesaid brother, that he, being now in that country, may consider well how he should arrange all things.

[Source: Pope Gregory the Great, *Epistle XI*, 56, trans. J. Barmby, *A Select Library of Nicene and Post-Nicene Fathers*, Second Series, XIII (Oxford and New York, 1898), pp. 84-5. The letter is also found in Bede's *Ecclesiastical History*, I.30.]

2. Bede the Venerable,[1] *Ecclesiastical History of the English People* II.13 (the Conversion of King Edwin of Northumbria).

[Edwin, already inclined towards Christianity by several miraculous events, submits the question of his conversion to his advisors:] When the king had heard his words, he answered that he was both willing and bound to accept the faith which Paulinus taught. He said, however, that he would confer about this with his loyal chief men and his counselors so that, if they agreed with him, they might all be consecrated together in the waters of life. Paulinus agreed and the king did as he had said. A

---

1   Bede, eighth-century historian, spent most of his life in the monastery of Wearmouth-Jarrow in Northumbria. His *Ecclesiastical History of the English People* tells the story of the conversion of the English, and the struggles between Roman and Irish missionaries in the newly-Christian land.

meeting of his council was held and each one was asked in turn what he thought of this doctrine hitherto unknown to them and this new worship of God which was being proclaimed.

Coifi, the chief of the priests, answered at once, 'Notice carefully, King, this doctrine which is now being expounded to us. I frankly admit that, for my part, I have found that the religion which we have hitherto held has no virtue nor profit in it. None of your followers has devoted himself more earnestly than I have to the worship of our gods, but nevertheless there are many who receive greater benefits and greater honour from you than I do and are more successful in all their undertakings. If the gods had any power they would have helped me more readily, seeing that I have always served them with greater zeal. So it follows that if, on examination, these new doctrines which have now been explained to us are found to be better and more effectual, let us accept them at once without any delay.'

Another of the king's chief men agreed with this advice and with these wise words and then added, 'This is how the present life of man on earth, King, appears to me in comparison with that time which is unknown to us. You are sitting feasting with your ealdormen and thegns in winter time; the fire is burning on the hearth in the middle of the hall and all inside is warm, while outside the wintry storms of rain and snow are raging; and a sparrow flies swiftly through the hall. It enters in at one door and quickly flies out through the other. For the few moments it is inside, the storm and wintry tempest cannot touch it, but after the briefest moment of calm, it flits from your sight, out of the wintry storm and into it again. So this life of man appears but for a moment; what follows or indeed what went before, we know not at all. If this new doctrine brings us more certain information, it seems right that we should accept it.' Other elders and counselors of the king continued in the same manner, being divinely prompted to do so.

Coifi added that he would like to listen still more carefully to what Paulinus himself had to say about God. The king ordered Paulinus to speak, and when he had said his say, Coifi exclaimed, 'For a long time now I have realized that our religion is worthless; for the more diligently I sought the truth in our cult, the less I found it. Now I confess openly that the truth shines out clearly in this teaching which can bestow on us the gift of life, salvation, and eternal happiness. Therefore I advise your Majesty that we should promptly abandon and commit to the flames the temples and the altars which we have held sacred without reaping any benefit.' Why need I say more? The king publicly accepted the gospel which Paulinus preached, renounced idolatry, and confessed his faith in Christ. When he asked the high priest of their religion which of them should be the first to profane the altars and the shrines of the idols, together with their precincts, Coifi answered, 'I will; for through the wisdom the true God has given me no one can more suitably destroy those things which I once foolishly worshipped, and so set an example to all.' And at once, casting aside his vain superstitions, he asked the king to provide him with arms and a stallion; and mounting it he set out to destroy the idols. Now a high priest of their religion was not allowed to carry arms or to ride except on a mare. So, girded with a sword, he took a spear in his hand and mounting the king's stallion he set off to where the idols were. The common people who saw him thought he was mad. But as soon as he approached the shrine, without any hesitation he profaned it by casting the spear which he held into it; and greatly rejoicing in the knowledge of the worship of the true God, he ordered his companions to destroy and set fire to the shrine and all the enclosures. The place where the idols once stood is still shown, not far from York, to the east, over the river Derwent. Today it is called Goodmanham, the place where the high priest, through the inspiration of the true God, profaned and destroyed the altars which he himself had consecrated.

[Source: *Bede's Ecclesiastical History of the English People*, ed. and tr. by Bertram Colgrave and R. A. B. Mynors (Oxford: Oxford UP, 1969), pp. 182-7.]

3. Boniface,[1] *Letter 46* (c. 738).

To all his reverend fellow bishops, to all those clothed with the grace of priesthood, deacons, canons, clerks, abbots, and abbesses set over the true flock of Christ, monks living in humble submission to God, virgins consecrated by vows to God, and all consecrated handmaids of Christ — and, in general, to all God-fearing catholics of the stock and race of the Angles, Boniface named also Winfred, born of that same race, German legate of the Church Universal, servant of the Apostolic See and called Archbishop for no merit of his own, sends greetings of humble communion and unfeigned love in Christ.

We earnestly beseech your brotherly goodness to be mindful of us, who are worth so little, in your prayers that we may be delivered from the snare of Satan the huntsman and from wicked and cruel men, that the word of God may make its way and be glorified. We beseech you to obtain through your holy prayers, that our Lord and God Jesus Christ, "who will have all men to be saved, and to come unto the knowledge of God," may turn the hearts of the pagan Saxons to the catholic faith, that they may free themselves from the snares of the devil in which they are bound and may be gathered among the children of Mother Church.

Take pity upon them; for they themselves are saying: "We are of one blood and one bone with you." Remember that the way of all the earth is at hand and that in hell no one will confess God, nor will death praise him.

Know also that in making this request I have the approval, the consent, and the blessing of two pontiffs of the Roman Church. Act now upon this our supplication so that your reward may shine with increasing splendor in the heavenly house of the angels.

---

1 St. Boniface (named in English Wynfrith), English churchman and martyr. Most of his life was devoted to missionary work on the Continent among the Saxons and Frisians, among whom he was martyred in 754. He is the author of numerous letters; this general letter to the English appeals to their sense of kinship with their continental pagan cousins to encourage support for their conversion.

May the Omnipotent Creator always keep the unity and communion of your affection in power and progress in Christ.

[Source: *The Letters of Saint Boniface*, translated with an introduction by Ephraim Emerton (New York: Columbia UP, 1940), pp. 74-5. The Latin text is found in *Briefe des Bonifatius, Willibalds Leben des Bonifatius*, ed. and tr. (into German) Reinhold Rau (Darmstadt, 1968), p. 134.]

4. Boniface, *Letter 73*[1] (c. 746)

To his dearest master, King Ethelbald, cherished in the love of Christ above all other kings and holding glorious sway over the realm of the Anglians [sic], Boniface, archbishop and legate of the Roman Church in Germany, and his fellow bishops, Wera, Burkhardt, Werbert, Abel, and Willibald, send greetings of unfailing love in Christ.

We acknowledge before God and the holy angels, that when we have heard through trustworthy messengers of your prosperity, your faith in God, and your good works before God and man we have returned joyful thanks to God, praying and beseeching the Savior of the world to keep you forever safe and steadfast in faith and works before God and in the leadership of the people of Christ. But when we hear that any harm befalls you, be it in the conditions of your government or the event of war or, worse yet, some peril to your soul's welfare, we are afflicted with pain and sorrow; for by God's will we rejoice with you in your joy and grieve with you in your sorrow.

We have heard that you are very liberal in almsgiving, and congratulate you thereon; for they who give to the least of their needy brethren shall hear at the day of judgment, according to Gospel truth, the gracious word of the Lord: "Inasmuch as ye have done it unto the least of these my brethren, ye have

---

1   This letter of advice from Boniface and other bishops to King Ethelbald of Mercia reproves a king whose evil conduct has caused widespread scandal; Boniface notes that even the pagans do not tolerate the kinds of vices Ethelbald is accused of practicing.

done it unto me. Come, ye blessed of my Father, inherit the kingdom prepared for you from the foundation of the world." We have heard also that you repress robbery and wrongdoing, perjury, and rapine with a strong hand, that you are famed as a defender of widows and of the poor, and that you have established peace within your kingdom. In this also we have rejoiced, because the Truth itself and our Peace, which is Christ, said, "Blessed are the peacemakers, for they shall be called the children of God."

But amidst all this, one evil report as to the manner of life of Your Grace has come to our hearing, which has greatly grieved us and which we could wish were not true. We have learned from many sources that you have never taken to yourself a lawful wife. Now this relation was ordained of the Lord God himself from the very beginning of the world and was repeatedly insisted upon by the Apostle Paul saying: "On account of fornication let every man have his own wife, and every woman have her own husband." If you had willed to do this for the sake of chastity and abstinence, or had refrained from women from the fear and love of God and had given evidence that you were abstinent for God's sake we should rejoice, for that is not worthy of blame but rather of praise. But if, as many say — but which God forbid! — you have neither taken a lawful spouse nor observed chastity for God's sake but, moved by desire, have defiled your good name before God and man by the crime of adulterous lust, then we are greatly grieved because this is a sin in the sight of God and is the ruin of your fair fame among men.

And now, what is worse, our informants say that these atrocious crimes are committed in convents with holy nuns and virgins consecrated to God, and this, beyond all doubt, doubles the offense.... We therefore, beloved son, beseech Your Grace by Christ the son of God and by His coming and by His kingdom, that if it is true that you are continuing in this vice you will amend your life by penitence, purify yourself, and bear in mind how vile a thing it is through lust to change the image of God created in you into the image and likeness of a vicious demon. Remember that you were made king and ruler over many not by your own merits but by the abounding grace of God, and now you are making yourself by your own lust the slave of an evil spirit, since, as the Apostle says, whatever sin a man commits, of that he becomes the slave.

This is held to be a shame and disgrace, not by Christians only but even by pagans. For the pagans themselves, although ignorant of the true God, keep in this matter the substance of the law and the ordinance of God from the beginning inasmuch as they respect their wives with the bond of matrimony and punish fornicators and adulterers. In Old Saxony, if a virgin disgraces her father's house by adultery or if a married woman breaks the bond of wedlock and commits adultery, they sometimes compel her to hang herself with her own hand and then hang the seducer above the pyre on which she has been burned. Sometimes a troop of women get together and flog her through the towns, beating her with rods and stripping her to the waist, cutting her whole body with knives, pricking her with wounds, and sending her on bleeding and torn from town to town; fresh scourgers join in with new zeal for purity, until finally they leave her dead or almost dead, that other women may be made to fear adultery and evil conduct. The Wends, who are the vilest and lowest race of men, have such high regard for the mutual bond of marriage that the wife refuses to survive her husband. Among them a woman is praised who dies by her own hand and is burned upon the same pyre with her husband.

If, then, heathen who know not God and have not the law do, as the Apostle says, by nature the things of the law and have the works of the law written upon their hearts, know you, beloved son, who are called a Christian and a worshipper of the true God — if in your youth you were ensnared in the filth of wantonness and involved in the mire of adultery and sunk in the whirlpool of lust as in an abyss of hell — it is now high time that you should remember your Lord, should rouse yourself from the snares of the devil, and wash your soul clean from the filthiness of lust. It is time for you in fear of your Creator no longer to venture to defile yourself by repeating such sins. It is time for you to have mercy upon the multitude of your people who are perishing by following the example of a sinful prince and are falling into the abyss of death. For, beyond a doubt, we shall receive from the eternal judge rewards for as many as we lead by good example into the life of our heavenly fatherland, and punishment for those whom we guide by evil example into perdition.

If the English people, as is reported here and as is charged against us in France and Italy and even by the heathen themselves, are scorning lawful marriage and living in wanton adultery like the people of Sodom, then we must expect that a degenerate and degraded people with unbridled desires will be produced. At last the whole race will become debased and finally will be neither strong in war nor steadfast in faith, neither honored among men nor pleasing in the sight of God. So it has been with the peoples of Spain and Provence and Burgundy. They turned thus away from God and lived in harlotry until the Almighty Judge let the penalties for such crimes fall upon them through ignorance of the law of God and the coming of the Saracens....

The riches of this world are of no avail in the day of requital if a man comes to the end of his life while still making bad use of them; for after the death of the body he shall fall into eternal punishment of the soul. Take these warnings to heart, my dear son, and, I pray you, yield to the prudent words of God's law and reform your life. Turn away from your vices and make an effort to acquire the sacred virtues; so shall you prosper in this world and receive eternal reward in the world to come.

May Almighty God so turn your life to better things that you may be worthy of the grace of our Lord himself forevermore.

[Source: *The Letters of Saint Boniface*, translated with an introduction by Ephraim Emerton (New York: Columbia UP, 1940), pp. 124-30. *Briefe des Bonifatius, Willibalds Leben des Bonifatius*, ed. and tr. (into German) Reinhold Rau (Darmstadt, 1968), pp. 212-27.]

5. Wulfstan[1] (d. 1023), *On False Gods*

Alas! Long ago it was that because of the Devil many things went wrong, and that mankind disobeyed God too much, and that heathenism all too widely caused great harm, and still widely causes harm. Yet we do not read anywhere in books that people raised up any heathen altars anywhere in the world during all the time that was before Noah's flood. But after that it came about that Nimrod and the giants made a marvelous tower after Noah's flood, and it came to pass that they had as many languages, as the book tells, as they had workmen.[2] Then afterwards they scattered into distant lands, and then mankind soon greatly increased. And then finally they were deceived by the ancient Devil who had betrayed Adam long before, so that perversely and heretically they made heathen gods for themselves, and scorned the true God and their own Creator, who formed them as men and fashioned them.

They also took it as wisdom, through the devil's teaching, that they ought to worship the sun and moon as gods because of their shining brightness; and finally, through the devil's teaching, they offered them sacrifices and abandoned their Lord who had made and fashioned them. Some men also said that the shining stars were gods, and began to zealously worship them, and some also believed in fire for its sudden heat; some in water, and some believed in the earth because it nourishes all things. But they might have readily realized, if they had had discernment, that he is the true God who made all these things for the enjoyment and use of us human beings, which he granted to mankind because of his great goodness. These created things, moreover, act just as their own Creator ordained for

---

1   Wulfstan, Bishop of London 996-1002 and Archbishop of York 1002-23, royal counselor and author of vigorous Old English homiletic prose. This brief sermon is an abridgement and adaptation of a piece by another writer, Ælfric, which in turn draws upon a still earlier source, the sixth-century archbishop Martin of Braga. It is found in only one copy, a manuscript in the Bodleian Library at Oxford (MS Hatton 113-14, ff. 58v-61).

2   The story of the Tower of Babel is told in the Bible, Genesis 11:1-9. The Bible does not call the builders of the tower 'giants', but apocryphal tradition ascribes incredible size to the generations before the Patriarchs. The Anglo-Saxons sometimes called great ruins *eald enta geweorc*, "the old work of giants."

them, and can do nothing except by our Lord's consent, because there is no other creator but the one true God in whom we believe, and Him alone above all other things we love and honour with certain faith, saying with our mouth and with the conviction of our heart that He alone is true God, who made and fashioned all things.

Yet the heathens would not be content with as few gods as they had previously, but finally took to worshipping various giants and violent men of the earth who became mighty in worldly power and were terrifying while they lived, and foully followed their own lusts. There was a man in days gone by living on the island that is called Crete, who was called Saturn, and he was so savage that he destroyed his own sons, all but one, and in an unfatherly way destroyed their lives early in their childhood. He uneasily left one alive, though he had destroyed all his brothers, and this one was called Jove, and he became a fierce enemy. He later drove his own father out of the aforesaid island called Crete, and would readily have slain him if he could. This Jove grew so lecherous that he took to wife his own sister, who was called Juno, and she became a very important goddess according to the heathen religion. Their two daughters were Minerva and Venus. These wicked men of whom we speak were considered the greatest gods in those days, and the heathens greatly worshiped them, through the Devil's teaching. And yet the son was worshipped among the heathens even more than the father had been, and he is considered most honorable of all those whom the heathens, in their error, took for gods in those days. He is called by another name, Thor, in some nations — the Danish people, in their error, love him greatly and worship him most diligently.[1] His son was called Mars, who always caused strife and trouble, and frequently stirred up conflict and hostility. The heathens also honoured this wretch, after his death, as an important god, and

---

1 Germanic and Roman pantheons were regarded as equivalent, as is seen in the days of the week (English Wednesday "Woden's Day" for the Latin day of Mercury (cf. French *mercredi*), English *Thursday* "Thor's Day" = the day of Jove (cf. French *jeudi*), English Friday "Frig's Day" = the day of Venus. The Germanic pantheon had no equivalent for Saturn, so they simply called the seventh day *Sæternesdæg* (I am indebted to Peter S. Baker for this footnote).

whenever they went to war or battle, they first offered their sacrifices in honour of this false god; and they believed that he would assist them with great strength in battle, because he loved battle and combat when he was alive.

There was also a certain man named Mercury while he was alive, who was very crafty and, though clever in speech, deceitful in his deeds and in falsehoods. The heathens also made him a great god, by their reckoning, and time and again they offered him sacrifices at crossroads through the devil's teaching, and often brought him various sacrifices of praise on high hills. This false god was also honoured among all heathens in those days, and in the Danish fashion he is called by the other name Odin. Now some of these Danish men, in their error, say that this Jove, whom they call Thor, was the son of Mercury, whom they call Odin, but they are not right because we read in books, both heathen and Christian, that the evil Jove is in fact Saturn's son. And a certain woman was called Venus, who was Jove's daughter, and she was very foul and so given over to lust that her own brother lay with her, as is said, through the devil's teaching, and the heathens also honour this evil one as an exalted woman.

Additionally, many other heathen gods were variously invented, and likewise many heathen goddesses held in great honour throughout the world for the ruin of mankind, but these are considered the most important in heathen religion, though they lived foully in the world. And the scheming devil, who always deceives mankind, brought the heathens into such deep error that they chose as gods such filthy people who had made their foul lusts a law for themselves and spent their whole life in uncleanness as long as they lived.

But blessed is he who scorns all this, and loves and honors the true God who formed and fashioned all things. Almighty God is one in three persons, that is, Father and Son and Holy Spirit; all three names enfold one divine power and one eternal God, ruler and maker of all creation. To him always be praise and honor forever and ever, world without end, amen.

[Source: Dorothy Bethurum, *Homilies of Wulfstan* (Oxford: Oxford UP, 1957), pp. 221-4. Translation RML.]

6. Laws against Paganism

i. Wulfstan, *Canons of Edgar* no. 16.[1]

And it is right that every priest eagerly teach Christianity and crush all heathenism; and forbid the worship of springs, and necromancy, and divination and incantations, and the worship of trees and stones, and the devilish trick people perform in which a child is dragged across the earth, and the superstitions practiced with various auguries on New Year's night and at pagan shrines and elder-trees, and a great many other errors which men practice much more than they should.

[Source: Roger Fowler, ed. *Wulfstan's Canons of Edgar* (EETS os 266. London, 1972), p. 26. Translation RML; the version of Oxford, Bodleian Lib. Junius 121 is translated here.]

ii. Laws of Cnut, 1-5.[2]

0.1 This is the secular law which I wish, with the advice of my counselors, to be held all across England:

1. First, that I wish that proper laws should be raised up and all outlawry should certainly be felled, and that one should weed out and root up all unrightfulness, as best one can, from this land, and raise up God's law.
   ...

3 And we command that Christian men ought not to be sold out of the country so often nor brought to heathen lands; but be on guard lest one's soul be destroyed, which Christ purchased with His own life.

---

1 The *Canons of Edgar*, a collection of ordinances of the late tenth century, was compiled by Wulfstan; the passage quoted here suggests a more immediate concern with pagan practices than that found in *On the False Gods*.

2 Perhaps drafted by Wulfstan (Liebermann 1903-16, I, 308-70), the laws of Cnut also forbid pagan practices, in the context of general law and order and the establishment of a Christian commonwealth.

4   And we command that everyone eagerly begin to clean this land in every part, and cease everywhere from sinful deeds.

4a   And if witches or sorcerers, murderers or whores are caught anywhere in this land, drive them out of the country immediately, or put them away, unless they desist and more fervently amend themselves.

4.1   And we command that traitors and outlaws from God and man depart from this land, unless they submit and more readily amend themselves.

4.2   And thieves and public criminals perish, unless they cease.

5.   And we strictly forbid all heathenism. Heathenism is the worship of idols, that is, when one worships heathen gods, and the sun or moon, fire or flood, watery springs or stones or any kind of forest tree, or prefers witchcraft or commits murder in any way, either by sacrifices or sorcery, or undertaking any such vain things.

[Source: Felix Liebermann, *Die Gesetze der Angelsachsen*. 3 vols. (Halle, 1903-16); I.312; translation RML.]

Appendix D: Contexts for reading Beowulf[1]

1. Wulfstan, *Sermo Lupi ad anglos*, 1014.[2]

The Sermon of 'Wolf' to the English, when the Danes were greatly persecuting them, which was in the 1014th year after the Incarnation of our Lord Jesus Christ.

Beloved men, recognize what is true: this world is in haste and it draws near its end. And therefore in this world things get worse and worse, and so it must be that because of the people's sins things will get very much worse before the coming of the Antichrist; and then it will indeed be terrible and grim widely throughout the world. Understand well, too, that the Devil has led this nation too far astray for many years, and there has been little loyalty among men, though they might speak well, and too many wrongs have ruled this land, and there were never many men who sought the remedy as eagerly as they should, but every day they added one evil to another, and raised up wrong and injustice too widely throughout this entire land.

And therefore we have also suffered many injuries and insults, and if we are to expect any remedy then we must deserve better of God than we have done previously. For with great demerit we have earned the miseries that oppress us, and with very great merits we must obtain the remedy from God, if things are to improve henceforth. Indeed, we know full well

---

1 The following selections were all circulating in manuscript at about the same time the manuscript of *Beowulf* was written. In this sense they may be regarded as 'contexts' for the reading of the poem and suggest different elements of the literary milieu in which *Beowulf* was copied and read. Moreover, each comments, in some way, on the central themes of the poem.

2 On Wulfstan, see Appendix C.5. In this vigorous sermon, written in a strongly rhythmical prose, Wulfstan considers the Viking attacks as divine retribution for the sins of the English. He adapts the historical attitude of the sixth-century British writer Gildas, whose *De excidio Britanniae* lamented the arrival of the English as a similar retribution upon the British; in doing so Wulfstan subscribes to a Biblical view of history which sees the rise and fall of nations as a reflection of their morality. Even pagans may be instruments of God's justice, and he notes as a rebuke to the English that pagans practice their religion more faithfully and with more morality than Christians do.

that a great breach requires a great remedy, and a great fire needs no little water, if one would quench that fire at all. And the necessity is great for every man henceforth diligently to heed God's law, and pay God's dues justly. Among heathen peoples no one dares withhold little or much of that which is pledged to the worship of false gods, and everywhere we withhold God's dues all too often. And among heathen people no one dares diminish, inside the temple or out, anything brought to the false gods and given over as an offering; and we have completely stripped the houses of God, inside and out, and the servants of God are everywhere deprived of respect and protection. And among heathen people no one dares abuse the servants of the false gods in any way, just as is now done too widely to the servants of God, where Christians ought to observe God's laws and protect God's servants.

But what I say is true: there is need of a remedy, because God's dues have decreased for too long in this land in every region, and the laws of the people have deteriorated all too much, and sanctuaries are commonly violated, and the houses of God are entirely stripped of ancient dues and are despoiled within of everything decent. And widows are wrongfully forced to take a husband, and too many are reduced to poverty and greatly humiliated; and poor men are sorely betrayed and cruelly defrauded, and widely sold out of this land into the power of foreigners, even though they are completely innocent; and with cruel injustice children in the cradle are enslaved for petty theft commonly throughout this nation; and the rights of freemen are taken away and the rights of slaves restricted, and the right to alms curtailed, and to speak briefly, the laws of God are hated and His teaching scorned; therefore through God's anger we all are frequently put to shame, let him know it who can. And although one might not imagine it, the harm will become common to all this nation, unless God protects us.

For it is clear and evident in us all that we have hitherto more often transgressed than we have amended, and therefore many things have fallen upon this nation. For a long time now, nothing has prospered either at home or abroad, but there has been plunder and famine, burning and bloodshed in nearly every region time and again. And stealing and slaughter, plague and pestilence, murrain and disease, slander and hatred, and the thievery of robbers has harmed us severely. And excessive taxes have greatly afflicted us, and bad weather has often caused crop failures; therefore there have been in this land, so it seems, many years now of injustices and unstable loyalties among men everywhere. Now very often a kinsman will not protect a kinsman any more than a foreigner, nor the father his children, nor sometimes the child his own father, nor one brother the other. Nor has any of us ordered his life as he should, neither the cleric according to the rule nor the layman according to the law. But all too frequently we have made lust into law for us, and have kept neither the teachings nor the laws of God or men as we should. Neither has anyone had loyal intentions toward others as justly as he should, but almost all men have betrayed and injured others by word and deed; and indeed almost everyone unjustly stabs the other in the back with shameful assaults: let him do more, if he can.

Therefore there are here in this land great disloyalties towards God and towards the state, and there are also in this country many who betray their lords in various ways, and the greatest of all betrayals of one's lord in the world is that a man betrays his lord's soul. And it is also a great betrayal of one's lord in the world when a man plots against his lord's life, or, living, drive him from the land, and both have happened in this country. They plotted against Edward and then killed, and afterwards burned him; and Æthelred was driven out of his country. And too many godparents and godchildren have been destroyed widely throughout this nation, and likewise too many other innocent people have been too commonly slain. And also far too many holy places have fallen down because previously certain men have been placed in them who ought not to have been, if one wished to show respect to God's sanctuary. And too many Christian people have been sold out of this land, all the time now, and all this is hateful to God, let him believe it who will. And it is shameful to speak of what happens too commonly, and dreadful to know what too many often do, who practice a wretched deed: they pool their money together and buy a woman in common as a joint purchase, and with the one woman commit foul sin, one after another and each after the other, just like dogs who do not care about filth, and then for a price they sell out of the land into the hands of the enemy this creature of God, His own purchase that He bought so dearly.

Also we know well where the crime has occurred that a father has sold his son for a price, and a son his mother, and one brother has sold another into the hands of foreigners; and all those are serious and terrible deeds, let him understand it who will. And yet that which is injuring this nation is still greater and more manifold: many are forsworn and greatly perjured, and vows are broken time and again, and it is evident in this nation that God's anger violently oppresses us, let him know it who can.

And indeed, how can greater shame befall men through the wrath of God than frequently does us for our own deeds? Though a slave should escape from his lord and, leaving Christendom become a Viking, and it afterwards happens that armed combat takes place between thane and slave, if the slave should slay the thane, he will lie without payment to any of his family; but if the thane kills the slave that he had previously owned, he must pay the price of a thane. Utterly shameful laws and disgraceful tributes are common among us, because of God's anger, let him understand it who is able; and many misfortunes befall this nation time and again. For a long time now nothing has prospered at home or abroad, but there has been devastation and hatred in every region time and again, and for a long time now the English have been entirely without victory and too much disheartened through God's wrath, and the pirates so strong through God's consent that often in battle one drives away ten, sometimes less and sometimes more, all because of our sins. And often ten or twelve, one after the other, will disgracefully put to shame a thane's wife, and sometimes his daughter or close kinswomen, while he looks on, he who considered himself brave and strong and good enough before that happened. And often a slave will bind fast the thane who had been his lord, and make him a slave through God's anger. Alas the misery, and alas the public shame that the English now suffer, all because of God's anger! Often two seamen, or sometimes three, will drive the droves of Christian men out from this nation from sea to sea, huddled together as a public shame for us all, if we could in earnest properly feel any. But all the disgrace we often suffer we repay with honour to those who shame us: we pay them continually, and they humiliate us daily. They ravage and they burn, plunder and rob and carry off to the ship; and indeed, what else is there in all these events than the wrath of God, clear and evident over this nation?

It is no wonder that misfortune should befall us, because we know full well that for many years now men have not cared what they did in word or deed. Rather it seems this nation has become thoroughly corrupted through manifold sins and many misdeeds: through acts of murder and evil, through avarice and greed, through theft and thievery, through slavery and pagan abuses, through treachery and trickery, through the breach of law and order, through mayhem upon kinsmen and manslaughter, through crimes against clergy and adulteries, through incest and various fornications. And everywhere, as we said before, by the breaking of oaths and by various lies many more than should be are lost and betrayed, and breaches of feasts and fasts are widely and frequently committed. And here in this land also there are far too many degenerate apostates, hostile enemies of the Church, and cruel tyrants, and widespread scorners of divine law and Christian custom, and everywhere in the nation foolish mockers, most often of those things that the messengers of God command, and especially those things which always by right belong to God's law. And therefore it has now come far and wide to such an evil state that men are nowadays more ashamed of good deeds than of misdeeds; because too often good deeds are dismissed with derision and God-fearing men are reviled all too much, and especially mocked and treated with contempt are those who love justice and fear God to any extent. And because men behave thus, blaming all that they should praise and hating too much all that they ought to love, they bring all too many to evil intentions and wicked deeds, so that they are never ashamed even though they sin greatly and commit wrongs against God himself. But because of idle assaults they are ashamed to atone for their misdeeds as the books teach, like those fools who for pride will not guard themselves against injury, until they cannot do so even though they wish to.

Here, so it seems, too many in this country are sorely injured by the stains of sin. Here there are slayers of men and slayers of kinsmen, and murderers of priests and enemies of monasteries, and here are perjurers and murderers, and here there are whores and child-killers and many foul fornicating adulterers, and here there are wizards and sorceresses, and here there are robbers and thieves and plunderers, and, to be brief, countless numbers of crimes and misdeeds. And we are not ashamed of it at all, but we are greatly ashamed to begin the remedy as the books teach us, and that is obvious in this wretched and sinful nation. Alas, many could easily call to mind much more in addition, which one man could not hastily devise, how wretchedly things have gone all the time now widely throughout this nation. And indeed let each one examine himself well, and not delay it all too long.

But lo!, in God's name, let us do what is necessary for us, defend ourselves as best we may, lest we all perish together. There was a historian in the time of the Britons named Gildas, who wrote about their misdeeds, how they with their sins angered God so exceedingly that He finally allowed the army of the English to conquer their land and completely destroy the nobility of the Britons. And this came about, he said, through robbery by the powerful and the coveting of ill-gotten gains, through the people's lawlessness and evil judgements, through the slackness of bishops and the abject cowardice of God's heralds, who too often kept silent from the truth and mumbled in their jaws when they should have shouted. Likewise, through the foul excesses of the people and through gluttony and manifold sins they destroyed their nation and themselves perished. But let us do what is needful — warn ourselves by such things; and what I say is true, we know of worse deeds among the English than we have ever heard of among the Britons. And therefore it is very necessary that we consider ourselves and earnestly plead with God Himself. And let us do what is necessary for us — bow to justice, and in some measure abandon injustice, and repair carefully what we have broken; and let us love God and follow God's laws, and earnestly practice what we promised when we received baptism, or those who were our sponsors at baptism; and let us arrange our words and deeds rightly, and cleanse our conscience thoroughly, and carefully keep our oaths and pledges, and have some faith between ourselves without deceit. And let us frequently consider the great judgment to which we all must come, and eagerly defend ourselves against the surging fires of the torments of hell, and earn for ourselves the glories and delights which God has prepared for those who do His will in the world. May God help us. Amen.

[Source: D. Bethurum, *Homilies of Wulfstan* (Oxford: Oxford UP, 1957), pp. 255-60. Tr. RML.]

2. Ælfric[1] (c. 950–c. 1020), *Life of St Edmund* (c. 995)

A certain very learned monk came from the south over the sea from St Benedict's place, in the days of King Æthelred, to Archbishop Dunstan three years before he died; the monk was named Abbo. Then they took to conversation, until Dunstan told the story of St Edmund, just as Edmund's sword-bearer had told it to King Athelstan, when Dunstan was a young man and the sword-bearer was a very old man. Then the monk set down that whole narrative in a book, and later, when the book came to us, within a few years, we translated it into English, just as it appears below. Within two years, the monk Abbo returned

---

1   Ælfric, abbot of Eynsham, prolific writer of homilies, sermons, and saints' lives. His *Life of St Edmund* commemorates a king of the East Angles who was killed by the Danes in 869. His martyrdom was celebrated on 20 November. Ælfric's source is the Latin *Passio Sancti Edmundi* by Abbo of Fleury (c. 945-1004), reworked by Ælfric in a more elaborate vernacular style as an example of a Christian ideal of kingship. See further Needham, *Lives of Three English Saints* 43-59, Whitelock, "Fact and Fiction." For a discussion of some ways in which the *Vita* of Edmund is a 'context' for *Beowulf*, see the Introduction, p. 40.

home to his monastery, and was immediately appointed abbot in the same monastery.

The blessed Edmund, king of the East Angles, was wise and honorable, and always worshipped the almighty God with noble customs. He was humble and virtuous, and continued so steadfastly that he would not turn to shameful sins, nor did he turn away on either side from his good practices, but was always mindful of that true teaching, "You are appointed ruler? do not exalt yourself, but be among men as one of them."[1] He was generous to the poor and widows like a father, and with benevolence always guided his people to righteousness, restrained the violent, and lived blessedly in the true faith.

It eventually happened that the Danish people went with their fleet, pillaging and killing throughout the land, as their custom is. The principal leaders of the fleet were Ivar and Ubbi, united by the devil, and they landed in Northumbria with warships, and wasted the land and killed the people. Then Ivar turned eastwards with his ships, and Ubbi remained in Northumbria, the victory having been won with savagery. Then Ivar came rowing to the East Angles in the year when Prince Alfred, who later became the famous king of the West Saxons, was twenty-one. And the aforesaid Ivar quickly stalked about the land like a wolf, and slew the people, men and women and innocent children, and shamefully tormented innocent Christians.

He then immediately sent to the king a boastful message that he must submit to his service, if he cared for his life. Then the messenger came to King Edmund and quickly announced Ivar's message: "Ivar our king, brave and victorious on sea and land, has command of many people, and has now suddenly come to land with an army here so that he might have winter quarters here with his troops. He now commands you to share your hidden treasures and your ancestral wealth with him without delay, and be his under-king, if you wish to live, for you do not have the power to resist him."

---

1 Ecclesiasticus 32:1.

Then King Edmund summoned the bishop who was nearest at hand, and considered with him how he should answer the fierce Ivar. The bishop was afraid for this sudden event and for the king's life, and said that it seemed advisable to him that he should submit to what Ivar demanded of him. Then the king fell silent and looked at the ground, and then said regally to him: "Alas, bishop! the wretched people of this land are treated too shamefully, and I would prefer to fall in battle, so long as my people could enjoy their native land." Then the bishop said, "Alas, dear king! your people lie slain, and you do not have the forces to be able to fight, and these pirates will come and bind you alive, unless you save your life with flight or save yourself by submitting to them." Then King Edmund said, very brave as he was: "I desire and wish in my heart that I alone should not remain after my dear thanes, who have been suddenly slain in their beds with their children and wives by these pirates. It has never been my custom to flee, but I would rather die, if I must, for my own land, and the almighty God knows that I will never turn away from his worship nor from His true love, whether I live or die."

After these words he turned to the messenger whom Ivar had sent to him and said to him, undaunted: "Indeed you were now worthy of death, but I will not defile my clean hands with your foul blood, because I follow Christ, who gave us such an example; and I will gladly be slain by you if God so decrees it. Go now very quickly and tell your fierce lord, 'Edmund will never in his life submit to Ivar, a heathen chieftain, unless he first submit with faith in this land to Christ the Savior.'"

Then the messenger went away quickly and met the blood-thirsty Ivar along the way, hastening to Edmund with all his band, and told the dishonorable man how he had been answered. Then Ivar boldly commanded the army that they should seize only the king, who had despised his commands, and immediately bind him. And Lo! then King Edmund, when Ivar came, stood within his hall, mindful of the Savior, and threw away his weapons; he wished to imitate the example of Christ, who forbade Peter to fight with weapons against the bloodthirsty Jews. And Lo! then the dishonorable men bound

Edmund and insulted him shamefully and beat him with rods, and afterwards led the faithful king to a tree set fast in the earth and tied him to it with strong bonds, and again beat him with whips for a long time; and he always cried out, between the strokes, with true faith to the Savior Christ. And then the heathens, because of his faith, became madly angry, because he called on Christ to help him. They shot at him with missiles, as if for their sport, until he was entirely covered by their shots like the bristles of a hedgehog, as Sebastian was.[1]

When Ivar, the wicked pirate, saw that the noble king would not forsake Christ, but with steadfast faith continually cried out to him, he commanded him to be beheaded, and the heathens did so. While he was still calling out to Christ, the heathens dragged the holy man to his death, and struck off his head with one blow, and his soul went blessed to Christ. There was a certain man nearby, kept hidden from the heathens by God, who overheard all this and afterwards told it, just as we tell it here.

Lo! then the pirates went back to their ship, and hid the holy Edmund's head in thick brambles, so that it would not be buried. Then after a while, when they had gone away, the people of that land — those who were left — came to the place where their lord's headless body lay, and they were very sorry in their hearts for his death, and moreso because they did not have the head for the body. Then the eyewitness who had seen it said that the pirates took the head with them, and it seemed to him, as indeed was very true, that they had hidden the head somewhere in the woods.

Then they all went together into the woods, searching everywhere through bushes and brambles, to see if they could find the head anywhere. It was indeed a great wonder that a wolf was sent by the guidance of God to guard the head day and night against other wild beasts. Then they went searching and continually crying out, as people who often go into the

---

1 St. Sebastian, whose feast is celebrated on January 20, was a Roman soldier martyred under the emperor Diocletian. According to legend he was riddled with arrows by a firing squad — a scene frequently depicted in Renaissance art — but recovered from this ordeal and returned to the Emperor, who then ordered him to be beaten to death with cudgels.

woods always do, "Where are you now, companion?", and the head answered them: "Here, here, here!" And so it called out frequently, answering them all whenever any of them called, until by means of that shouting they all came to it. The gray wolf that watched over the head lay there, with the head clasped between his two paws, greedy and hungry, and did not dare, for God's sake, to taste the head but guarded it against wild beasts. They were amazed at the wolf's care, and carried the holy head home with them, thanking the Almighty for all his wonders. But the wolf followed along with the head until they came to the village, as if he were tame, and then he turned back to the woods. The people of the land afterwards lay the head beside the holy body and buried it as best they could in such haste, and immediately built a church above it.

Eventually, many years later, when the pillaging stopped and peace was granted to the afflicted people, they banded together and built a church worthy of the saint, because miracles had frequently taken place at his grave in the chapel where he was buried. They wished to transport the holy body with public ceremony and lay it inside the church. It was great wonder then that he was just as whole as if he were alive, with an uncorrupted body, and his neck was healed which had been severed, and there was something like a red silken thread around his neck, to show people how he had been slain. Likewise the wounds which the bloodthirsty heathens had made on his body with their repeated shots had been healed by the heavenly God; and he lies uncorrupted like this until this present day, awaiting the resurrection and eternal glory. His body, which lies undecayed, shows us that he lived here in the world without fornication, and journeyed to Christ with a pure life. A certain widow named Oswyn dwelt at the saint's tomb in prayers and fasting for many years afterwards; she would cut the saint's hair every year and pare his nails carefully with devotion, and keep them in a shrine as relics on the altar. So the people of that region faithfully venerated the saint, and Bishop Theodred richly endowed the church with gifts of gold and silver, in honour of the saint.

Then at a certain time eight unlucky thieves came one night to the venerable saint, wishing to steal the treasures people had brought there, and craftily conniving how they might get in. One struck the hasps hard with a sledgehammer, one of them filed around them with a rasp, one even dug under the door with a spade, one of them with a ladder wanted to unlock the window, but they toiled in vain and fared miserably, for the holy man miraculously bound them, each as he stood there struggling with his tool, so that none of them could commit his crime nor escape, but they stood in that manner until morning. People were amazed at how the criminals were hanging — one on a ladder, one bending down to dig, and each was bound fast in his labor. Then they were all brought to the bishop, and he commanded that they should all hang on a high gallows, but he was not mindful how the merciful God spoke through his prophet these words that stand here, *Eos qui ducuntur ad mortem eruere ne cesses* "do not fail to save those who are led to death";[1] and also the holy canons forbid those in holy orders, both bishops and priests, to concern themselves with thieves, for it is not fitting that those who are chosen to serve God should have a hand in any man's death, if they are the Lord's servants. Then after Bishop Theodred had examined his books, he repented with lamentation that he had passed such a cruel sentence on the unfortunate thieves, and he always regretted it until the end of his life, and earnestly asked the people if they would fast with him fully for three days, asking the Almighty to have mercy on him.

In that region was a certain man named Leofstan, powerful in the world and foolish before God, who rode to the saint's shrine with great arrogance, and very insolently commanded them to reveal to him whether the holy saint was uncorrupt; but as soon as he saw the saint's body, he immediately went mad and roared savagely, and wretchedly ended with an evil death. This is similar to what the faithful Pope Gregory said in his narrative about Saint Lawrence, who lies in the city of Rome — that men, both good and evil, were always wanting to examine how he lay, but God restrained them, so that once in the examination seven men died there together, and then

---

1 Prov. 24:11.

others stopped examining the martyr with their human foolishness.

We have heard many miracles in popular report concerning the holy Edmund, which we will not set down in writing, but everyone knows them. By this saint and by others like him, it is clear that almighty God is able to raise man again on doomsday uncorrupted from the earth, He who keeps Edmund whole in his body until the great day, though he came from the earth. The place is honored because of that worthy saint, that men should honor it and provide it well with pure servants of God in the service of Christ, because the saint is greater than men may conceive.

The English nation is not lacking in the Lord's saints, since in England there lie such saints as this holy king, and the blessed Cuthbert, and Æthelthryth in Ely, and also her sister, sound in body as a confirmation of the faith. There are also many other saints in the English nation who perform many miracles, as is widely known, for the praise of the Almighty in whom they believed. Christ declares to mankind through His famous saints that He is almighty God who does such miracles, though the wretched Jews completely rejected him, wherefore they are accursed, just as they wished upon themselves.[1] No miracles are performed at their tombs, because they do not believe in the living Christ, but Christ makes clear to mankind where the true faith is, when He works such miracles through His saints widely throughout this earth. Wherefore to Him be glory forever with His heavenly father and the Holy Ghost. Amen.

[Source: Bruce Mitchell and Fred C. Robinson, *A Guide to Old English* (Oxford: Blackwell, 1992), pp. 195-203 (editing London, BL Cotton Julius E.vii). Translation RML.]

---

1   Matthew 27:25.

3. Vainglory[1]

Listen! An old advisor long ago
told me, wise messenger, of many marvels:
he opened his word-hoard of the prophets' wisdom,
the old sayings of the saints, this scholarly man,
so that afterwards I might truly recognize   5
by these sayings the true son of God,
a welcome guest, and the weaker one too
I might discern, cut off by his sins.
    Every man can easily understand this,
who does not let a lecherous mind   10
mar his reason in this fleeting world
or drunkenness drown all his days:
when many men meet in the assembly,
proud warmongers in their cities of wine,
they sit at the feast singing old songs,   15
exchanging words, and try to determine
what field of strife may find its dwelling
among the men in the hall, when wine whets
their thoughts. The clamor rises,
a din in the company; in discord   20
they shriek their words. So the minds of men
are differently divided; men of honor
are not all alike. One in his arrogance
vaunts his glory, within him swells
an immoderate mind — there are too many like this!   25
He is entirely filled with envy,

---

1   Anonymous and undated poem of homiletic instruction, found in the Exeter Book
    of Old English poetry immediately before *Widsith*. The author has drawn heavily
    upon the wisdom and thought patterns of the Church Fathers, particularly Augus-
    tine and Cassiodorus, for his understanding of the workings and consequences of
    pride, but the poem is also a moral reflection on the boasting and feasting inherent
    in the heroic life, a Christian condemnation of the life in the hall. Pride, envy, and
    malice are described as a kind of spiritual combat; compare Hrothgar's similar
    description in *Beowulf* 1740-46. The vocabulary of heroic verse is turned around,
    and the world of the hero is seen in the unflattering light of Christian humility. See
    further Bernard F. Huppé, *The Web of Words* (Albany, NY, 1970), pp. 1-26; Cather-
    ine Regan, "Patristic Psychology and the Old English *Vainglory*," *Traditio* 26 (1970),
    324-335.

the flying darts and schemes of the devil;
he shouts and belches, boasts of himself
much more than does a better man,
30 thinks that his ways will seems to everyone
utterly unblemished. It will turn out otherwise
when he sees the result of that wickedness.
He shifts and he cheats and imagines deceits,
so many snares, shoots his mental darts,
35 lets them fly in showers. He feels no guilt
for the crimes he has committed, hates the better
man with envy, lets the arrows of malice
break the castle wall which his Maker commanded
him to protect, that place of battle.
40 He sits proud at the feast, foggy with wine,
with wily cunning he lets a word
slip out in provocation, leavened with pride,
inflamed with envy, glutted with vainglory,
malice and treachery. Now you can know,
45 if you should meet such a thane
living in the dwellings, learn from these
few declarations that this is the devil's child
incarnate, with a corrupt life,
his spirit bound for hell, empty of God,
the King of Glory.
50   The prophet sang of this,
ready of speech, and spoke this verse:
'He who exalts himself in arrogance,
advances himself in an evil time
in haughty pride, he will be humbled,
55 brought down after his journey of death
to dwell in torments, entangled in serpents.'
It was long ago in the Kingdom of God
that pride arose among the angels,
a notorious struggle; they raised up strife,
60 a hard campaign, polluted heaven,
betrayed their better when they tried with treason
to steal the kingdom and the King of Glory's
royal throne — as was not right —

and then to occupy just as they pleased
the fair land of glory. The Father of creation   65
stopped them in battle — too bitter was the fight for them.
   It will not be the same for the other one,
who lives his life humbly here on earth,
and always keeps with all his neighbors
peace in the land, and loves his enemy,   70
though he has often done him offense
willfully in this world. In wonderful joy
he may ascend hence from the earth
to the land of the angels. Not so the other,
who in his pride and wicked deeds   75
lives in his sins; the reward will not be the same
from the King of Glory. Keep this in mind,
if you meet a modest prince,
a thane in the nation — to him is always
joined as a guest God's own son,   80
delight of the world, if the prophet did not lie.
Therefore always considering the counsel of salvation,
we must remember at every moment
the truest good, the God of victories. Amen.

[Source: *The Exeter Book*, ed. G. P. Krapp and E. V. K. Dobbie
(New York: Columbia UP, 1936); translation RML.]

Appendix E: *Translations of* Beowulf

Since its rediscovery at the turn of the nineteenth century, *Beowulf* has attracted scores of translators. The history of the poem in modern English reflects not only progress in linguistic and historical knowledge but changes in attitudes towards the poem's meaning and style. The passage below, chosen for its relative lack of textual difficulty or highly-wrought 'poetic' effect, may represent the course of this history of translation. Some early translators tried to recreate the poem in an idiom their contemporaries would recognize as 'heroic' (nos. 2, 4, 6, 8); others have tried to reproduce the aural effect of the poem's alliteration and stress (notably nos. 7, 18, 20); still others avoid imitation or archaism and have tried to recreate the poem in a modern poetic idiom (nos. 12, 17, 19), while others, beginning with Kemble (no. 3) have foregone verse altogether and presented the poem in prose. In all cases the translation of the poem suggests the tension and interplay between an older verse-form and a modern ear, and an ancient poem and modern society.

Beowulf 229-257 (Mitchell and Robinson text).

Þa of wealle geseah   weard Scildinga
se þe holmclifu   healdan scolde
beran ofer bolcan   beorhte randas
fyrdsearu fuslicu,   hine fyrwyt bræc
modgehygdum   hwæt þa men wæron.
Gewat him þa to waroðe   wicge ridan
þegn Hroðgares,   þrymmum cwehte
mægenwudu mundum,   meþelwordum frægn:
'Hwæt syndon ge   searohæbbendra
byrnum werede   þe þus brontne ceol
ofer lagustræte   lædan cwomon
hider ofer holmas?   Hwæt, ic while wæs
endesæta,   ægwearde heold
þe on land Dena   laðra nænig

mid scipherge   sceðþan ne meahte.
No her cuðlicor   cuman ongunnon
lindhæbbende   ne ge leafnesword
guðfremmendra   gearwe ne wisson,
maga gemedu.   Næfre ic maran geseah
eorla ofer eorþan   ðonne is eower sum,
secg on searwum,   nis þæt seldguma
wæpnum geweorðad.   Næfre[1] him his wlite leoge,
ænlic ansyn!   Nu ic eower sceal
frumcyn witan   ær ge fyr heonan
leassceaweras   on land Dena
furþur feran.   Nu ge feorbuend
mereliðende   minne gehyrað
anfealdne geþoht: Ofost is selest
to gecyðanne   hwanan eowre cyme syndon.'

1. **Sharon Turner,**[2] *The History of the Manners, Landed Property, Government, Laws, Poetry, Literature, Religion and Language of the Anglo-Saxons* **(London: Longman, Hurst, Rees & Orme, 1805), p. 404.**

Then from the wall
He that the sea-cliff should guard
Beheld the warder of Scyldingi
Bear over the hills
The bright shields,
The instruments of battle.
Instantly he broke the fire vessel
In the doubts of his mind
What these men were.
The Thegn of Hrothgar with his host
Went straight then
To ride to the shore of the conflict.

---

1   Most editors emend the word *næfre* 'never' to *næfne* 'unless'. The text of Mitchell and Robinson would be translated "May his looks never belie him."

2   Sharon Turner (1768-1847), English antiquary. His work has the distinction of being the first version of any part of the poem in modern English, but it is highly inaccurate, and was only lightly and partially corrected in subsequent editions.

The powerful wood
He shook in his hands,
He asked counsel by his words.
"What are the designs
of this mail-clad host
That thus have brought this warlike ship
Over the streets of the sea?
Come they hither over the ocean,
Injuring every where the settled people?
The land of the Danes
Holds nothing more odious
Than ship-plunderers. —
How I will your origin know
Before that far hence,
Like false spies
On this celebrated land,
You shall further go now,
Band of sea-dwellers.
Hear my simple thought;
It will be best to tell with speed
Why you have come here."

2. John Josias Conybeare,[1] *Illustrations of Anglo-Saxon Poetry*
(London: Harding and Lepard, 1826), 39. Ellipses in the
original.

Nor was it long, ere he who held in charge
To guard each inlet of the rocky coast,
The Scylding's warden, from his tower descried
The prompt and well train'd band in fair array
Bearing their bright shields onwards. Then arose

---

1   John Josias Conybeare (d. 1824), Professor of Anglo-Saxon and Poetry of Oxford
    from 1809 to 1812. His translations were made around 1820 but not published until
    two years after his death. His blank-verse rendering is notably Miltonic, to suit the
    expectations of his age: "Manifestly he feared the roughness, the remoteness of the
    poem in its natural state. He feared to offend a nation of readers reveling in the
    medievalism of Scott and Byron. A literal Latin translation was inserted to appease
    the scholar" (Tinker 31).

Care in his heart, and question, who might be
That stranger host; and straight he flew to horse
And sought the shore, and high uplifted shook
His herald staff, and thus in solemn guise
Bespoke them: "Whence and what ye are, declare,
Who thus in arms o'er ocean's watery path
Have urged to Denmark's coasts your rapid keel.
'Tis mine, the warden of the seas, to hold
with loyal care these outposts of the Dane,
Lest pirate force assail them. ★ ★ ★
★ ★ ★ ★ ★ ★ ★ ★ ★ ★
And sure, methinks, mine eyes ne'er yet beheld
A chief of nobler port than him that leads you;
No stranger (if his bright and beauteous aspect
Belies him not) to the proud garb of war,
Nor in its toil unhonour'd. Speak ye then,
Ere yet your further march explore our realm,
Or friend or foe, your names and kindred speak.
Hear, ye far-faring tenants of the wave,
My full and clear demand — soonest were best
To give me answer — whence and what ye are."

3. J. M. Kemble,[1] *A Translation of the Anglo-Saxon Poem of Beowulf, with a Copious Glossary, Preface, and Philological Notes* (London: William Pickering, 1835; vol. 2 appeared in 1837).

Then from the wall, the warder of the Scyldings, whose duty it was to keep the sea-cliffs, beheld bear over the balks *their* bright shields, *their* ready implements of war. Curiosity overcame him in the thoughts of his mind, what the men might be. He then set out to ride upon *his* horse to the sea-shore; Hrothgar's thane brandished a mighty spear in his strong hands: he spake with prepared words; "What are ye, of armed men, guarded with mailed coats, that thus have come to lead a foaming keel, over

---

1   Kemble was the first Anglo-Saxonist in England to embrace the new philological methods of Germans like Jacob Grimm. His translation accompanied an edition of the poem, indebted in many respects to Thorkelin but notably more accurate.

the lake paths, hither over the deeps of the sea? I on this account placed here at the extremity *of the territory* have kept an ocean-watch, that on the land of the Danes no foe might do injury with a sea-force. Hither no shield-bearers have begun to come more openly, who knew not already the password of *our* warriors, the due observances of kinsmen. I never saw throughout the earth a larger champion than one of you is, a warrior in his trappings. That man is not *one* seldom dignified in *feats of* arms, unless his face, his comely countenance, belie him. Now must I know your origin, before ye proceed farther hence into the land of the Danes, false spies *as ye are.* Now ye dwellers afar off; ye sailers over the sea, *ye* hear my simple thought: Speed were best to reveal whence is your coming."

4. Henry Wadsworth Longfellow, from "Anglo-Saxon Literature," *North American Review* 47 (1838): 90-143; Rptd. in *Poets and Poetry of Europe* (Philadelphia: Carey and Hart, 1845).

Then from the wall beheld
The warden of the Scyldings,
he who the sea-cliffs
Had in his keeping,
Bear o'er the balks
The bright shields,
The war-weapons speedily.
Him the doubt disturbed
In his mind's thought,
What these men might be.
  Went then to the shore,
On his steed riding,
The Thane of Hrothgar.
Before the host he shook
His warden's-staff in hand,
In measured words demanded:
    "What men are ye
War-gear wearing,

Host in harness,
Who thus the brown keel
Over the water-street
Leading come
Hither over the sea?
I these boundaries
As shore-warden hold;
That in the Land of the Danes
Nothing loathsome
With a ship-crew
Scathe us might....
Ne'er saw I mightier
Earl upon earth
Than is your own,
Hero in harness.
Not seldom this warrior
Is in weapons distinguished;
Never his beauty belies him,
His peerless countenance!
Now would I fain
Your origin know,
Ere ye forth
As false spies
Into the Land of the Danes
Farther fare.
Now, ye dwellers afar-off!
Ye sailors of the sea!
Listen to my
One-fold thought.
Quickest is best
To make known
Whence your coming may be."

5. John Earle, *The Deeds of Beowulf* **(Oxford: Clarendon, 1892).**

Then from his rampart did the Scyldings' warden, he who had to guard the sea-cliffs, espy men bearing over bulwark bright shields, accoutrements ready for action; — curiosity urged him with impassioned thoughts (to learn) who those men were. Off he set then to the shore, riding on horseback, thane of Hrothgar; powerfully he brandished a huge lance in his hands, and he demanded with authoritative words — "Who are ye arm-bearing men, fenced with mail-coats, who have come thus with proud ship over the watery highway, hither over the billows? Long time have I been in fort, stationed on the extremity of the country; I have kept the coast-guard, that on the land of the Danes no enemy with ship-harrying might be able to do hurt: — never have shield-bearing men more openly attempted to land here; nor do ye know beforehand the pass-word of our warriors, the confidential token of kinsmen. I never saw, of eorlas upon ground, a finer figure in harness than is one of yourselves; he is no mere goodman bedizened with armour, unless his look belies him, his unique aspect. Now I am bound to know your nationality, before ye on your way hence as explorers at large proceed any further into the land of the Danes. Now ye foreigners, mariners of the sea, ye hear my plain meaning; haste is best to let me know whence your comings are."

6. William Morris and A. J. Wyatt,[1] *The Tale of Beowulf Sometime King of the Folk of the Weder Geats* **(London: Longmans, Green, 1895; originally published Hammersmith: Kelmscott Press, 1895).**

But now from the wall saw the Scylding-folks' warder,
E'en he who the holm-cliffs should ever be holding,
Men bear o'er the gangway the bright shields a-shining,
Folk-host gear all ready. Then mind-longing wore him,

---

1   In this joint venture Wyatt was responsible for a preliminary prose translation which Morris then converted to verse.

And stirr'd up his mood to wot who were the men-folk.
So shoreward down far'd he his fair steed a-riding,
Hrothgar's Thane, and full strongly then set he a-quaking
The stark wood in his hands, and in councilspeech speer'd he:
What men be ye then of them that have war-gear,
With byrnies bewarded, who the keel high upbuilded
Over the Lake-street thus have come leading,
Hither o'er holm-ways hieing in ring-stem?
End-sitter was I, a-holding the sea-ward,
That the land of the Dane-folk none of the loathly
Faring with ship-horde ever might scathe it.
None yet have been seeking more openly hither
Of shield-havers than ye, and ye of the leave-word
Of the framers of war naught at all wotting,
Or the manners of kinsmen. But no man of earls greater
Saw I ever on earth than one of you yonder,
The warrior in war-gear: no hall-man, so ween I,
Is that weapon-beworthy'd, but his visage belie him,
The sight seen once only. Now I must be wotting
The spring of your kindred ere further ye cast ye,
And let loose your false spies in the Dane-land a-faring
Yet further afield. So now, ye far-dwellers,
Ye wenders o'er sea-flood, this word do ye hearken
Of my one-folded thought: and haste is the handiest
To do me to wit of whence is your coming.

7. Francis B. Gummere, *The Oldest English Epic: Beowulf,*
Finnsburg, Waldere, Deor, Widsith, and the German Hildebrand
(New York: Macmillan, 1909).

Now saw from the cliff a Scylding clansman,
a warden that watched the water-side,
how they bore o'er the gangway glittering shields,
war-gear in readiness; wonder seized him
to know what manner of men they were.
Straight to the strand his steed he rode,
Hrothgar's henchman; with hand of might
he shook his spear, and spake in parley.

"Who are ye, then, ye armed men,
mailed folk, that yon mighty vessel
have urged thus over the ocean ways,
here o'er the waters? A warden I,
sentinel set o'er the sea-march here,
lest any foe to the folk of Danes
with harrying fleet should harm the land.
No aliens ever at ease thus bore them,
linden-wielders: yet word-of-leave
clearly ye lack from clansmen here,
my folk's agreement. — A greater ne'er saw I
of warriors in world than is one of you, —
yon hero in harness! No henchman he
worthied by weapons, if witness his features,
his peerless presence! I pray you, though, tell
your folk and home, lest hence ye fare
suspect to wander your way as spies
in Danish land. Now, dwellers afar,
ocean-travellers, take from me
simple advice: the sooner the better
I hear of the country whence ye came."

8. William Ellery Leonard, *Beowulf* (New York: Century Co., 1923; Heritage Club, 1939).

Then from the wall the Watchman,   the Scylding set to guard
The water-cliffs, espied them   over the gangway bear
Their glittering shields of linden,   their ready fighting-gear.
His wits were seized with wonder,   what men were these indeed!
Down to the strand he gat him,   riding on a steed;
Henchman, he, of Hrothgar, —   mightily did shake
With his hands his spear-shaft,   and in parlay spake:
"What are ye, ye mail-clad,   what armor-bearing braves,
Who lead a keel so high-prowed   hither o'er the waves,
O'er the ocean causeway?   I've been out-post long,
Long I've held the sea-watch,   lest a pirate throng
In their fleet might sometime   do our Daneland wrong.
Here have strangers never   made them more at home;

Yet to you no word-of-leave   from my kin hath come,
No consent from braves here.   Never did I view
O'er earth a mightier jarlman,   than is one of you, —
That Hero in his harness: yon Man in weapons dight,
He is no mere retainer,   if tells his face aright,
His peerless port and presence!   But know I must your kin,
Your home, before from hence ye   (as if some spies ye bin)
Farther fare on Daneland.   Ye boatmen of the brine,
Ye far-off dwellers, hear now   this simple thought of mine:
'T'were best forthwith ye tell me   whence your coming be!"

9. R. K. Gordon, *The Song of Beowulf* (London: Dent, 1923).

Then the watchman of the Scyldings whose duty it was to
guard the sea-cliffs saw from the height bright shields and bat-
tle-equipment ready for use borne over the gangway. A desire
to know who the men were pressed on his thoughts. The thane
of Hrothgar went to the shore riding his steed; mightily he
brandished his spear in his hands, spoke forth a question: "What
warriors are ye, clad in corslets, who have come thus bringing
the high ship over the way of waters, hither over the floods? Lo!
for a time I have been guardian of our coasts, I have kept watch
by the sea lest any enemies should make ravage with their sea-
raiders on the land of the Danes. No shield-bearing warriors
have ventured here more openly; nor do ye know at all that ye
have the permission of warriors, the consent of kinsmen. I
never saw in the world a greater earl than one of your band is, a
hero in his harness. He is no mere retainer decked out with
weapons, unless his face belies him, his excellent front. Now I
must know your race rather than ye should go further hence
and be thought spies in the land of the Danes. Now, ye far-
dwellers, travellers of the sea, hearken to my frank thought. It is
best to tell forth quickly whence ye are come."

10. Charles W. Kennedy, *Beowulf: The Oldest English Epic* (New York: Oxford UP, 1940).

Then the Scylding coast-guard watched from the sea-cliff
Warriors bearing their shining shields,
Their gleaming war-gear, ashore from the ship.
His mind was puzzled, he wondered much
What men they were. On his good horse mounted,
Hrothgar's thane made haste to the beach,
Boldly brandished his mighty spear
With manful challenge: 'What men are you,
Carrying weapons and clad in steel,
Who thus come driving across the deep
On the ocean-lanes in your lofty ship?
Long have I served as the Scylding outpost,
Held watch and ward at the ocean's edge
Lest foreign foemen with hostile fleet
Should come to harry our Danish home,
And never more openly sailed to these shores
Men without password, or leave to land.
I have never laid eyes upon earl on earth
More stalwart and sturdy than one of your troop,
A hero in armor; no hall-thane he
Tricked out with weapons, unless looks belie him,
And noble bearing. But now I must know
Your birth and breeding, nor may you come
In cunning stealth upon Danish soil.
You distant-dwellers, you far sea-farers,
Hearken, and ponder words that are plain:
'Tis best you hasten to have me know
Who your kindred and whence you come.'

11. Edwin Morgan, *Beowulf: A Verse Translation into Modern English* **(Aldington, Kent: Hand and Flower, 1952. Rptd. Berkeley: U of California P, 1962).**

But the Scyldings' coastguard gazing from his rock,
He whose duty was to watch the sea-cliffs,
Saw shining shields borne across the gangplank,
Saw bared battle-gear; and his thoughts were pricked
With desire to discover the strangers' business.
So he came to the shore, mounted on horseback,
Hrothgar's man, brandishing with force
A formidable spear, and uttered these words:
'What men would you be, here in your armour,
Mail-coat-protected, in that tall ship
Brought through the paths and acres of ocean
Here, to our land? Long have I been
A watcher on these coasts, my vigil the sea,
Lest any enemy with warship-convoy
Should come to plunder the country of the Danes.
Never more openly have shield-armed men
Made harbour here, yet where is your permission,
Pass of any kind from our commanders,
Consent from the court? I never looked on
A finer man living than one of you seems,
He there in his armour: no mere retainer
Tricked out with weapons, unless looks belie him,
Looks without equal. Now I must know
Who you are, and from where, in case from this point
You push forward into Denmark and are taken as spies
As you move on inland. So now far-sailers
From homes sea-hidden, bend your attentiveness
To my plain request: promptly to tell me
Where you have come from, in courtesy is best.'

12. Burton Raffel, *Beowulf* (New York: New American Library, 1963).

        High on a wall a Danish watcher
Patrolling along the cliffs saw
The travelers crossing to the shore, their shields
Raised and shining; he came riding down,
Hrothgar's lieutenant, spurring his horse,
Needing to know why they'd landed, these men
In armor. Shaking his heavy spear
In their faces he spoke:
                    "Whose soldiers are you,
You who've been carried in your deep-keeled ship
Across the sea-road to this country of mine?
Listen! I've stood on these cliffs longer
Than you know, keeping our coast free
Of pirates, raiders sneaking ashore
From their ships, seeking our lives and our gold.
None have ever come more openly —
And yet you've offered no password, no sign
From my prince, no permission from my people for your landing
Here. Nor have I ever seen,
Out of all the men on earth, one greater
Than has come with you; no commoner carries
Such weapons, unless his appearance, and his beauty,
Are both lies. You! Tell me your name,
And your father's; no spies go further onto Danish
Soil than you've come already. Strangers,
From wherever it was you sailed, tell it,
And tell it quickly, the quicker the better,
I say, for us all. Speak, say
Exactly who you are, and from where, and why."

13. E. Talbot Donaldson, *Beowulf* (New York: W. W. Norton, 1966).

Then from the wall the Scyldings' guard who should watch over the seacliffs, saw bright shields borne over the gangway, armor ready for battle; strong desire stirred him in mind to learn what the men were. He went riding on his horse to the shore, thane of Hrothgar, forcefully brandished a great spear in his hands, with formal words questioned them: "What are you, bearers of armor, dressed in mail-coats, who thus have come bringing a tall ship over the sea-road, over the water to this place? Lo, for a long time I have been guard of the coast, held watch by the sea so that no foe with a force of ships might work harm on the Danes' land: never have shield-bearers more openly undertaken to come ashore here; nor did you know for sure of a word of leave from our warriors, consent from my kinsmen. I have never seen a mightier warrior on earth than is one of you, a man in battle-dress. That is no retainer made to seem good by his weapons — unless his appearance belies him, his unequalled form. Now I must learn your lineage before you go any farther from here, spies on the Danes' land. Now you far-dwellers, sea-voyagers, hear what I think: you must straightway say where you have come from."

14. Kevin Crossley-Holland, *Beowulf* (London, 1968; Rptd. Cambridge, 1977).

Then, on the cliff-top, the Danish watchman
(whose duty it was to stand guard by the shore)
saw that the Geats carried flashing shields
and gleaming war-gear down the gangway,
and his mind was riddled with curiosity.
Then Hrothgar's thane leaped onto his horse
And, brandishing a spear, galloped
down to the shore; there, he asked at once:
'Warriors! Who are you, in your coats of mail,
who have steered your tall ship over the sea-lanes
to these shores? I've been a coastguard here

for many years, kept watch by the sea,
so that no enemy band should encroach
upon this Danish land and do us injury.
Never have warriors, carrying their shields,
come to this country in a more open manner.
Nor were you assured of my leaders' approval,
my kinsmen's consent. I've never set eyes
on a more noble man, a warrior in armour,
than one among your band; he's no mere retainer,
so ennobled by his weapons. May his looks never belie him,
and his lordly bearing. But now, before you step
one foot further on Danish land
like faithless spies, I must know
your lineage. Bold seafarers,
strangers from afar, mark my words
carefully: you would be best advised
quickly to tell me the cause of your coming.'

15. Howell D. Chickering, Jr. *Beowulf: A Dual-Language Edition* (Garden City, NY: Anchor Books, 1977).

From high on a wall   the Scylding watchman
whose duty it was   to guard the sea-cliffs
saw glinting shield-bosses   passed hand to hand
down the gangplank,   an army's war-gear.
His mind was afire   to know who they were.
He rode his horse   straight down to the shore,
retainer of Hrothgar,   brandished his spear,
shook the strong wood,   mighty in his hand,
spoke out stiffly: "Who are you armored men,
protected by mail,   who thus come sailing
your high ship   on the sliding wave-roads,
overseas to this shore?   [Long have I] held
the sea-watch in season,   as the king's coast-guard,
that none of our enemies   might come into Denmark,
do us harm with an army,   their fleet of ships.
Never more openly   have warriors landed
when carrying shields,   and you have no leave

from our men of battle,   agreement with kinsmen.
Never have I seen   a mightier noble,
a larger man,   than that one among you,
a warrior in armor.   That's no mere retainer
so honored in weapons —   may that noble bearing
never belie him!   I must know your lineage,
now, right away,   before you go further,
spies scouting out   the land of the Danes.
Now, you far strangers   from across the sea,
ocean-travelers,   hear my simple thought:
haste is needed,   and the sooner the better
it is best to be quick   and say whence you come."

16. S. A. J. Bradley, *Anglo-Saxon Poetry* (London: Dent, 1982).

Then the sentinel of the Scyldings, who was required to keep guard over the sea-cliffs, observed them carrying gleaming shields and serviceable fighting-gear down the gangplank. An urgency to know what men these might be obsessed his thoughts. Hrothgar's thane, then, went riding down to the shore on horseback, forcefully brandished the sturdy wooden shaft in his hands and demanded with formal words:

'What sort of armour-bearing men are you, protected by corselets, who have come here in this manner, steering your tall ship over the seaways and over the deeps? I have long been the installed custodian of the land's extremity and maintained the coast-guardianship so that no enemy with a ship-borne army might cause damage within the land of the Danes. No shield-bearing warriors have ever arrived here more openly. Yet you were not absolutely sure of the permission and consent of the warrior-kinsmen. Never have I seen a greater nobleman on earth than is that notable person in your midst, that man in his accoutrements. He is no ordinary member of the hall enhanced by his weapons: may his face, a peerless countenance, never belie him.

'Now I must know your extraction before you go any further beyond this point into the land of the Danes as dissembling spies. Now, you inhabitants of far-off places, you voyagers of ocean, listen to my straightforward mind: haste is best in declaring what lies behind your coming here.'

17. Stanley B. Greenfield, *A Readable Beowulf: The Old English Epic Newly Translated* (Carbondale, IL: Southern Illinois UP, 1982).

Then from the wall the Scyldings' warden,
whose task was to keep the sea-cliffs safe,
saw bright shields, battle-ready armor,
carried down the gangway. Curious,
he wondered who and what those men were.
So, riding his horse, right to the shore
went Hrothgar's thane; in his hand he shook
his great spear, spoke to them formally:
"What kind of men are you, armor-clad
in your coats of mail, who have thus come
hither in so tall a ship, taking
the sea-paths in your stride? For some time
have I guarded this land's end, held sea-watch
so that no foes with a force of ships
could launch a raid in our Danish land.
No other band has come so openly
with shields, yet you have no leave to land,
have not received consent of kinsmen,
our noble leaders. Never have I seen
such greatness as one of you suggests:
that warrior so worthily armed
is no plain hall-thane, else peerless looks
deceive. Come now: I must know the source
of your coming, and why, so that you'll
not be held as spies hastening further
into Denmark. Now mark well my thought,
you who dwell afar and dare the sea:
it were best for you to be in haste
to make quite clear whence you've come, and why."

18. Ruth P. M. Lehmann, *Beowulf: An Imitative Translation*
(Austin: U of Texas P, 1988).

Then the Scyldings' watch,   who on shore kept guard
along the coastal wall,   saw from the cliffsummit
bucklers on the bulwarks,   bright shields hanging,
casques and mail ready.   Questions assailed him,
tormented his mind,   who these men might be.
Hrothgar's watchman   rode to the seastrand,
his steed striding;   stoutly he brandished
a weighty war-spear   and, well-mannered, asked:
"Who may ye be,   having armor,
defensive corslets,   who have fared hither
over the waterways,   the windswept vessel
guided across ocean?   Guard of the seashore
for a time am I,   trusted watchman,
so that on Danish lands   no dreaded foemen
could inflict damage   with a fleet of ships.
Targe-bearing men   have not touched this land
more openly,   nor have you met, surely,
leave of warriors,   license of kinsmen.
Never have I noted   among noble men
a greater on ground   than that grand fellow,
a warrior in war-gear.   He is no waiting-man,
honored by his armor,   unless his aspect lies,
his peerless appearance.   Now I propose to know
your ancestry   before you enter here,
faring further   as informers hence
on the strand of Danes.   For you strangers all,
seavoyagers,   a simple question:
whence come you now?   I call for answer.
Recount to us clearly,   for quickest is best."

19. Marc Hudson, *Beowulf: A Translation and Commentary* (Bucknell University Press, 1990).

Then the Scylding guard gazed out from the wall,
he who must patrol the sea-beaten cliffs
saw bright shields, cunning war-gear
borne over the gang-plank; he was feverish
with desire to know who the men were.
Spurring his horse, he rode down to the shore,
Hrothgar's man, brandishing a spear
fiercely in his hand, and spoke these formal words:
"Who are you, in your steel harness,
your coats of mail, that have dared steer
your tall ship over the sea-ways,
hither on uncertain currents. Listen well:
I've kept sea-watch for a long time now,
making sure no raiders come ashore
to pillage and plunder the Danish land.
None have beached their ships more brazenly
than you men-at-arms and yet you await
no word of leave from our warriors,
consent from my kinsmen. Never have I seen
a greater man than that one there,
a champion in war-gear: nor is he someone's servant,
possessed of such weapons, unless his face belies him,
that singular visage. Now I must know
your lineage before you take another step —
spies that you may be — onto Danish soil.
You seafarers, strangers from afar,
hear now my naked thought:
you'd best make known straightway
whence you are come."

20. Frederick Rebsamen, *Beowulf: A New Verse Translation* (San Francisco: HarperCollins, 1991).

Watching above them   the warden of the shores
glimpsed from the cliff-top   a glinting of armor
as they bore from their boat   bright shields and spears
rich with war-weapons.   He wrenched his thoughts
groped within his mind   who these men might be.
He roused his horse then   rode to the seashore —
Hrothgar's cliff-guardian   heaved up his spear
shook it to the sky   and spoke this question:
"Who might you be   in your burnished mailcoats
shining with weapons?   Who steered this warboat
deep-running keel   across the waveswells
here against this shore?   I assure you now
I've held this guard-post   hard against sailors
watched over Denmark   down through the years
that no hateful shipband   might harbor unfought.
Never have boatmen   beached more openly
shield-bearing thanes   unsure of your welcome
hoisting no signal   to hail peace-tokens
friendship to the Danes.   I doubt that I've challenged
a loftier shieldman   than your leader there
hale in his war-gear — no hall-lounger that
worthied with weapons — may his wit not belie
so handsome a swordman.   I will hear quickly
first where you came from   before you move on
you possible pirates   pushing further
into Danish land.   Now let me advise you
horseless sailors   hear my counsel
my heartfelt words: Haste will be best
in letting me know   the land you came from."

Works Cited/Recommended Reading

Editions and Translations

Alexander, Michael. *Beowulf: A Verse Translation*. Harmondsworth: Penguin, 1973.

Alexander, Michael. *Beowulf*. London: Penguin, 1995.

Bradley, S. A. J. *Anglo-Saxon Poetry*. London: Dent, 1982.

Chickering, Howell D. *Beowulf: A Dual-Language Edition*. Garden City, NY: Anchor Books, 1977.

Donaldson, E. Talbot. *Beowulf*. Ed. Joseph F. Tuso. New York: W. W. Norton, 1975.

Earle, John. *The Deeds of Beowulf: An Enlgish Epic of the Eighth Century Done into Modern Prose*. Oxford: Clarendon, 1892.

Gordon, R. K. *The Song of Beowulf*. London: Dent, 1923.

Greenfield, Stanley B. *A Readable Beowulf: The Old English Epic Newly Translated*. Carbondale, IL: Southern Illinois UP, 1982.

Hudson, Marc. *Beowulf: A Translation and Commentary*. London: Associated University Presses, 1990.

Jack, George. *Beowulf: A Student Edition*. Oxford: Oxford UP, 1994.

Kemble, John M. *A Translation of the Anglo-Saxon Poem of Beowulf, with a Copious Glossary, Preface, and Philological Notes*. Vol. 2. London: William Pickering, 1835.

Kennedy, Charles W. *Beowulf: The Oldest English Epic*. New York: Oxford UP, 1940.

Klaeber, F. *Beowulf and the Fight at Finnsburg*. 3rd. ed., with First and Second Supplements. Boston: D. C. Heath, 1950.

Lehmann, Ruth P. M. *Beowulf: An Imitative Translation*. Austin: U of Texas P, 1988.

Mitchell, Bruce and Fred C. Robinson. *Beowulf: An Edition*. Oxford: Blackwell, 1998.

Morgan, Edwin. *Beowulf: A Verse Translation into Modern*

English. Aldington, Kent: Hand and Flower, 1952. Rptd.
Berkeley: U of California P, 1962.

Raffel, Burton. *Beowulf*. New York: New American Library,
1963.

Rebsamen, Frederick. *Beowulf: A New Verse Translation*. San
Francisco: HarperCollins, 1991.

Turner, Sharon. *The History of the Manners, Landed Property,
Government, Laws, Poetry, Literature, Religion and Language
of the Anglo-Saxons*. London: Longman, Hurst, Rees &
Orme, 1805.

Critical Studies

Amodio, Mark. "Affective Criticism, Oral Poetics, and
Beowulf's Fight with the Dragon." *Oral Tradition* 10
(1995): 54–90.

Amos, Ashley Crandell. *Linguistic Means for Determining the
Dates of Old English Literary Texts*. Cambridge: Medieval
Academy of America, 1981.

Baker, Peter S. *Beowulf: Basic Readings*. Basic Readings in
Anglo-Saxon England I. New York: Garland, 1995.

Barnes, Daniel. "Folktale Morphology and the Structure of
'Beowulf'." *Speculum* 45 (1970): 416–34.

Bately, Janet. "Linguistic Evidence as a Guide to the Authorship of Old English Verse: A Reappraisal, with Special
Reference to *Beowulf*." *Learning and Literature in Anglo-
Saxon England: Studies Presented to Peter Clemoes on the
Occasion of his Sixty-Fifth Birthday*. Ed. Michael Lapidge
and Helmut Gneuss. Cambridge: Cambridge UP, 1985.
409–32.

Benson, Larry D. "The Literary Character of Anglo-Saxon
Formulaic Poetry." *PMLA* 81 (1966): 334–41.

———. "The Originality of Beowulf." *The Interpretation of
Narrative: Theory and Practice*. Ed. Morton W. Bloomfield.
Harvard English Studies 1. Cambridge, MA: Harvard UP,
1970. 1–43. Rprt. L. D. Benson, *Contradictions: From
Beowulf to Chaucer*. Ed. Theodore M. Andersson and
Stephen A. Barney. Aldershot, Hants: Scolar Press, 1995.
32–69.

————. "The Pagan Coloring of *Beowulf.*" *Old English Poetry: 15 Essays.* Ed. Robert Creed. Providence: Brown UP, 1967. Rptd. Baker 35-50.

Bjork, Robert. "Digressions and Episodes." Bjork and Niles 193-212.

————. "Grímur Jónsson Thorkelin's Preface to the First Edition of *Beowulf,* 1815." *Scandinavian Studies* 68 (1996): 291-323.

Bjork, Robert E. and John D. Niles, ed. *A Beowulf Handbook.* Lincoln, NE: U of Nebraska Press, 1997.

Bonjour, Adrien. *The Digressions in Beowulf.* Oxford: Blackwell, 1950.

Brodeur, Arthur. "Variation." *The Art of Beowulf.* Berkeley: U of California P, 1959. Rptd. Fulk, *Interpretations* 66-87.

Bruce-Mitford, R. L. S. *The Sutton Hoo Ship Burial: A Handbook.* 3rd ed. London: British Museum, 1979.

Bullough, Donald A. "What has Ingeld to do with Lindisfarne?" *Anglo-Saxon England* 22 (1993): 93-125.

Cabaniss, Alan. "*Beowulf* and the Liturgy." *JEGP* 54 (1955): 195-201.

Calder, Daniel G. "The Study of Style in Old English Poetry: A Historical Introduction." *Old English Poetry: Essays on Style.* Ed. Daniel G. Calder. Berkeley: U of California P, 1979. 1-65

Cameron, Angus. "Saint Gildas and Scyld Scefing." *Neuphilologische Mitteilungen* 70 (1969): 240-6.

Campbell, Joseph. *The Hero with a Thousand Faces.* 2nd ed. Princeton: Princeton UP, 1968.

Carver, Martin. *Sutton Hoo: Burial Ground of Kings?* Philadelphia: U of Pennsylvania P, 1998.

Chambers, R. W. *Beowulf: An Introduction to the Study of the Poem with a Discussion of the Stories of Offa and Finn.* 3rd. ed., with a supplement by C. L. Wrenn. Cambridge: Cambridge UP, 1959.

Chase, Colin, ed. *The Dating of Beowulf.* Toronto: U of Toronto P, 1981. Rpt. 1997.

Cherniss, Michael. *Ingeld and Christ: Heroic Concepts and Values in Old English Christian Poetry.* The Hague: Mouton, 1972.

Clark, Francelia Mason. *Theme in Oral Epic and in 'Beowulf'*.
New York: Garland, 1995.

Creed, Robert P. "The Making of an Anglo-Saxon Poem."
ELH 26 (1959): 445-454.

Damico, Helen. *Beowulf's Wealhtheow and the Valkyrie Tradition*.
Madison: U of Wisconsin Press, 1984.

Davis, Craig. *'Beowulf' and the Demise of Germanic Legend in
England*. New York: Garland, 1996.

Dean, Paul. "*Beowulf* and the Passing of Time." *ES* 75 (1994):
193-209 and 293-302.

Deskis, Susan. *'Beowulf' and the Medieval Proverb Tradition*.
Tempe, AZ: Medieval and Renaissance Texts and Studies,
1996.

Dobbie, E.V.K., ed. *The Anglo Saxon Minor Poems*. Anglo-
Saxon Poetic Records VI. New York: Columbia UP,
1942.

Donahue, Charles. "*Beowulf*, Ireland, and the Natural Good."
Traditio 7 (1949-51): 263-277.

Dronke, Ursula. "Beowulf and Ragnarok." *Saga-Book* 17
(1969): 302-25.

Dümmler, E., ed. *Alcuini Epistolae*. Monumenta Germaniae
Historica, Epistolae Aevi Carolini, vol. 2. Berlin, 1895.

Dumville, David. "Kingship, Genealogies and Regnal Lists."
Early Medieval Kingship. Ed. P.H. Sawyer and I.N. Wood.
Leeds: Leeds UP, 1977. 72-104.

———. "The Anglian Collection of Royal Genealogies and
Regnal Lists." *Anglo-Saxon England* 5 (1976): 23-50

Duncan, Ian. "Epitaphs for Æglæcan: Narrative Strife in
Beowulf." *Beowulf*. Ed. Harold Bloom. New York: Chelsea
House, 1987. 111-30.

Earl, James W. *Thinking about 'Beowulf'*. Stanford: Stanford UP,
1994.

Ettmüller, Ludwig. *Beowulf: Heldengedicht des achten
Jahrhunderts*. Zurich, 1840.

Evans, A.C. *The Sutton Hoo Ship Burial*. London: British
Museum Publications, 1986.

Evans, Jonathan D. "Episodes in Analysis of Medieval Narrative." *Style* 20 (1986): 126-41.

Farrell, Robert T. "Beowulf, Swedes, and Geats." *Saga-Book* 18 (1972): 225-86.

Farrell, Robert and C. Neuman de Vegvar, eds. *Sutton Hoo: Fifty Years After.* Kalamazoo, MI: Medieval Institute, 1992.

Fell, Christine. "Paganism in *Beowulf*: a Semantic Fairy-Tale." *Pagans and Christians: the Interplay Between Christian Latin and Traditional Germanic Cultures in Early Medieval Europe.* Ed. T. Hofstra et al. Mediaevalia Groningana 16 (1995): 9-34.

Foley, John Miles. "Texts That Speak to Readers Who Hear: Old English Poetry and the Languages of Oral Tradition." *Speaking Two Languages: Traditional Disciplines and Contemporary Theory in Medieval Studies.* Ed. Allen J. Frantzen. Albany: State U of New York P, 1991. 141-156.

———. "Tradition and the Collective Talent: Oral Epic, Textual Meaning, and Receptionalist Theory." *Cultural Anthropology* 1 (1986): 203-22.

———. *Immanent Art: From Structure to Meaning in Traditional Oral Epic.* Bloomington: Indiana UP, 1991.

———. *The Theory of Oral Composition: History and Methodology.* Bloomington: Indiana UP, 1988.

———. *Oral-Formulaic Theory and Research: An Introduction and Annotated Bibliography.* New York: Garland, 1985.

Fontenrose, Joseph. *Python: A Study of Delphic Myth and Its Origins.* Berkeley: U of California P, 1959.

Frank, Roberta. "Beowulf and Sutton Hoo: The Odd Couple." in *Voyage to the Other World: The Legacy of Sutton Hoo.* Ed. Calvin B. Kendall and Peter S. Wells. Minneapolis: U of Minnesota P, 1992. 47-64.

———. "The *Beowulf* Poet's Sense of History." *The Wisdom of Poetry: Essays in Early English Literature in Honor of Morton W. Bloomfield.* Ed. Larry D. Benson and Sigfried Wenzel. Kalamazoo, MI: Medieval Institute Publications, 1982. 53-65.

Fry, D. K. *Finnsburh: Fragment and Episode.* London: Methuen, 1974.

Fulk, R. D. *A History of Old English Meter.* Philadelphia: U of Pennsylvania P, 1992.

Fulk, R. D., ed. *Interpretations of Beowulf: a critical anthology.*

Bloomington, IN: Indiana UP, 1991.

Georgianna, Linda. "Hrethel's Sorrow and the Limits of Heroic Action in *Beowulf*." *Speculum* 62 (1987): 829-50.

Glosecki, Stephen O. *Shamanism and Old English Poetry*. New York: Garland, 1989.

Goldsmith, Margaret. *The Mode and Meaning of Beowulf*. London: Athlone, 1970.

Greenfield, Stanley B. "Geatish History: Poetic Art and Epic Quality in *Beowulf*." *Neophil* 47 (1963): 211-17. Rptd. in Fulk, *Interpretations* 120-126.

———. "The Formulaic Expression of the Theme of 'Exile' in Anglo-Saxon Poetry." *Speculum* 30 (1955): 200-206.

Hanning, Robert W. "*Beowulf* as Heroic History." *Medievalia et Humanistica* 5 (1974): 77-102.

Helterman, Jeffrey. "*Beowulf*: The Archetype Enters History." *ELH* 35 (1968): 1-20.

Hill, John M. *The Cultural World in 'Beowulf'*. Toronto: U of Toronto P, 1995.

Hill, Thomas. "The Christian Language and Theme of *Beowulf*." *Companion to Old English Poetry*. Ed. H. Aertsen and R. Bremmer. Amsterdam: Vrije UP 1994. 63-77.

Hills, Catherine M. "*Beowulf* and Archaeology." Bjork and Niles 291-310.

Hobsbawm, Eric J. and Terence Ranger, ed. *The Invention of Tradition*. Cambridge: Cambridge UP, 1983.

Howe, Nicholas. *Migration and Mythmaking in Anglo-Saxon England*. New Haven: Yale UP, 1989.

Irving, Edward B. *A Reading of Beowulf*. New Haven: Yale UP, 1968.

Kaske, Robert E. "*Sapientia et Fortitudo* as the Controlling Theme of *Beowulf*." *SP* 55 (1958): 423-56. Rptd. *An Anthology of Beowulf Criticism*. Ed. Lewis Nicholson and D. W. Frese. Notre Dame: Notre Dame UP, 1963. 269-310.

Kelly, Birte. "The Formative Stages of *Beowulf* Textual Scholarship." Part One *ASE* 11 (1983): 247-274. Part Two *ASE* 12 (1984): 239-275.

Kiernan, Kevin. *'Beowulf' and the 'Beowulf' Manuscript*. 1981. Revised ed. Ann Arbor: U of Michigan P, 1996.

————. *The Thorkelin Transcripts of 'Beowulf'*. Anglistica 25. Copenhagen: Rosenkilde and Bagger, 1986.

Leake, Jane. *The Geats of Beowulf: A Study in the Geographical Mythology of the Middle Ages*. Madison: U of Wisconsin P, 1967.

Lerer, Seth. "Grendel's Glove." *ELH* 61 (1994): 721-51.

Levine, Robert. "Ingeld and Christ: A Medieval Problem." *Viator* 2 (1971): 105-28.

Leyerle, John. "The Interlace Structure of Beowulf." *University of Toronto Quarterly* 37 (1967): 1-17. Rptd. Fulk, *Interpretations* 146-67.

Liberman, Anatoly. "Beowulf — Grettir." *Germanic Dialects: Linguistic and Philological Investigations*. Ed. Bela Brogyanyi and Thomas Krömmelbein. Amsterdam Studies in the Theory and History of Linguistic Science 38. Amsterdam: John Benjamins, 1986. 353-401.

Lionarons, Joyce. "*Beowulf*: Myth and Monsters." *ES* 77 (1996): 1-14.

Liuzza, R. M. "On the Dating of *Beowulf*." Baker, *Beowulf: Basic Readings*. 281-302.

Lord, Albert B. *The Singer of Tales*. Cambridge, MA: Harvard UP, 1960.

Magoun, F. P. "*Beowulf* A´: a Folk Variant." *Arv: Journal of Scandinavian Folklore* 14 (1958): 95-101.

————. "*Beowulf* B: A Folk-poem on Beowulf's Death." *Early English and Norse Studies Presented to Hugh Smith in Honour of His Sixtieth Birthday*. Ed. Arthur Brown and Peter Foote. London: Methuen, 1963. 127-40.

————. "The Oral-Formulaic Character of Anglo-Saxon Narrative Poetry." *Speculum* 28 (1953): 446-67. Rptd. Fulk, *Interpretations* 45-65.

————. "The Theme of the Beasts of Battle in Anglo-Saxon Poetry." *NM* 56 (1955): 81-90.

Malone, Kemp. "Grendel and His Abode." *Studia Philologica et Litteraria in Honorem L. Spitzer*. Ed. A.G. Hatcher and K.L. Selig. Bern: Francke, 1958. 297-308.

————. "King Alfred's Geatas." *Modern Language Review* 20 (1925): 1-11.

McNamee, M. B. "*Beowulf:* an Allegory of Salvation?" *JEGP* 59 (1960): 190-207. Rptd. Fulk, *Interpretations* 88-102.

Meaney, Audrey. "Scyld Scefing and the Dating of *Beowulf* — again." *Bulletin of the John Rylands Library* 75 (1989): 7-40.

Mellinkoff, Ruth. "Cain's Monstrous Progeny in *Beowulf*: Part I, Noachic Tradition." *ASE* 8 (1979): 143-62. "Part II: Post Diluvian Survival." *ASE* 9 (1981): 183-97.

Mitchell, Bruce. "*Beowulf,* line 1020b: *brand* or *bearn*?" *Studi sulla cultura germanica (Romanobarbarica* 10). Ed. M. A. D'Aronco et al. Rome: Herder, 1988-9. 283-92.

Mitchell, Bruce and Fred C. Robinson. *A Guide to Old English.* 5th ed. Oxford: Blackwell, 1997.

Moffat, Douglas. "Anglo-Saxon Scribes and Old English Verse." *Speculum* 67 (1992): 805-27.

Moisl, H. "Anglo-Saxon Royal Genealogies and Germanic Oral Tradition." *Journal of Medieval History* 7 (1981): 215-48.

Moorman, Charles. "The Essential Paganism of *Beowulf.*" *MLQ* 28 (1967): 3-18.

Müllenhoff, Karl. "Der Mythus von *Beovulf.*" *Zeitschrift für deutsches Altertum* 7 (1849): 419-41.

———. "Die innere Geschichte des *Beovulfs.*" *Zeitschrift für deutsches Altertum* 14 (1869): 193-244.

Murray, Alexander Callander. "*Beowulf,* the Danish Invasions, and Royal Genealogy." Chase 101-12.

Nagler, Michael. "*Beowulf* in the Context of Myth." *Old English Literature in Context.* Ed. John Niles. Cambridge: D. S. Brewer, 1980. 143-56.

Needham, G. I. *Lives of Three English Saints.* London: Methuen, 1966.

Newton, Sam. *The Origins of 'Beowulf' and the Pre-Viking Kingdom of East Anglia.* Woodbridge, Suffolk: D. S. Brewer, 1993.

Niles, John D. "Understanding *Beowulf:* Oral Poetry Acts." *Journal of American Folklore* 106 (1993): 131-55.

———. "Locating *Beowulf* in Literary History." *Exemplaria* 5 (1993): 79-109.

———. "Myth and History." Bjork and Niles 213-32.

O'Keeffe, Katherine O'Brien. "Diction, Variation, and the Formula." Bjork and Niles 85-104.

———. *Visible Song: Transitional Literacy in Old English Verse.* Cambridge: Cambridge UP, 1990.

Orchard, Andy. *Pride and Prodigies: Studies in the Monsters of the Beowulf Manuscript.* Cambridge: D. S. Brewer, 1995.

Page, Amy and V.H. Cassidy. "*Beowulf:* the Christologers and the Mythic." *Orbis Litterarum* 24 (1969): 101-11.

Page, R. I. "The Audience of *Beowulf* and the Vikings." Chase 113-122.

Panzer, Friedrich. *Studien zur germanischen Sagengeschichte, I: Beowulf.* Munich: Beck, 1910.

Pasternak, Carol Braun. *The Textuality of Old English Poetry.* Cambridge: Cambridge UP, 1995.

Prescott, Andrew. "The Ghost of Asser." *Anglo-Saxon Manuscripts and their Heritage.* Ed. P. Pulsiano and E. Treharne. Aldershot: Ashgate Publishing, 1998. 255-91.

———. "'Their Present Miserable State of Cremation': The Restoration of the Cotton Library." *Sir Robert Cotton as Collector: Essays on an Early Stuart Courtier and his Legacy.* Ed. C. J. Wright. London: British Library Publications, 1997. 391-454.

Robinson, Fred C. *'Beowulf' and the Appositive Style.* Knoxville: U of Tennessee P, 1985.

———. "Beowulf." *The Cambridge Companion to Old English Literature.* Ed. Malcolm Godden and Michael Lapidge. Cambridge: Cambridge UP, 1991. 142-43.

———. "Why is Grendel's Not Greeting the *gifstol* a *wræc micel?*" *Words, Texts, and Manuscripts.* Ed. Michael Korhammer. Cambridge: D. S. Brewer, 1992. 257-62.

Rosenberg, Bruce. "Folktale Morphology and the Structure of 'Beowulf': A Counterproposal." *Journal of the Folklore Institute* 11 (1975): 199-202.

Russom, Geoffrey. "Artful Avoidance of the Useful Phrase in *Beowulf, The Battle of Maldon,* and *Fates of the Apostles.*" *SP* 75 (1978): 371-390.

Schaefer, Ursula. "Rhetoric and Style." Bjork and Niles 105-124.

Schrader, Richard. "Succession and Glory in *Beowulf.*" *JEGP* 90 (1991): 491-504.

Scowcroft, R. Mark, "The Irish Analogues to *Beowulf.*" *Speculum* 74 (1999): 22-64.

Shippey, Thomas A. "Structure and Unity." Bjork and Niles 149-174.

Sisam, Kenneth. "Anglo-Saxon Royal Genealogies." *Proceedings of the British Academy* 39 (1953): 287-348.

———. "Notes on Old English Poetry: The Authority of Old English Poetical Manuscripts." *Studies in the History of Old English Literature.* Oxford: Clarendon, 1953. 148-98.

———. *The Structure of Beowulf.* Oxford: Clarendon, 1965.

Stanley, E.G. "The Germanic 'Heroic Lay' of Finnesburg." *A Collection of Papers with Emphasis on Old English.* Publications of the Dictionary of Old English 3. Toronto: Pontifical Institute of Medieval Studies, 1987. 281-97.

Stanley, Eric G. *"Beowulf." Continuations and Beginnings.* London: Thomas Nelson, 1966. Rptd. Baker 3-34.

Stitt, J. Michael. *Beowulf and the Bear's Son: Epic, Saga, and Fairytale in Northern Germanic Tradition.* New York: Garland, 1992.

Tinker, Chauncey B. *The Translations of Beowulf: A Critical Bibliography.* Yale Studies in English XVI. New York: Henry Holt, 1903.

Tolkien, J.R.R. *"Beowulf:* The Monsters and the Critics." *Proceedings of the British Academy* 22 (1936): 245-95. Rptd. Fulk, *Interpretations* 14-44.

———. *Finn and Hengest: The Fragment and the Episode.* Ed. Alan Bliss. London: Allen and Unwin, 1982.

Turville-Petre, J. *"Beowulf* and *Grettis saga:* an excursion." *Saga-book* 19 (1977): 347-57.

Whitelock, Dorothy. "Fact and Fiction in the Legend of St Edmund." *Proceedings of the Suffolk Institute of Archaeology* 31 (1970): 217-33.

———. *The Audience of Beowulf.* Oxford: Clarendon, 1951.

Wormald, Patrick. "Bede, *Beowulf,* and the Conversion of the Anglo-Saxon Aristocracy." *Bede and Anglo-Saxon England: Papers in Honour of the 1300th Anniversary of the Birth of*

Bede, Given at Cornell University in 1973 and 1974. Ed. Robert T. Farrell. London: British Archaeological Reports, 1978. 32-95.